THE BUREAU
AND
THE MOLE

Also by the author

Eagle on the Street

(with Steve Coll)

THE BUREAU

AND

THE MOLE

The Unmasking of Robert Philip Hanssen,
the Most Dangerous Double Agent
in FBI History

DAVID A. VISE

Atlantic Monthly Press
New York

Published simultaneously in Canada
Printed in the United States of America

PHOTO CREDITS—Page 231: Howard Hanssen with young Bob (personal photograph); Robert Philip Hanssen and Jack Hoschouer (1962 Taft High School Yearbook). Page 232: Hanssen at dental school (personal photograph); Bonnie Hanssen (personal photograph); Russian embassy (Susan Biddle/*The Washington Post*). Page 233: Priscilla Galey (personal photograph); Louis Freeh with President Clinton (Frank Johnston/*The Washington Post*). Page 234: Aldrich Ames (Frank Johnston/*The Washington Post*); Viktor Cherkashin (Pete Earley); Vladimir Kryuchkov (FBI file photo). Page 235: Dmitri Polyakov (Pete Earley); Valery Martynov and Sergei Motorin (FBI file photos); Hanssen in dark suit (personal photograph). Page 236: Freeh with Janet Reno (Robert A. Reeder/*The Washington Post*); FBI stakeout house (Mark Malseed); FBI SIOC (Bill O'Leary/*The Washington Post*). Page 237: Bridge in Foxstone Park and Foxstone Park sign (Mark Malseed); Cash and black garbage bag (FBI file photos). Page 238: Hanssen at sentencing (Arthur Lien, illustrator); Freeh with John Ashcroft and George Tenet (Jahi Chikwendiu/*The Washington Post*).

Library of Congress Cataloging-in-Publication Data

Vise, David A.
    The bureau and the mole : the unmasking of Robert Philip Hanssen, the most dangerous double agent in FBI history / David A. Vise.
        p. cm.
    Includes bibliographical references.
    ISBN 0-87113-834-4
    1. Hanssen, Robert. 2. Spies—Russia (Federation)—Biography. 3. Intelligence agents—United States—Biography. 4. United States. Federal Bureau of Investigation—Biography. I. Title.

    UB271.R92 H372 2002
    327.1247073'092—dc21   2001053872

DESIGN BY LAURA HAMMOND HOUGH

Atlantic Monthly Press
841 Broadway
New York, NY 10003

02 03 04 05   10 9 8 7

To our daughters, Lisa, Allison, and Jennifer
And especially to Lori

CONTENTS

AUTHOR'S NOTE

Mark Malseed and Matthew Obernauer were my partners in virtually every aspect of this book. Together, they gave new meaning to the title "research assistant," tackling reporting, writing, and editing with extraordinary dedication and care. They displayed a tremendous commitment to fairness and accuracy and transformed the supposedly lonely task of writing a book into a high-energy collaboration imbued with a shared sense of mission.

Mark, a Phi Beta Kappa graduate of Lehigh University, is a computer maven whose sophisticated use of technology led us to many important discoveries. He is a detail-oriented journalist of the first order who made an invaluable contribution through his literary skills, organizational abilities, and iconoclastic approach.

A graduate of Yale University in 2000, Matt brought the passion and relentlessness of an old-fashioned gumshoe reporter—and the intelligence and ear of a well-read wordsmith—to this endeavor. Through his friendly demeanor, talent for brainstorming, and reporting skill, he made an immense contribution.

I have been fortunate to work with Mark and Matt as we pierced the veil of secrecy that kept Bob Hanssen's spying and the FBI's role hidden from the public. I will forever be grateful to them for helping me shine some light on this mysterious, global tale of character and intrigue.

David A. Vise

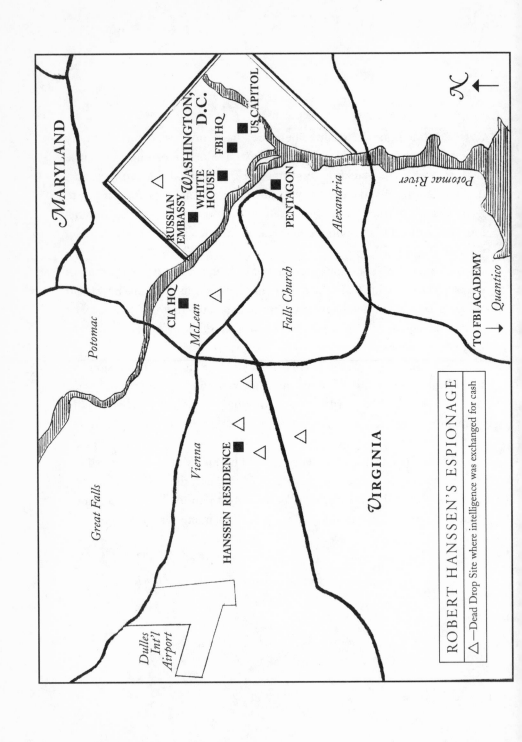

ROBERT HANSSEN'S ESPIONAGE

△—Dead Drop Site where intelligence was exchanged for cash

A NOTE TO
THE READER

All correspondence between FBI Special Agent Robert P. Hanssen and his handlers in the KGB and Russian intelligence appears in this book as originally written. Letters have not been edited for clarity or for errors in spelling and grammar. The same is true of the stories, e-mails, and texts authored by Hanssen and others. In some cases, letters and other items have been excerpted or shortened. In addition, I have included brief explanatory notes in some passages where references are made to names, organizations, or events that are not widely known; these notes are enclosed within brackets.

—D.A.V.

He who walks in the way of integrity
shall be in my service.

No one who practices deceit
can hold a post in my court.

No one who speaks falsely
can be among my advisors.

Psalm 101

Selected by FBI Director Louis Freeh to begin
A Report to the American People on the Work of the FBI, 1993–1998

PROLOGUE

On the morning of February 18, 2001, FBI Special Agent Bob Hanssen woke up, got out of bed, ate breakfast, and followed his regular Sunday morning routine. Accompanied by his wife and children, Hanssen drove out to St. Catherine of Siena Church in Great Falls, Virginia. There were numerous Roman Catholic churches closer to the Hanssens' home in Vienna, but they had a special reason for traversing the rolling hills of the Washington, D.C., suburbs to attend St. Catherine's. Various high-ranking government officials also attended the church, including FBI Director Louis Freeh. They were all drawn to it, according to its pastor, Father Franklyn Martin McAfee, because of its traditional approach. The Hanssens also relished the church's close ties to Opus Dei, an elite and influential movement within the Catholic Church, and delighted in praying alongside some of the most powerful people in Washington. More members of Opus Dei attended St. Catherine's than any other church in the region. And several of its parishioners sent their boys to The Heights School in Potomac, Maryland, an Opus Dei academy where both Freeh and Hanssen enrolled their sons and had crossed paths recently.

Worship is serious business at St. Catherine's. "In the Washington area, we are the most traditional, the most High church," Father McAfee said. "We detest mediocrity." On Sunday mornings, High Mass, the Mass of Paul XI, is celebrated in Latin, with the choir singing Mozart, the priest facing a wooden altar shrouded in white linens, and a sculpted crucifix illuminated by sunlight streaming in from a hidden skylight. "There is an emphasis on devotions and spirituality and an emphasis on confessions," McAfee said. "We get a lot of confessions here."

The Hanssens always sat on the left side of the airy church near the statue of Mary, Mother of Sorrows. The Freeh family always sat on the right side of the church, close to the organ and choir. In addition to St. Catherine's and The Heights, Hanssen and Freeh had other things in common: both were married with six children, lived in northern Virginia, regularly dealt with sensitive matters of Russian counterintelligence, and had decided long ago to devote themselves to careers in law enforcement.

Back at home following church that day, Hanssen struck up a conversation with his old pal Jack Hoschouer, a career soldier turned munitions salesman who was preparing to leave after visiting for several days. Hoschouer went outside with "Sundae," the Hanssens' black Labrador, and played Frisbee for about fifteen minutes. Then, the two friends, whose relationship dated back more than thirty years to high school in Chicago, launched into one of their philosophical discussions about ethics. One point led to another until Hanssen went to get *The Man Who Was Thursday*, a book by his favorite author, G. K. Chesterton.

"Here, read this," Hanssen said, handing his friend the novel— originally published in 1908—he had read and reread many times. "You will probably enjoy it. Things are not always the way they seem."

Hoschouer had to put a rubber band around the tattered book to keep it from falling apart. He was used to such exchanges with Hanssen and didn't consider it out of the ordinary. The two had shared many books and secrets over the years, often talking about the nature of clandestine operations and the kinds of people who carried them out. After Hoschouer finished packing, Hanssen drove him to Dulles International Airport, where he got out of the car at the curb, and the two bid each other farewell.

Fifteen minutes later, a phalanx of armed FBI agents swarmed Hanssen after he deposited a black garbage bag filled with U.S. intelligence secrets at the base of a footbridge in a northern Virginia park. In exchange for the promised secrets, the Russians had left $50,000 in cash for him nearby. At the moment of the arrest, Hanssen's fellow parishioner Louis Freeh sat at the controls of the FBI's sleek, ultramodern crisis operations center, choreographing Hanssen's downfall and raising the curtain on a series of puzzling questions about why this churchgoing family man and FBI sleuth had become a double agent who sold more closely guarded national security secrets than anyone in the Bureau's ninety-year history.

Two days later when the story broke, Hoschouer was stunned by the news. After all they had shared, Hoschouer thought that he really knew Bob Hanssen. In time, to better understand his complex friend, Hoschouer would follow Hanssen's suggestion by reading *The Man Who Was Thursday*. But while sitting with his parents in Arizona and watching the initial TV news reports about Hanssen's arrest and the allegations of espionage, Hoschouer had a sick feeling in his stomach. His head was swimming with questions.

Who is the real Bob Hanssen? he wondered. What caused such a patriotic American to spy? Why had he risked it all? The only thing Hoschouer was now sure of was what Hanssen had told him a few days earlier when he had handed him the book.

Things are not always the way they seem.

1

ALONE

Ever since his childhood days in the Norwood Park neighborhood of Chicago, Bob Hanssen had been something of a loner. His mother, Vivian, noticed that whenever something upset him, Bob would head for the safety of his room in their modest, two-bedroom bungalow on Neva Street and immerse himself in books. Bob—an only child born just before the end of World War II—seemed too quiet for a healthy growing boy, and Vivian didn't understand why her son acted the way he did.

At the time, however, Vivian wasn't preoccupied by Bob's taciturn demeanor. He was a dutiful son, his teachers at Norwood Park Elementary said he was a good student, he participated in Cub Scouts at the Lutheran church, and he didn't get into the kind of mischief that led many other boys in the leafy neighborhood astray. Bob walked home daily during the noon break at school. "My son appreciated coming home from school for lunch and having me there. He has told me that time and time again," Vivian recalled.

While the pair enjoyed a loving mother-son relationship, Vivian would have been happier if Bob had not turned inward so much. "He was a loner as a kid. He had friends, but when he was home he would be in his room reading or out watching TV with us. But there were never too many deep conversations."

One of Bob's favorite books was *The Code Breakers* by David Kahn, a thick volume about secret codes and intercepts that fueled his boyhood fascination with the technical aspects of intercepting confidential communications. "If you write the word CLANDESTINE on a piece of paper and think of everything you can imagine, there it is. From bugs to eavesdropping to spying to lock picking to false identities to code breaking to secret messages. Pick up a book on spies, and run through the list, and he had some interest in it," a friend of Bob Hanssen's said.

Vivian met Howard Hanssen in 1929, the year of the stock market crash on Wall Street when both of them were working in retail, trying to help their families scrape by during tough times. The two native Chicagoans got to know each other downtown at the city's best-known department store, Marshall Field's, after initially meeting at a much smaller shop that went under.

"Howard and I went together for a long time before getting married," Vivian explained. "I was left with my mom, he was left with his mom, and we were the sole support. . . . My mother's husband had died, and she was alone. Earning fifteen dollars a week, or from twelve to twenty dollars a week, doesn't stretch that far."

In 1935 Vivian and Howard wed in a modest ceremony that took place in the pastor's house beside the Lutheran church Howard attended, rather than in the church itself. "We had a small party afterward that my sister arranged at her home, in keeping with the times. It was a desperate time for a lot of people."

The couple began their married life in an apartment on the south side of Chicago. Howard was not content sitting behind a desk and considered becoming a cop, a job he believed would be exciting. "It was hard to get on the police force in those days," Vivian said. Decisions about who would get every city job, from trash collector to police officer to health worker, were imbued with the politics and patronage of the Daley machine. But the family had the right political connections for Howard to be hired as a police officer. "He took an exam and passed it and didn't need anything else," Vivian said.

In the early 1940s, with World War II raging, Howard enlisted in the Navy rather than taking the risk of being drafted into the Army and dispatched on a dangerous assignment. "I have friends whose husbands were in that D-Day massacre," Vivian said. "Howard thought the Navy was a little easier than the Army might have been. I imagine he would have gone overseas if he had been in the Army." Instead, Howard stayed far from the battle front, working in the United States as a shore patrolman searching for Americans who had gone AWOL. Eventually, he ended up with a Navy assignment in the Chicago area, permitting him to spend weekends with his bride, who soon became pregnant.

"My son was born in April 1944 and that was a good thing," Vivian said.

The Hanssens became a family of three, eligible for some additional benefits from the federal government because of Howard's service in the Navy. "There were allowances for families and we had a little more money," Vivian said. "Things did get better." Vivian devoted herself to keeping house and caring for their infant son.

After the war, Howard returned to his job on the Chicago police force, and the couple moved to the northwest part of the city. With the help of the G.I. Bill, they bought a modest home on an L-shaped lot in Norwood Park, a popular neighborhood for police officers and their families. They picked the house, built at an angle to Neva Street, largely because the public schools in the area had a good reputation.

Bob was exposed to religion as a youngster, attending a Lutheran church on Sunday mornings with his mother, who felt it was an important part of raising her son. "The Lutheran church fit in because I think every child should have that kind of upbringing at the beginning of life," Vivian said. "Every child should have religion and know the Bible and get a good start in that respect. I would go and Bob would go to church, but my husband not as often. He was working or whatever."

On the Chicago police force, Howard Hanssen tackled a variety of assignments, including working for a special unit that hunted down suspected communist sympathizers. Some of his assignments stirred up ill will, but he told himself that was just part of the job. After many years on the force, the truth was he didn't particularly enjoy the work the way he once did, but it paid the bills. And that was one notch up the ladder from his younger brother, Edward, who could not seem to hold a steady job for long. Howard was street-smart to be sure, but his choices for career alternatives were limited severely by his lack of a formal education. So Howard remained a Chicago cop, even after his promotion to lieutenant left him in the type of job he loathed, behind a desk.

But Howard Hanssen did have an abiding passion in life, something that lifted his spirits and kept him going through the day-to-day monotony. He loved to go to the track and bet on the horses. The pastime became the focal point of the couple's social life, and Vivian enjoyed going with him. "That is where we spent all of our spare time, watching the races," Vivian recalled. "Howard had friends who owned horses. That made it interesting. It makes a difference when you know the horses and jockeys."

Vivian emphasized that Howard's affinity for the horses did not mean he was an addicted gambler or an irresponsible bettor. Instead, she described it as an outlet for his energy and a place where he felt comfortable, whatever the town. "We took a vacation once," Vivian said, "and I didn't realize we were hitting every race track in Canada and the East Coast. I didn't realize it until after the third race track. He had planned it out that way. It gives you something to do in strange towns."

Howard Hanssen also had an agenda for his son that Vivian failed to recognize from its inception. Howard spoke of a better life for Bob. He wanted him to go to college, get an advanced degree, and become a doctor. But in the course of raising his son with an extremely firm hand, he succeeded in destroying Bob's confidence. Instead of praising his schoolwork and encouraging him to succeed, Howard Hanssen's approach was to criticize and berate his son repeatedly. It wasn't tough love; it was tough luck. And, according to Vivian Hanssen, her son came to feel emotionally abused by his father.

"Sometimes people make themselves feel better by not allowing someone else to feel too good," she said. "Maybe Howard had been treated that way. Maybe I just looked at things as the way I hoped they were. . . . I think [Howard] had the idea that if he complimented someone too much, they might get bigger than they should."

Bob was both physically and emotionally abused by his father, according to family members and others.

On at least two occasions, Howard Hanssen physically abused his son while exhorting him to "be a man." When Bob was six or seven years old, his father wrapped him in blankets and twirled him around and around until he became so dizzy that he vomited. Another time, Howard grabbed one of Bob's legs by the ankle, forcefully pulling it into the air and stretching his son's hamstring until he urinated on himself involuntarily. The torture left Bob feeling helpless and humiliated.

"The person you are supposed to trust and identify with is doing everything from hurting to humiliating you, and it is confusing. It creates the beginning of negative feelings about individuals who are supposed to be your protector and authority figures," said Dr. Stephen Hersh, a longtime Washington psychiatrist who has treated FBI agents and many senior federal officials. "He is swung until he gets sick and vomits. Vomiting is a loss of control of your body in the context of extreme distress and fear. This is a child who had repeated experiences that totally destroyed his capacity to identify in a healthy way with male authority figures."

When Bob became old enough, his father took him to get his driver's license. Bob was ready for the road test and excited about the freedom and independence driving would bring. But his father had other ideas. He bribed the official administering the test to fail his son. Bob was aware of what his father did, and it left him feeling that the world was crooked and set up to deny him any sense of control over his own destiny. "I didn't approve of it," Vivian Hanssen said. "[Howard] thought Bob was too cocky and thought he believed he was too good a driver."

Although they could do little or nothing about it, some of the parents of students in Hanssen's grade school were mortified by the way Howard publicly belittled his son to anyone who would listen. "My mom would apparently run into Mr. Hanssen in the grocery store shopping," one classmate recalled. "Howard Hanssen used to say terrible things about Bob."

The problems were exacerbated, Vivian Hanssen said, because her son never raised objections with her about the way he was treated. And so the pattern of abuse, of being rebuked and put down again and again, continued throughout his childhood. Bob suffered enormously, but quietly. "He wouldn't come out and say anything to his dad about it, and would harbor that inside, and it gnaws at you," she said. "That was the kind of thing Howard did that I didn't notice enough of. I thought that they were far enough apart and isolated incidents. I didn't know they were so important to [Bob]. He must have brooded on them."

Vivian caught a glimpse of Bob's resentment of his father one day, when Howard received the results of an exam he had taken. "Howard took a test for something, and he was not a real educated man," Vivian said. "His grade was not too hot and Bob, when he saw that, he laughed and said, 'Look at that,' as if he had been told to get good grades and Howard hadn't done so well himself."

While growing up, Bob did find some joy at home. Vivian remembers holidays as special times around the Hanssen household, especially Christmas, when her relatives from Indiana often visited. A neighbor regularly dressed up as Santa Claus when Bob was young and the house would be alive with festive decorations. After his paternal grandparents moved in, Bob also found some companionship with them. Having divorced years earlier, his grandparents stayed in separate makeshift bedrooms. The attic was converted into a bedroom for Bob's grandmother; his grandfather, at times, stayed in the basement. Bob spent time with his grandfather, an engineer, playing with a train set and learning how to put things together and take them apart. He also enjoyed using a ham radio with his father and grandfather.

Bob's serious and melancholy nature can be seen in his 1962 yearbook from Chicago's Taft High School. Most of the graduating class members had glib or light remarks beside their photographs. Beside Robert Albert Heroux: "If I ever became rich with too much green, I would pledge to build a monument for the late James Dean." Beside Carolyn Marie Hinds: "Of all 57 varieties, this 'Hinds' is the best." Beside Anthony Gutilla: "Leader of men, follower of women." Beside Robert Philip Hanssen: "Science is the light of life."

The few high school classmates who remember Hanssen recall an extraordinarily quiet boy, awkward in his interpersonal skills, unusually bright in science, and talented in the nuts and bolts of how things work. "My chemistry teacher looked out at him and said, 'There is old slipstick Hanssen,' and Bob was using a slide rule," a classmate recalled. "He was always on the cutting edge. In those days, slide rules were cutting edge technology. He seemed to automatically grasp things like that, the guy who sees relationships very quickly and clearly in a scientific way. I'm not so sure he has it down sociologically."

Others had recollections of Hanssen participating in the ham radio club, talking to operators from around the world even as he remained quiet amid his fellow students. Tom Kozel, a fellow member of the club, said Hanssen enjoyed the four-member group immensely. Yet there is no photo for the ham radio club in the school yearbook—Hanssen's photo appears only in his official graduating class portrait. "We were kind of considered geeky, the ham radio guys," Kozel said. "That's probably how our friendship started. That was a common interest and then it branched out into other areas, an interest in cars, girls, careers."

Hanssen, who was not athletic himself, attended many of Taft High School's football games but usually didn't socialize with the kids who were playing sports, either at school or informally, and did not date much. That placed him on the periphery of life at Taft, which had school spirit and a championship football team that included a fullback, Jim Grabowski, who went on to play for the Green Bay Packers.

"WHAT IS TAFT?" Bob Hanssen's high school yearbook asks—"bewildered Freshies? a desperate game? carefree Seniors? college hopes? a rough Chem test? career dreams? safe drivers? 7:30 chorus practice? tears at graduation? Taft is all of these, but, most of all, Taft is friends, the ones you share yourself with."

Hanssen didn't share himself with many of his Taft classmates. Kozel's clearest recollection of Hanssen concerns the way he just went about his business and did things, without boasting. "I remember him as someone who did not brag about things; he just did them," Kozel emphasized. "He did things and showed up with the evidence afterward. And I kind of admired him, because I was not that way and most people were not that way."

Various classmates' memories of Hanssen are mixed, mostly due to his quiet, inward nature. "People would say he is weird," one classmate recalled. "That is just the way he is. I remember a girl I was dating thought Bob was really strange."

Kozel disputed that assessment, saying Hanssen was "reticent" and awkward around people he didn't know, leaving a false impression that he was that way all the time. He said that Hanssen loosened up around friends. Kozel also remembered Hanssen as the "most conservative" member of their clique. And he blamed Bob's parents for being overprotective when they refused to allow him to join Kozel and two other friends on a backpacking trip to Rocky Mountain National Park after high school graduation.

If she could turn back the clock, if she had another chance to raise her son, Vivian Hanssen would do some major things differently. She would take a firmer stance against her husband's heavy-handed treatment. She would take steps to encourage Bob to get more involved with people and spend less time locked away in his room. She would encourage Bob to speak up for himself, rather than letting problems fester. And she would pay more attention to what was taking place all around her as her son struggled to develop his own personality and identity.

As she reflects on it, Vivian Hanssen wishes she would have done more to protect her son from his father. "I had a good relationship with Howard and could have told him to cut out whatever he was doing. I think he would have paid attention."

There was another side to Bob Hanssen's personality, a side that scared his friends and was concealed from his parents. It would manifest itself in an instant, leaving Hanssen feeling exhilarated and in control. His friends weren't sure where it came from or what caused it, given his normally quiet and straitlaced approach. Sometimes it was fun, but other times it could rattle them so much that they feared for their own lives. From his friends' vantage point, the hardest part involved its unpredictable nature. "When he got a crazy idea in his head, he was going to do it," one high school friend said. There was no talking him out of it. And Hanssen's friends never knew how, when, or where this other side of Bob would take charge.

On the surface, Hanssen's penchant for taking enormous risks belied everything that surrounded the rest of his personality and demeanor. He never exhibited a need to be the center of attention—to the contrary, he generally seemed at ease with life on the fringe of the social milieu. As he moved through his high school years, he appeared content reading books, especially anything dealing with secret codes, clandestine modes of operation, or deception. Often, he enjoyed getting together with his friend Jack Hoschouer, whom he met during freshman biology class. The two would sit for hours in a room, silently reading and only occasionally exchanging ideas. Together, they delved further into science, teaming up as chemistry lab partners during their sophomore year of high school. But mostly they enjoyed being in each other's company and entering the world of images, ideas, and fantasy that reading provided. In that world, Hanssen felt inferior to no one.

Yet one day Jack Hoschouer also saw the other side of Bob Hanssen. The two were firing Hoschouer's father's rifles at point-blank range into a bullet trap in the basement. Suddenly, Bob took one of the guns, went about a dozen feet away from the trap, and took aim. "I can shoot that!" he shouted. Before anyone could stop him, Hanssen fired the rifle, hitting the wall two feet above the target and sending shards of concrete flying into the air.

After Hanssen studied the physics of Grand Prix auto racing in high school, he would climb into his 1962 Dodge Dart and test its limits by trying to find out the maximum speed his car could reach when turning a corner. "We would challenge guys to races," said a high school friend. "Not drag races. We would find twisty, turny streets and challenge someone to follow us through them. We were screaming through a residential street and went around the corner with two guys following us in a Buick. They ended up in the middle of some guy's front yard." Bob did not stop to ask his friends if they minded taking wild rides whenever his daredevil streak overcame him. Instead, he would get the impulse to act and just take off. "It scared the crap out of me a couple of times," one said.

Hanssen's tendency to push things to the edge didn't reveal it-self much at Knox College, a small liberal arts school in Illinois. Bob respected his father's job and thought he wanted to pursue a career in law enforcement. Police work had an unpredictable element that kept things interesting and fresh. "I think Bob was proud of Howard's job," Vivian Hanssen said. "He liked having a policeman for a father." But his father pushed Bob to take premed courses, along with math and Russian. After a while, Hanssen's resentment began to build to the point where he did not want his parents, especially his father, to visit him at college. Bob feared the kinds of things his father would say to his professors and friends. Living on his own, Hanssen was feeling somewhat better about himself, dating a bit and relishing the freedom he had out from under his father's day-to-day control.

Hanssen's fears were confirmed when his parents came to see him at Knox. His father sought out Bob's professors and undercut him.

His mother Vivian said: "I'm afraid Howard wasn't the best one to come to college and visit. You are on your own, and if a professor likes you, that is great. But if somebody belittles you just a bit, that is going to hurt. Howard would say, 'He has good grades, but next time, he won't be so hot.' He had the idea that Bob would work real hard and then slide." The more accurate description of Bob's work habits was that he was naturally bright but didn't focus much on subjects or courses that didn't interest him. "Some things he didn't care about, he didn't worry about," one former college classmate said.

Despite the anger he felt toward his father, Bob stayed on the premed track at Knox and worked during his summer break from college as a recreational therapist at a state mental hospital in Chicago. Bob found the job intriguing; the work involved interacting with mental patients and trying to get them outside for games and activities on the grounds, including volleyball and badminton. "[In addition to] the student nurses, he enjoyed dealing with the people and trying to figure out what made them tick and understand them," a coworker said.

One of the student nurses Bob met in the summer of 1965 was an attractive, vivacious woman named Bonnie Wauck, who admired the way he carried himself and made the patients feel comfortable. "She was very much impressed at how effective he was with the patients," recalled her father, Leroy Wauck. "He was very effective, very nice and kind and considerate." Bob's relationship with Bonnie played a pivotal role in the decisions he made in the years immediately after they met. Their courtship proceeded slowly, with exchanges of letters and holiday visits in Chicago. Bob was attracted to Bonnie's friendly, outgoing manner, and with her light brown hair and big brown eyes, Bonnie reminded him of the actress Natalie Wood. The second oldest of eight children, she had grown up in a large family, often caring for her younger siblings in their 1920s four-bedroom, Dutch Colonial house on Vine Street in Park Ridge, one of Chicago's northern suburbs. The daughter of a psychology professor at Loyola University and a deeply religious homemaker, Bonnie had had a happy childhood, which included summers living on a private lake with her family where they enjoyed canoeing, sailing, bike riding, gardening, and just spending time together. "Bonnie was perfectly normal," said her mother, Fran Wauck. Bonnie attended a Catholic high school in Evanston, Illinois, and then went on to college tuition free at Loyola, majoring in sociology at the Catholic university. After returning to Knox College, Bob thought about Bonnie often.

Bob encountered difficulty with medical-school admissions, so he applied to dental school instead. He didn't want to be a dentist any more than he wanted to be a doctor. But his father was still pushing him to go into medicine. Bob applied, and was accepted, to Northwestern University's dental school. He studied there from 1966 to 1968, even though it became clear to him early on that dentistry was not what he wanted to do with his life. His first-year roommate, Jerald Takesono, said that while everyone else dressed casually, Hanssen wore a coat and tie daily, even to human anatomy lab. "I was really glad to get rid of my anatomy outfits because they smelled. And I joked with Bob, 'Now you can get rid of your suits too.'" Hanssen kept his negative feelings about dental school largely to himself, declining to tell family members and friends how much he hated it. Along the way, he kept himself amused as a devoted reader of *Mad* magazine, which Takesono said "we all loved because it flouted authority."

On August 10, 1968, during the same summer that violence and rioting disrupted the Democratic National Convention in Chicago, Bob married Bonnie Wauck. The Catholic wedding ceremony was performed by Bonnie's uncle, Monsignor Robert Hagarty, Vice Chancellor of the Archdiocese. Tom Kozel, who attended the wedding and reception, recalled the entire celebration as joyous and first-rate in every way. There were guests of all ages, a range of music for all tastes, and an abundance of food, drinks, and happy people. "It was a great reception," Kozel said. "Everyone that I saw seemed like they were having a great time. I've been to few that have equaled it. There was a huge wedding cake."

Bonnie married Bob even though Howard Hanssen told her it was a bad idea. "Why are you marrying this guy?" Howard Hanssen asked her before the wedding. Within a few weeks, Bob dropped out of dental school. Though he had completed much of the course work necessary to become a dentist before the wedding, his marriage to Bonnie gave him a fresh perspective, as well as the strength to make a break from the medical path his father had chosen for him. "He didn't like dentistry, didn't like working on people's mouths," Vivian said.

Howard Hanssen was furious. How could Bob have allowed the family to spend all that money on dental school and then quit? How could he throw away all those years of study that had prepared him to become a medical professional? After all that he had done as a father, this seemed to Howard Hanssen the ultimate betrayal, and it left him extraordinarily disappointed in Bob. After years of struggling on the salary of a Chicago police officer and the sacrifices that went along with it, Howard Hanssen angrily expressed his remorse to family, friends, neighbors, and coworkers.

Friends of Bob Hanssen remember the trouble he had making his own decision, given the pressure he was under from his father. At the same time, Bob seemed elated over his marriage to Bonnie. "Bob seemed happy, getting married to a beautiful girl and a smart girl," one friend recalled. Meanwhile, Bonnie was enraptured with her man, whose knowledge and understanding of the world seemed to her to be limitless. During dinner, Bob typically wouldn't say much, focusing on his food rather than conversation and continuing a habit he had picked up from his family of tilting his glass to indicate he wanted more to drink. Bonnie quickly grew exasperated with this practice, telling her husband, "You're going to have to speak up around here." But once the plates were cleared, Bob would break his silence, opening up a world of ideas and sophisticated thought for family and friends, and Bonnie would sit and listen, hanging on every word.

Even though the young couple's parents lived in Chicago, the two families didn't mesh well. "There was not much interaction," one friend said. "Different interests, different levels of education, perhaps. I would say different fundamental interests. A philosopher [psychologist] in one house and a policeman in another. They wouldn't mix and meet on that kind of level."

There were other, darker problems as well. Within days of their marriage, Bonnie received a nasty jolt that destroyed her postwedding bliss. The telephone rang, and Bonnie answered; the voice on the other end of the line sounded familiar. It was an old girlfriend of Bob's he had met while working at the state mental hospital. She bluntly told Bonnie that she and Bob had just made love and that she was the one he really had wanted to marry. The woman staked her claim on Bonnie's new husband, saying that Bob was her man and urging Bonnie to back off. Bonnie hung up the phone and burst into tears. This was a bride's worst nightmare—but to Bonnie, the wedding vows they had made were sacred and immutable. Her faith in Bob, at least momentarily, had been shaken, but her conviction about the holiness of their marriage remained intact. If Bob had committed adultery, he would have to face up to it and seek forgiveness, or he would compound the problem further by lying.

Bonnie confronted Bob about the disturbing phone call later that day. She told him she wanted to know the truth and had to know the facts, no matter how painful. Bob, stunned by the brash nature of the surprise phone call Bonnie described, admitted his sin and begged Bonnie for forgiveness. He said he wasn't worthy of her love. He also promised repeatedly that nothing like that would ever happen again. He was not in love with the other woman, and he said there was no truth to the notion that he had really wanted to marry her. Bob had been preyed upon and had given in to temptation. He couldn't explain it any other way. Maybe, he said, the woman wanted to marry him, but those feelings were not reciprocal and he would sever all ties to her.

Over and over, Bob told Bonnie that he loved her. Again and again he said he felt ashamed and did not deserve to have such a wonderful wife. Bonnie, a woman of extraordinary religious conviction, reassured him of her love, and they agreed to keep his indiscretion a secret, a pattern that would repeat itself in later years. Thanks to Bonnie, the young couple had survived the first major test of their nascent marriage, but her faith in Bob would never be the same. While Bonnie could forgive, she couldn't forget. Bonnie would worry about their relationship from this point forward and remain suspicious of her husband's fidelity. But she would do so stoically, silently, and, for the most part, alone.

Bob's marriage to Bonnie, its early triumph over temptation, and his decision to forgo becoming a dentist marked seminal moments in his life. Though the path ahead was not entirely clear, Bob had found the will to break away from his father. Yet at another level, the career move away from dentistry introduced additional complexity into his life and his already strained relationship with Howard. Bob felt guilty that he wasn't living up to the goals his father had established for him years earlier, leaving him with a sense of emptiness and a belief that he could not measure up, could not make his father proud. His father may have had a quiet demeanor, but on the subject of his son "the failure," it didn't take much prompting to get him to speak up.

Bob's decision to abandon dentistry as a career naturally raised the question: What was he going to do next? He had majored in both math and chemistry as an undergraduate, and ultimately decided to continue his studies at Northwestern University's business school. Building on his natural aptitude for numbers, Bob played to his strengths, earning a master's degree in Business Administration with a dual specialization in accounting and information systems. He liked the meticulousness, the internal consistency, and logic inherent in these fields. In accounting, there was a right way and a wrong way to do things, and Bob felt very comfortable with that degree of certainty.

"When he graduated from high school or college, he had his first electronic watch . . . and he said, 'It really is nice to know what time it *really* is,'" a friend recalled with amazement. Years later, Bob would seek absolute precision in numerous aspects of his life, feeling a strong inner need to be exacting. He would even put a program on his computer that frequently dialed up the mega-clock at the U.S. Naval Observatory to synchronize its settings.

Bob received his MBA in 1971, and it appeared that the false starts in his studies, career, and marriage were behind him. Ready to head out into the world of work, Bob joined one of the big accounting firms in Chicago and was assigned to the mammoth Sears, Roebuck and Co. account. It sounded prestigious, but he found it hopelessly mind-numbing and mundane. For someone with an active imagination, the work seemed downright drab.

Once again, Bob had ventured forward only to find himself where he didn't want to be. Without Bonnie's support, it was possible Bob would have undergone a personal crisis. Even with her backing, it was tough for Bob to overcome what was beginning to feel like one misstep after another. Maybe it was time to listen to his gut, rather than trying to meet the expectations of others. Deep down, Bob knew exactly what he wanted to do with his life, and he had known for years—work in law enforcement. Despite the litany of problems he had had with his father on a personal level, Bob always respected that his dad was a cop. Howard Hanssen wielded real power, did interesting things, and was making a difference. When he carried his badge, he was one of the good guys.

But could Bob make the leap, given his abundance of education and his father's negative feelings? There were two things Howard Hanssen had made clear for many years—he wanted his son to become a doctor and he did not want him to become a cop. To his father, Bob had had the chance for a better life and career based on a sound education. In the face of those pressures, the loyal son was haltingly trying to break away and blaze his own trail.

2

MAD DOG

From the time he was ten years old, Louis (pronounced "Louie") Freeh knew he wanted to be an FBI agent. The danger and intrigue of the Bureau's work, as portrayed on television and in movies, captured young Louis's imagination. While his friends dreamed about being Mickey Mantle or Willie Mays, Louis wanted to fight crime. To him, nothing seemed more exciting than a life of stakeouts and undercover operations to track down fugitives, capture bank robbers, and snare communist spies.

Family members wondered where the boy's notions originated. "It had to be from the media," Louis would later muse. "I didn't have anybody in the family in law enforcement, so I remember Saturday afternoon movies about the FBI." The Bureau of Louis's childhood dreams was an aggressive, well-oiled crime-fighting machine led by J. Edgar Hoover. The longtime director, who was obsessed with the Bureau's image, launched a public relations campaign that made the FBI a household name and depicted its Special Agents as paragons of justice who always got "their man."

Born on January 6, 1950, in Jersey City, New Jersey—a gritty, blue-collar town across the Hudson River from lower Manhattan—Louis was the second of three sons of William and Bernice Freeh. Louis's parents were both New York natives. His mother's parents had emigrated from Naples and settled in the Bronx, while his father, raised in Brooklyn, was of German and Irish stock. Louis's father was a mildly successful real estate salesman and the son of a city garbage collector who later became the sanitation supervisor for Coney Island.

Louis had a good relationship with both his mother and father, bonds strengthened by the cramped conditions in which they lived. The family of five occupied just three rooms on the bottom floor of a small house for most of Louis's childhood. His parents were able to afford the home only by renting out the upstairs. "I still remember when we were able to afford to move into the second floor," Freeh recalled.

It was in the living room of this house where Louis and his two brothers sprawled on the floor to watch television. One of the family's favorite shows was a hit ABC program that aired on Sundays beginning in 1965 called *The F.B.I.* The program—which starred Efrem Zimbalist, Jr., as an agent who tracked down murderers, thieves, and gangsters in a very matter-of-fact way—was based on real FBI cases and received the Bureau's full cooperation.

Without the necessary skills and talents, Louis's dream of joining the Bureau would have gone unfulfilled. But he had the right stuff. In school, Louis was a no-nonsense kid who worked hard and got good grades. He was an altar boy and an Eagle Scout and not known to back down from a fight. Though only 5'9", Freeh was athletic and well built.

Louis's combination of brains and brawn served him well in northern New Jersey, where stickball was king in the neighborhood's back alleys and abandoned lots and games often ended in scuffles. "I had a lot of scraps growing up," Freeh said. "I remember getting involved with people who I thought were picking on other kids. Not that I was a champion or anything, but I remember a couple of fights where I thought somebody was getting picked on. It was something that always bothered me."

A cautious fourth-grade teacher thought Freeh was getting in with the wrong crowd of boys who were likely to get into trouble, as Louis amusingly recalled. In those days, "Trouble meant tying somebody's shoe to the chair or something." Freeh remembers the concerned teacher telling his father who he should and should not associate with, and his father following the advice, even though it made things awkward because the school was small.

Louis's staunchly Roman Catholic upbringing stressed community service as an important part of the faith—service that went beyond protecting kids from bullies on the playground lot. Louis would accompany his father, who served his country as an Army infantryman in Europe during World War II, on visits to the homes of the elderly and needy families on behalf of a Catholic aid organization. William Freeh's unfailing dedication to helping others made an impression on his son. "He'd visit old people who couldn't make it down the stairs, and do homework with children whose parents didn't speak English," Louis recalled. "As busy as he was with work and taking care of his family, he found time to do all that, and I was very impressed with that. Still am."

Freeh's mother Bernice recounted a story to him at the kitchen table one day that he would later say affected him deeply. Bernice's maiden name was Chinchiolo, and when she tried to get a job during the Great Depression, she had to change her name to avoid being discriminated against. Newspaper want ads in those days commonly said "Anglo-Saxon Preferred." She had listed her last name as Chinsley and eventually got a job as a bookkeeper for a Wall Street brokerage house. "It just shocked me. It made me angry. It made me a little bit embarrassed for her," Louis said.

During the summer between his junior and senior years at St. Joseph of the Palisades High School, Louis took a trip to Appalachia that opened his eyes. As part of a church youth-group mission, he taught English to children and worked on a cucumber farm started by a local priest in rural Kentucky. "One of the things I remember very starkly from that experience," Louis said, "is that we did a census of the hollows—these little sort of off-the-road, off-the-mainstream places. We had a series of questions we would ask the people, and it was incredible. Many of the people did not know what country they were living in. Or they knew what country, but not what state. They had no concept—no television, no radio, no communications. We asked who the president was and some would say Franklin Roosevelt. This was in 1966."

Louis attended Rutgers, the mammoth state university located in New Brunswick, New Jersey. He put himself through college by working a series of jobs to pay the bills and also receiving a scholarship. Freeh largely ignored the tumult and distractions of campus life in the late 1960s, earning a degree in American Studies and graduating Phi Beta Kappa. On days when classes were canceled for antiwar protests, Freeh went to the Manpower office downtown, where he was hired as a "temp" for all sorts of odd jobs. "When I couldn't go to school, I would just go there," he said. "Any kind of job you can imagine, I'd probably do it." That included loading trucks for the Teamsters Union in North Jersey during the summers, where he experienced firsthand the impact of Mafia corruption. Seeing the Mob's influence reinforced his desire to join the FBI.

While Freeh was not energized by the protest movements that were changing American society at the time, he was interested in the well-being of his fellow man. A college roommate remembers Louis inviting a homeless man inside for a meal and talking with the stranger—a drifting former college professor—late into the night before putting him on a bus the next morning.

After earning his undergraduate degree, Louis went to Rutgers law school at night. A year after getting his law degree, the twenty-five-year-old Freeh was accepted into the FBI Academy in Quantico, Virginia, for a sixteen-week training program. Al Whitaker, one of Freeh's instructors, remembers his charge as an outstanding recruit. "A quiet fellow, obviously intelligent, in excellent physical condition," said Whitaker. "But I'm also remembering that he wasn't a good shot."

Freeh's questionable marksmanship would not interfere with his first important assignment after graduating from Quantico in 1975. Louis worked undercover out of the FBI's New York field office on a waterfront corruption case involving the Longshoremen's Union

and major Mafia families. Louis's assignment was to buddy up to a
noted racketeer in his preferred "working environment"—a steam
room in a dingy Brooklyn gym called the Shelton Health Center. The
mobster, Mike Clemente, insisted on doing business in the steam
room, sans clothing, so potential undercover agents and stool pigeons
could not conceal a wire. Beginning in the summer of 1977, Freeh,
posing as an unemployed law school graduate, struck up a casual
friendship with Clemente, a capo in the Genovese crime family who
was the undisputed boss of the Manhattan waterfront. The old man
and the kid hit it off so well that Clemente offered Freeh help in landing a job as a lawyer.

Freeh spent four years on the waterfront case, monitoring
Clemente and the Mafia in a variety of surveillance and undercover
operations. The young lawyer quickly gained respect in the New
York office for his thorough understanding of the complex but vital
new Racketeer Influenced and Corrupt Organizations Act (RICO)
statute. The law gave prosecutors a powerful weapon to go after organized crime syndicates by freeing law enforcement officials to pursue the legitimate and quasi-legal businesses the Mob used to support
criminal activities.

In March 1979, Clemente and eleven mob associates were indicted
for racketeering, extortion, tax evasion, and other crimes. At the arraignment, the old man thought he would try to do his young pal another
favor. Clemente saw Freeh standing up front in the courtroom and
ordered his attorney, Paul A. Victor, to find out what they were charg-
ing the kid with. As Victor approached, he saw Freeh huddled with
prosecutors and got the sinking feeling he wasn't in need of help at all.

"You're an FBI agent?" Victor asked.

"Yeah," said Freeh.

"Oh shit!" said Victor.

"What do you mean?" asked Freeh.

Victor laughed as he explained his orders from Clemente, and
Freeh turned to see the old man smiling and waving. "I felt as low, I
guess, as I could possibly feel, like a little snake," Freeh recalled.

During the trial, particularly when the lawyers went off to the side to have a private discussion, Clemente would yell out, "Hey, Freeh! Let's go get a steam! Get me outta here, I need a steam!" The dogged pursuit that Freeh employed to nab Clemente and his associates, and the comments he'd fire off about bureaucratic roadblocks, earned the young agent the nickname "Mad Dog." Years later, it was a nickname that Freeh would laugh off. "When I get my teeth into something, sometimes I don't let go," he said. "Maybe that was it."

Oddly enough, it was "Mad Dog" Freeh's ability to subdue and train a mobster's vicious guard dogs that led to a big break in the waterfront corruption investigation. Freeh and his partner, Bob Cassidy, had been surveilling William "Sonny" Montella, one of Clemente's associates. Montella, who regularly sent payoffs to Clemente, operated a contracting business out of Red Hook, New Jersey. The agents had been monitoring Montella's activities through wiretapping, bugs, and stakeouts for seven months. As the FBI prepared to close in on Mafia operatives all along the East Coast, Freeh and Cassidy needed to convince Montella that they had a mountain of evidence against him, and that he ought to cut a deal and become a witness for the prosecution.

The investigators knew they had a strong case but felt they needed Montella's testimony to ensure convictions. "We were prepared to make arrests in about five or six different cities, conduct dozens of searches," Freeh said. "We had the warrants, everything was going to go down at once. We were confident that if we could get [Montella's] attention we could convince him to cooperate. On the other hand, if we didn't, the whole house of cards was going to come down."

On the evening of May 17, 1978, Freeh and Cassidy paid a visit to Red Hook. They found Montella in his office, sitting behind his desk. When they introduced themselves as FBI agents, Montella recognized Cassidy from a supposedly bona fide business dinner a few months before and exploded. "You have the nerve to break bread with me and then come here like this?" Montella barked. "Fuck you!"

As the agents explained the situation to Montella, he remained incredulous that his office had been bugged. "You'd never get past my dogs," Montella said.

But they had. The dogs, half-Doberman and half–German shepherd, were ferocious, but they hadn't been well trained. During their stakeout, Freeh and Cassidy regularly brought the dogs Big Macs. "We'd bring them about five or six Big Macs a night, and they'd start eating out of our hand. And pretty soon they'd see us and they'd lick us." Montella still doubted the agents' story, so Freeh insisted that Sonny bring in the dogs. "He brings the dogs in, and they start licking us, and then he goes, 'Oh shit!'"

Freeh and Cassidy closed the deal with Montella over dinner that night, and for the next two years they worked with him almost daily on the case. Thanks in large part to Montella's testimony, the government won convictions and lengthy jail terms for a host of top Mob associates, including the head of the Longshoremen's Union and Clemente, who got twenty years for his 103 counts of racketeering, extortion, and other crimes. Sonny Montella disappeared into hiding with his family under the federal Witness Protection Program, but his wife still calls Freeh occasionally to say how they're coping.

In 1980, after working for the FBI in New York for five years, Freeh received a commendation from FBI Director William Webster for his work in the waterfront investigation and was promoted and transferred to FBI headquarters' organized crime section. The move to Washington would alter Freeh's life in profound and unexpected ways.

Freeh would continue waterfront-related work while in Washington, helping Senator Sam Nunn of Georgia conduct hearings on the landmark case. Freeh liked the committee work, but quickly became disenchanted with the culture at headquarters. He had deplored the bureaucracy before he arrived. While working in New York, the fast-moving Freeh had been repeatedly stifled by delays in Washington. When his requests for wiretaps and warrants were not processed quickly, Freeh would exclaim, "I really *need* this shit!" Most of all, Freeh missed life in the field—the stakeouts, the debriefings of Mafia informants, the steam sessions with Clemente.

"I was restless," Freeh said of his new supervisory role. "It was a bureaucratic, nonoperational job, and I was very frustrated." He began looking for a new position outside his beloved FBI and landed a challenging new job at the U.S. Attorneys' Office in Manhattan. Freeh quit the FBI, but not before meeting Marilyn Coyle, a paralegal at headquarters, who was eight years younger. "I met Marilyn in this building, somewhere on the third floor between Organized Crime and Civil Rights. And we fell right in love," he said. "And then I left, and we carried on a long-distance romance."

Freeh was headed back to New York. That's where the action was, that's where the Mafia was, and that's where Louis wanted to be.

3

A G-MAN

When Bob Hanssen joined the Chicago police department in the early 1970s, he didn't go to work as a cop on the beat. Instead, he joined a special internal affairs unit, known as C5, which had as its mission ferreting out crooked cops on the force. While it was the sort of work that most police officers would eschew, Hanssen gravitated toward the unit without hesitation. It played to his strong interest in intelligence gathering and clandestine operations, and it immediately put him, as a rookie, in a position of far greater power and influence than he would have experienced as a junior police officer on patrol. He sensed he was brighter than other police officers, and far more educated; working in C5 would enable him to put some of his knowledge to use.

Bob joined the force without his father's long-coveted blessing, and with an assignment that sent the following message to Howard Hanssen: too many cops are crooks, and I'm going to do something about it. Joining C5 provided an outlet to release all the deep-seated feelings of resentment toward his father. It didn't bother Hanssen that many of the officers on the force hated the snitches that joined C5. Bob finally had what he'd longed for: the badge of a Chicago cop and a challenging job that interested him. He also had Bonnie's unfailing love, a counterbalance to the lack of support from his dad.

At the time C5 was created, many people in Chicago no longer trusted those who were charged with protecting them. In the aftermath of rioting during the 1968 Democratic National Convention, negative stories about the police department were regularly finding their way onto the front page of the *Chicago Tribune*. In the early 1970s, three separate criminal probes and public hearings about police brutality highlighted the widespread problems in the department. Bribery had become so commonplace and organized that traffic cops on Lakeshore Drive knew exactly how much they could expect from motorists they pulled over, and how much of their spoils were to be passed up the line. Faced with institutionalized corruption, Chicagoans no longer believed that the department's internal affairs unit could, or would, discipline its own. The C5 unit brought in a wave of new blood to police the police, and set up sting operations and anonymous tip lines in an attempt to flush out the "thieves in uniform." By detecting problems themselves and projecting an image of integrity, the hope was that public confidence in the force would be restored.

With his strong accounting background, Hanssen joined C5 as a financial investigator, not long after the unit was formed in 1972. The assignment was quite different from the cases his father had pursued during his career of hunting suspected communists. Like Bob, the handful of younger recruits who went straight into C5 tended to be willing to incur the wrath of fellow officers. Those who worked with Hanssen recalled his deep interest in politics and his unusual knowledge of the way various parts of the city's municipal machine operated.

Numerous police districts at that time had a "bag man," a plainclothes officer who went around the neighborhood accepting payoffs from bar owners and others who routinely broke the law. To keep things in check, the bag man typically passed the bribes up the ladder to his commanding officer and other cops who worked in the precinct. A favorite question for potential new recruits to C5 was, "Who's the bag man in your district?" When the question was posed to Hanssen, he stunned his superiors by offering more than he had been asked to deliver. "When Hanssen comes in, he not only knew

who the bag man in his district was, but he knew the bag men in sur-
rounding districts. I said, 'We ask for Fords, and we get a Mercedes,'"
Jack Clarke, a supervisor for the C5 squad, recalled. Hanssen's edu-
cational background, varied interests, and aloof manner made some
people suspect that he might have been planted in the unit. "He's an
accounting graduate. I thought he's either working for the police brass
or the FBI, so we kept him on a tight leash."

While the unit struggled to crack the "thin blue line"—the police force's unwritten code of honor that says you don't rat on your
fellow cop—Mitchell Ware, the architect of C5, remembers that its
mere existence had a deterrent effect on corruption. "We caught some
bad cops," Ware said, recalling the phony drug deals and makeshift
gambling parlors that were used to nail some officers. "A lot of cops
did not like it."

After he hired Bob Hanssen, Ware recalls a judge who happened
to be a neighbor of Hanssen's telling him he had made an "excellent"
choice. Hanssen found the stings and undercover operations deployed
by C5 engaging. He and others in C5 saw themselves as the white
knights, the honest police officers who wanted to rid the department
of crooked cops. Some who worked with Hanssen say he displayed a
sense of elitism as part of the special unit, but others don't recall him
making a strong impression.

New recruits like Hanssen who joined C5 straight out of the
police academy had the advantage of anonymity, which was particularly important when trying to nab narcotics officers who were dealing drugs themselves or taking payoffs and who "would smell another
cop a mile away," according to James W. Reilley, who served as a
prosecutor in Chicago until the mid-1970s. Reilley recalls that in recruiting for C5, the number one character trait being sought was "integrity."

"They were straight, honest guys," Reilley said of the officers
who served in C5. "We trusted them. There wasn't going to be corruption on top of corruption." In addition to exuding honesty, Bob
Hanssen stood out as an unusually bright recruit straight out of the

academy. But C5 cops had rough edges, and many of their attempted undercover operations seemed amateurish. "They strip-searched some officers out in the street and they ended up getting sued," said Richard Brzyczek, a former head of the Chicago police department. After several years in the unit, Hanssen's supervisors told him he had too much potential for the career track he was on and ought to apply to become an FBI agent. "Hanssen was very glib, asking a lot of questions and answering very few," Clarke said. "He came to me a couple of times for so-called information. I told him to write down the questions, and he never did. One day, after I got tired of him bouncing around, asking all these questions, I said, 'I have an assignment for you. Go to the FBI and fill out an application.'"

And that is exactly what Hanssen did. Though his initial application to the FBI was rejected due to poor eyesight, he was accepted on his second try. On January 12, 1976, Robert Philip Hanssen began sixteen weeks of intensive training at the FBI Academy in Quantico. As a new recruit, he pledged his loyalty, a quality valued within the Bureau above all else.

The FBI that Hanssen stepped into traced its roots back to the appointment of a small group of federal agents under President Theodore Roosevelt. The special investigative group, renamed the Bureau of Investigations as part of the Justice Department in 1909, came into existence at a time when there were few federal criminal statutes on the books to be enforced. But the dramatic growth of interstate commerce through transportation, national banking, and other major changes made it increasingly clear that there was an important role for law enforcement at the federal level.

As a student of the FBI and its history, Hanssen had a deep respect for J. Edgar Hoover, who served as head of the Bureau of Investigations and director of the FBI from 1924 until his death in 1972. Presidents and members of Congress came and went, but Hoover remained and was considered by many the most powerful man in Washington. Although numerous questions arose after Hoover's death about his heavy-handed tactics and investigative practices, Hanssen remained a fan. He especially admired the FBI's larger-than-life image that had become embedded in the nation's consciousness. After gangsters and crime dominated during Prohibition in the 1920s, Hoover's FBI achieved a series of major successes with cases in the 1930s, including gunning down the notorious bank robber John Dillinger, tracking the kidnapper of the Lindbergh baby, and gaining fame by arresting George "Machine Gun" Kelly. After being surrounded by a cadre of FBI agents, Kelly exclaimed, "G-men, don't shoot!" He later explained that "G-men" was slang for "government men"; Hoover loved it, the press picked up on it, and the name stuck. The G-man came to symbolize the bold, brave FBI agent in the dark suit, and Hoover himself appeared in newsreels and movies promoting the Bureau's image.

Hoover ran the Bureau with tight rules of conduct for agents, careful recruiting, and a clear message that he—and he alone—was to receive credit for important FBI accomplishments. In his dress as an FBI agent, Hanssen seemed a throwback to the Hoover era, when all FBI agents were expected to wear dark suits with white shirts, emulating the director. Hanssen admired Hoover's strong leadership and reputation for integrity, and dismissed the damaging revelations about the director that emerged after his death. These included monitoring leaders of the civil rights movement with secret wiretaps and the spread of misinformation about his political enemies. It also involved illegal intelligence-gathering techniques, such as unauthorized phone taps and mail intercepts against suspected communists and antiwar protesters, and maintaining files on prominent Americans as a means of blackmail.

Hanssen liked the way Hoover had created a fiercely independent culture for the FBI, even though the director ostensibly reported to the attorney general. He also relished the image of elitism projected by Hoover's FBI, and it was one of the things that attracted him to the Bureau even after the late director's death. "He loved Hoover," a Hanssen associate said of him. "He liked his autocratic way of dealing with things."

Under Hoover, photos of criminals on the FBI's "Ten Most Wanted Fugitives List" began appearing in post offices across the nation around 1950. In addition to warning people to beware and getting input to help track down criminals at large, the Ten Most Wanted List conveyed the message to millions of Americans that the FBI was on their side.

In the decades that followed, Hoover's FBI, comprised completely of male agents, proceeded to investigate as he saw fit, with relatively little oversight or checks on his authority. He made major advancements in the field of criminology—including training agents in using scientific techniques to examine evidence. But he also built the FBI's reputation for "Fidelity, Bravery and Integrity" in part by squelching publicity about corruption or rogue agents. And while the FBI focused on easier targets including bank robbers, it avoided going after organized crime aggressively, allowing it to flourish for decades without Hoover so much as acknowledging the Mafia's existence. Most troubling of all, it turned out that the immense power Hoover wielded generated mammoth investigative excesses that betrayed the trust placed in the Bureau by the American people.

When he died, Hoover's long-term achievements overshadowed the most egregious abuses that took place on his watch. He received an honor accorded very few Americans when his body was placed in the Rotunda of the Capitol to lay in state, with dignitaries coming to pay their last respects. The FBI's new, oddly shaped maze of a headquarters—directly across the street from the Justice Department and stationed in between the White House and the Capitol along Pennsylvania Avenue—was named for Hoover in 1974.

After his burial, however, anger over the FBI's abuses on his watch took hold in Washington and the nation. It would be up to future directors to restore the Bureau's gilt-edged reputation.

Bob Hanssen didn't see the need for anyone to be an apologist for the Bureau's aggressive efforts under Hoover to keep the nation safe from communist infiltration or other threats. From Hanssen's perspective, the FBI simply had been doing its job. He said the United

States needed new laws, like Britain's Official Secrets Act, banning publication of books and articles that contained too much sensitive intelligence information. And he challenged friends and associates who voiced liberal perspectives or disagreed sharply with White House policy, accusing them at times of being disloyal citizens. On national holidays, Bob Hanssen proudly flew an American flag at his home, a symbol of his staunch patriotism. With those close to him, he left no doubt about where he stood.

"He had a strong feeling that since Hoover left the Bureau, it was all downhill."

As he had in high school and college, Hanssen stood out among the budding agents at the FBI Academy as a classroom whiz. Fellow agents remember how the former Chicago cop handled the most difficult problems effortlessly, while the rest of the recruits struggled. Although he disliked manual labor and hadn't spent much time playing sports, Hanssen's proficiency as a marksman was heralded within the class. "He could shoot the hell out of a target, I'll tell you that," a recruit in his class remembered. "He was really good." But Hanssen did not measure up to the other agents in the physical tests. After failing the initial physical training test, he was put on "the weak squad," and throughout his time at Quantico, his athletic shortcomings risked keeping him from becoming a Special Agent. "He just wasn't an athlete. He wasn't a workout guy," one classmate said. "If I didn't kick his ass verbally, saying 'If you don't do it Bob, you're not going to make it,' then I don't think he would have made it."

Hanssen didn't get along well with his roommate, Bruce Harford, the son of a sheriff, who according to one recruit gave Hanssen a particularly hard time. Yet Bob refused to engage in a war of words, and apparently never spoke negatively about Harford. He was not so tight-lipped, however, about the brash, cocksure agents he met who favored a self-serving FBI culture. Instead of doing what was best for the Bureau, they appeared to be looking out for themselves. "Hanssen was not the guy who'd knock the door down, but he'd be there," one classmate said. "He didn't respect guys who were in the Bureau on a program of self-promotion. Most of the guys that end up going up the ladder in the Bureau are not so much serving their country as they are serving their own program."

A few weeks into new-agent training, the recruits were allowed off the Academy grounds for the weekend. Hanssen and a handful of others made the trip from Quantico to Washington, D.C., where he led his compatriots to one final stop on the sight-seeing tour—the Soviet Embassy on Sixteenth Street. Hanssen spoke of having a first-class radio license and equipment, noting that the Soviets, who were strategically located behind *The Washington Post* and only blocks from the White House, could pick up signals at will. "He tells us what kind of [communications] they can intercept because they're up on a hill," a friend on the trip recalled. "He knew all this stuff. The first time I ever heard of KGB Center was from him."

After sixteen physically grueling weeks, the Bureau formally opened its doors to Robert Philip Hanssen in the spring of 1976. Having successfully completed the necessary training, he was sworn in as a Special Agent in April, putting him closer to the prospect of living out his childhood fantasies and dreams. The FBI was the most elite law enforcement organization in the world. Hanssen liked the idea of being part of that, and relished the potential for getting involved in the handling and processing of secret information. When he was sworn in, Hanssen signed the oath of office:

> I do solemnly swear that I will support and defend the Constitution of the United States against all enemies, foreign and domestic; that I will bear true faith and allegiance to the same; that I take this obligation freely, without any mental reservation or purpose of evasion; and that I will well and faithfully discharge the duties of the office on which I am about to enter, so help me God.

He also signed the FBI's pledge for law enforcement officers and received his initial TOP SECRET security clearance, agreeing to uphold the sacred trust bestowed upon him and refrain from using confidential information for his own benefit:

> In the performance of my duties and assignments, I shall not engage in unlawful and unethical practices. . . . I shall wage vigorous warfare against the enemies of my country, of its laws, and of its principles.

> I shall always be loyal to my duty, my organization, and my country.

As a newly minted FBI agent, Hanssen received his initial assignment on the white-collar-crime squad in the Bureau's Indianapolis field office. But he soon asked for a transfer from Indianapolis to the satellite office in Gary, Indiana. The depressed industrial town was a Siberia of sorts for most agents, so the Bureau was happy to have someone volunteer for duty there. Bob and Bonnie, meanwhile, were content to move closer to family in Chicago. The Hanssens settled in the small town of Dunster and Bob began his career as a G-man. His mother Vivian recalls that her husband appeared pleased to see their son get out of the Chicago Police Department.

Hanssen also worked in the white-collar-crime unit in Gary, making at least one large case during his stint. Given his financial background, he was highly valued within the office, which did not often see agents of Hanssen's superior intelligence and credentials. His unit supervisor, according to one former agent, "thought Bob Hanssen walked on water." With his skills, Hanssen was not going to languish in a small midwestern office. He had not joined the FBI so he could spend his life chasing money launderers and tax cheats. He wanted a job with excitement, like the one his father had back in Chicago. As one friend said, "He wanted to work the Russians." Hanssen had an excessive fascination with the Soviets, who were masters in secrecy. It had been a key factor in his decision to join the FBI, and would lead him to seek an assignment in foreign counterintelligence.

Among those few he trusted, Hanssen spoke of his passion for secrecy. He told his wife, Bonnie, and a friend, about a movie, *Investigation of a Citizen Above Suspicion*, which he had fallen in love with in the early 1970s and which had won an Academy Award for Best Foreign Film. Hanssen's fascination with the movie revolved around the secrecy concerning a high-ranking official who committed a crime. "Because he was so high up in the government," Hanssen explained to a friend, "he deliberately left all these clues saying, 'I'm the guy who did this.' And every time people looked at him, they would say, 'No. It can't be. He is too high up in the government.'"

He was also captivated by the story of high-ranking British intelligence officer Kim Philby, who spied for the Soviets for years before fleeing to Moscow. "Philby, they just figured he couldn't be, or couldn't *possibly* be, what he turned out to be," Hanssen told another friend. Hanssen had encyclopedic knowledge of Philby's spying. He also seemed to know everything about the Rosenbergs, the American couple who had been executed in 1953 for selling atomic secrets to the Soviets.

In 1978, after two years in Indiana, the Bureau transferred Hanssen to the FBI field office in New York City, cradle of Soviet spies. According to former KGB major general Oleg Kalugin, there were roughly 220 spies working for the U.S.S.R. in the United States. Many of them were based in New York, where they worked under the diplomatic cover of the Soviet delegation to the United Nations.

Finally, Hanssen had found work that excited him, that gave him a sense of purpose. He figured out that the Soviet intelligence officers carried out many illegal acts on weekends when FBI agents didn't work. So he organized a group of his colleagues to work one Sunday and catch KGB agents in the act. "His task was to watch the Russians in the UN Mission and log in who comes and goes," a friend of Hanssen's said. "He figured they did all their illegal stuff on Sundays and said, 'We are going to set up this big net and we know the directions they go generally, and we will follow them and catch them in the act.'" But Hanssen was disappointed by his fellow agents, who were not the dedicated team of sleuths he had imagined they would be. "He set up this squad. And the Russians took off and well over half of the FBI guys called in from home. They didn't want to work on Sunday. . . . The Russians got away."

Hanssen's attitude changed from that experience. "He had some great disappointments with the Bureau," a colleague said. "He went in extremely idealistic and found out to his dismay that it is made up of fallible human beings who sometimes screw up and don't do things right. This is one of his triggers. I don't think he ever really accepted that."

The episode left Hanssen dejected and ready to give up on the FBI in its struggle with the Soviets. He knew what needed to be done but, as far as he was concerned, his fellow agents lacked his insight and drive. His instinct was to do things his own way and forget about the others. On a certain level, Hanssen's reaction was reminiscent of an incident during his residency training program in dental school when he avoided confrontation despite the high stakes. He was working in the hospital one day along with a physician when a patient having a heart attack was rushed into the emergency room. As the doctor prepared to give the patient a shot of adrenaline, Hanssen stopped him, saying the injection needed to be given directly into the heart to be effective. When the doctor said a shot directly into the heart was too radical, Hanssen coolly walked out rather than intervening more aggressively, and the patient died.

Bob felt he was being ostracized by inferior agents and began to resent the FBI, just as he had come to resent his father. That feeling intensified over time, even as Hanssen slowly rose through the ranks based on what he was convinced was his superior intellect. He helped establish an automated database of foreign intelligence officials based in the United States, a treasure trove that was classified SECRET. (In the classification system used by the U.S. intelligence community, information that would cause "serious" damage to national security if compromised is labeled SECRET, and information that would cause "exceptionally grave" damage is labeled TOP SECRET.) However, he developed virtually no real friendships at the FBI, where his increasingly dour personality and demeanor made him unappealing for others to be around. When the guys went out for a beer after work, they didn't bother inviting Bob Hanssen, certain he would not join them. Hanssen felt overlooked and unappreciated in an organization that, in his view, valued the macho, door-kicking lawman even as it increasingly relied on analytical minds like his to solve complex, technical cases.

Despite the FBI's shortcomings and his negative feelings, Bob Hanssen was where he wanted to be, on the front lines of his country's silent war. Yet already he was sowing the seeds of his own betrayal.

4

A CHARITABLE
CONTRIBUTION

Through the miscarriages, the fertility drugs, the births of three children, and the move away from their hometown of Chicago, Bonnie Hanssen had been a loyal, loving spouse and homemaker who kept a neat and clean house, baked delicious fresh bread and cinnamon rolls, and always had dinner on the table at 5:30 P.M. Bonnie thought of her marriage to Bob as a covenant blessed by the Holy Spirit. A medical condition had forced her to have one of her ovaries removed when she was a teenager, leaving her overjoyed each time she gave birth to a healthy child. Her faith and Bob's support helped her through multiple miscarriages along the way. She emulated her parents, who remained dedicated to each other and to the Church. But Bonnie had done more than inherit the religious convictions of her parents. She had embraced Catholicism and joyfully passed on her passion to Bob.

Bob made changes in his spiritual life that coincided with his move from municipal to federal law enforcement. It was a conversion that would profoundly affect his outlook and behavior. Four months after his completion of FBI training, with his fellow new agent Patrick Hogan serving as his godfather and with Bonnie's full support, Bob was baptized as a Catholic in Chicago.

Within a few years, Hanssen also joined Opus Dei, the lay Catholic organization that played a major role in Bonnie's life. In its purest form, the concept of Opus Dei is that Catholics need not join the clergy to find God or to live saintly lives. Rather, people can find their "individual call to holiness" and serve God at their desk, in their kitchen, and in the ordinary course of the day. Describing Opus Dei, Father Franklyn McAfee, pastor for both Hanssen and FBI Director Louis Freeh, said, "God is found in the pots and pans."

Bob's decision to join Opus Dei (Latin for "Work of God") was influenced not only by Bonnie, but also by Patrick Hogan at the FBI Academy. According to an agent in Hanssen's class, the two went to Mass every Sunday, and while they rarely talked about "churchy stuff," Hogan spoke with Hanssen and others about a book called *On the Theology of Work*, written by an Opus Dei cleric.

Hanssen appreciated Opus Dei's high standards. Just as he strove to be a stellar FBI agent, Hanssen had a sense of devotion to the Lord unmatched by the average Catholic. The same man who, as a high school senior, wrote under his yearbook photograph "Science is the light of life" now celebrated the light of God and His Word. As his career in the FBI progressed, Hanssen became known for his denunciations of immorality. "Bob would walk into my office and tell me that without religion, man is lost, and the Soviet Union would ultimately fail because it was run by godless Communists. And I believe he was sincere," said Hanssen's FBI colleague David Major. Other FBI coworkers sometimes bristled at Hanssen's self-righteous nature, evident in his condemnation of going-away parties at nearby strip clubs, events he termed "occasions of sin."

It was Bonnie's mother, Fran Wauck, who first had gotten the family involved in Opus Dei, which is often referred to as "the Work." She remains zealous, jokingly referring to herself as "the family's prayer." Bonnie had found that Opus Dei imbued her life with a depth of meaning, and like her mother she became a teacher of religion at an Opus Dei school.

"Opus Dei is the best thing that ever happened to the world," Fran Wauck said. "All of our children have been influenced by Opus Dei. Now they are better than they ever were. God did this, believe me. They send their kids to schools Opus Dei runs. People like the excellence in Opus Dei schools. Teachers get input to do things for the love of God and not just the monetary reward."

The Hanssens' six children have attended schools in the Washington area affiliated with Opus Dei—Oakcrest School for girls and The Heights School for boys. The latter is the same institution chosen by Louis Freeh and his wife Marilyn for their sons. The schools have an Opus Dei chaplain, daily Mass, and an Opus Dei priest who hears confessions. Most of the teachers are members of the movement.

Opus Dei requires its adherents to abide by a strict set of duties, including attendance at Mass daily, prayers at noon and in the afternoon, weekly confession, spiritual reflection, evenings of recollection, and a hefty dose of proselytizing. As Bob Hanssen adopted Opus Dei, he was drawn to that strict sense of order, as well as to the absolutist manner in which the movement viewed religious and secular issues in a world increasingly filled with moral relativism. Critics of Opus Dei argue that the rigidity of the organization runs counter to Catholic teachings and is harmful to those who follow its edicts. Some people close to the Hanssen family have wondered whether the rigorous movement was precisely the wrong influence for a compulsive personality like Bob's. They view Opus Dei as dangerous, cultlike, and highly secretive.

The mystique of Opus Dei is caught up in intra-Church politics and Vatican power plays, and in the end there exist two distinct perceptions of the movement—the "good" and the "bad" Opus Dei—a stark duality mirrored in the personality of Robert Hanssen himself.

Opus Dei, which has power in the Catholic Church despite its relatively small number of 80,000 adherents worldwide, was founded in Spain in 1928 by a young priest named Josemaria Escriva. According to Father McAfee, "Opus Dei is an approach to spiritual life for people who want to go deeper. How do I become holy and get more out of daily life? Opus Dei provides the answers."

Hanssen and other Opus Dei members are devout Catholics who hold a firm belief in the pope and his infallibility. For these men and women, there are no gray areas. The Bible has the answers, and the pope's interpretation is absolute.

For his followers, Escriva changed the centuries-old roles of the Catholic clergy and laity. Rather than being the gatekeepers to salvation or the interpreters between God and man, Opus Dei priests are seen as assistants to individual lay Catholics who are responsible for their own holiness. With this responsibility come strict guidelines for living, including performing every task as if it were an offering to God.

The stated mission of "the Work" sounds appealing and constructive, and provides consistency in life for many who answer the call to holiness. But some Catholic clergy and parishioners, academics, and psychologists say Opus Dei members end up feeling and acting as if they are superior to others, a feeling that is reinforced as they spend time together. Family members and friends say Hanssen displayed that sense of superiority.

"Opus Dei is elitist," McAfee said. "[Its followers] tend to be intellectual. Truck drivers can't be intellectual. You find Opus Dei members in the more prominent urban-suburban settings. In order to change the world, you get [important] people in different occupations." Freeh himself has had family connections to "the Work" through his brother, John, who according to Opus Dei leaders has been a member.

The Hanssens and numerous other Opus Dei members in the Washington area attend St. Catherine's, where Father McAfee and other parish priests celebrate a traditional Latin mass while standing before the altar with their backs to the congregation. Opus Dei, as a movement, took a strong stance against the Catholic Church's move away from such tradition. The schism has often caused tension between Opus Dei and non–Opus Dei Catholics. Many within the Church regard "the Work" as radical, while followers of the movement argue that the traditional liturgy has been perverted by liberal Church factions. Nonmembers are often characterized as "grocery-cart Catholics" who choose only those pieces of Catholic dogma that fit their needs while leaving the rest on the shelf.

While Opus Dei regards itself as a religious and not a political movement, others within the Church argue that the two are inextricably linked. The movement had initially been seen as controversial in part because it rose to prominence during the emergence of Francisco Franco's fascist regime in Spain just before World War II. Many have argued that the rise of Opus Dei was directly related to the group's close ties to the conservative Roman Catholic Franco and his government. "It is and always has been very right wing politically," said Richard McBrien, professor of theology at the University of Notre Dame. Most Opus Dei members are staunchly antiabortion, including cases of rape, incest, and risk to the life of the mother. Bonnie Hanssen sees abortion as "the evil in the world," friends and acquaintances have said, adding that she nearly came to blows with a neighbor once over the issue. In the name of saving lives, Bonnie has said it is okay to kill doctors who perform abortions and to bomb clinics, though she would leave such actions to others.

Numerous anti–Opus Dei organizations and groups have been created by self-described "survivors" of the movement, who have created Web sites and written books to explain how they were brainwashed into becoming Opus Dei members and had to be rescued. Most of these outspoken adversaries have come from the ranks of former "numeraries," celibate members of Opus Dei who agree to go wherever "the Work" takes them. Opus Dei is made up mostly of "supernumeraries" like Bonnie and Bob Hanssen, who are married with children.

Throughout its history, Opus Dei has maintained an organizational hierarchy that relies heavily on numeraries, lay Catholics who voluntarily turn over their entire lives to the movement. Their existence evokes an image of nonclerical monasticism—Opus Dei numeraries take vows of celibacy and poverty, and some live in special all-male or all-female housing. Opus Dei seeks to eliminate virtually all of their contact with the opposite sex outside a work environment. One former numerary says she was forbidden to spend time with a childhood friend to avoid even the appearance of an intimate relationship. Within the Catholic Church, which has its own hierarchy of priests, monks, and nuns, many look with suspicion on the numeraries, seeing them as part of Opus Dei's desire to place itself as "first among equals."

Sex, among both numeraries and supernumeraries, is a taboo subject, and discussion of homosexuality in any form is considered dangerous because it can poison the soul. Opus Dei itself is tight-lipped about the lives and roles of numeraries. One of the Hanssens' daughters, Sue, is a numerary who, as required by Opus Dei, sleeps on a wooden board every night and without a pillow once a week. (Women are treated more harshly than men in Opus Dei in order to quell their passions, officials say.) When Sue's sister, Jane, got married a number of years ago, Sue turned down her invitation to be a bridesmaid. Opus Dei would not allow Sue to take a man's arm and walk down the aisle in a wedding.

Yet while many second-guess Opus Dei and its practices, Pope John Paul II is a supporter. Members of Opus Dei occupy some of the most powerful positions in the Vatican, and in 1982 the pope conferred special status on Opus Dei and subsequently put its founder on the fast track to sainthood. Later, the pope proclaimed before 300,000 people in St. Peter's Square, including members of the Hanssen family, that Josemaria Escriva was an "exemplary priest who succeeded in opening up new apostolic horizons of missionary and evangelizing activity."

Many have argued, however, that the lofty principles of Opus Dei often become distorted when put into practice. Tammy DiNicola, a student at Boston College, became an Opus Dei numerary at the urging of a friend. Soon, her daily schedule had to be approved, she had to account for all of her purchases, turn over her earnings to Opus Dei, have all of her mail reviewed by the Opus Dei spiritual director, and get permission whenever she wanted to journey out of the house. As part of her daily regimen, she was instructed to whip her buttocks and wear a small, spiked chain around her thigh for two hours each morning to cleanse her spirits through pain and to remind her of the agony that Christ endured on the cross. During the spring of her junior year, Tammy wrote a letter to her family saying she would not be home for Easter because she had a "new family." The DiNicolas sought help from Opus Dei leaders, to no avail, and eventually retained mind-control experts to intervene after Tammy DiNicola's graduation from college. Within days, she began to reconnect with family members.

Bob Hanssen prompted complaints from some junior FBI officials after he tried to persuade them to join him at Opus Dei meetings. Jim Bamford, a former producer for ABC's *World News Tonight with Peter Jennings*, also remembered being aggressively recruited by Hanssen. As a journalist with a major television network, Bamford was an inviting target, a member of the media elite who could aid Opus Dei by influencing public opinion. Bamford had dealt with many FBI and CIA agents, but he had never experienced anything quite like this. No matter how many times Bamford turned him down, Hanssen refused to give up, until Bamford finally agreed to go to an Opus Dei meeting, just to get Hanssen to stop haranguing him. "I never had anybody try to save my soul before, especially not an FBI agent," Bamford said. "It was somewhat unusual. He really did have this missionary complex."

Bob and Bonnie had faced problems in their marriage ever since she received that call from one of Bob's ex-girlfriends and found out that her new husband was cheating on her. Still, Bonnie never gave up, preferring instead to treat Bob as a canvas on which she painted the portrait of a model husband. That was the image she clung to and projected to her family and community.

In private, she could not always maintain the facade. Anxious that Bob might be having an affair with his secretary at the FBI, Bonnie

would pepper her children—who had internships at the Bureau—
with questions about whether his assistant was pretty and whether
the two were flirtatious. Once, after teaching a class at Oakcrest School
in McLean, Virginia, about the importance of good communication
in marriage—leaving her students in awe of their instructor and the
married life she described—Bonnie privately broke down and cried.
Later, she told one of her sisters that her relationship with Bob lacked
the very honesty and dialogue that she espoused. Despite it all, she
never dreamed of abandoning the union that God had blessed.

But nothing in her experience could have prepared Bonnie for
what she encountered in the basement of their Scarsdale home one
day in 1980. Bonnie walked in on Bob, who awkwardly covered something up. Based on her earlier experiences, Bonnie immediately suspected that Bob was having an affair and that he was trying to hide a
love letter to another woman. She was wrong.

Working for the FBI in counterintelligence, Bob had made
contact with the Russian military intelligence agency, *Glavnoye
Razvedyvatelnoye Upravlenie* (GRU) and sold them information in exchange for about $20,000. He told Bonnie that he had tricked the
Soviets, selling data that was of no value in exchange for thousands
of dollars in cash. In fact, Hanssen compromised valuable U.S. intelligence, including the identity of Dmitri Polyakov, a Soviet general
code-named TOPHAT who worked as a valued double agent for
more than two decades before the Russians executed him.

Bonnie Hanssen was shocked and confused as she listened to
Bob explain what he had done. Was her husband spying for the Soviet Union? Was he lying to her? No, he promised. He was being truth-
ful, and, in any event, he would break off his contacts with the Soviets.

They both knew that one option was for Bob to reveal what he
had done to his superiors—but the mere thought of confessing to the
FBI brass was frightening to both Bonnie and Bob, who feared that
any perceived breach would end his Bureau career and wreak havoc
on their family life. If there was one thing Bob Hanssen didn't need—
after his failure to go to medical school, dropping out of dental school,

and quitting accounting—it was another setback. He could just imagine what his father, who thought very little of him anyway, would have to say. For her part, Bonnie believed she had married a good man. The consequences that would flow from Bob turning himself in seemed out of proportion to this momentary lapse, especially if all he had done was use bad judgment. Bob vowed never to do anything like it again, and Bonnie believed him. Yet as a woman of faith, Bonnie knew that Bob could not absolve himself of his actions; true forgiveness came from God alone. She insisted that her husband speak with a priest, confess his sins, and seek confidential guidance about his misdeeds. They would put their future in the Lord's hands. Whatever the priest told them to do, they would abide.

Father Robert P. Bucciarelli had heard many stories of marital woe, but nothing like this one. Bucciarelli, an Opus Dei priest, listened intently as Bob repeated the story he had told Bonnie. The father said he would think about the matter before anyone took irreversible steps. After meeting with the priest, Bonnie prayed for her husband and their family, including the baby she was carrying. She knew it was impossible to turn back the clock, but she found solace in prayer. Her faith left her convinced that God listened to those who called upon Him with reverence and contrition. She could only hope for a miracle, something to pull her husband and her family out of this mess.

At the same time, Bob's head was spinning. He thought he knew how to handle Bonnie. According to a friend of Bob's, "He has a little theory that every day you have to tell a woman a certain amount of positive things, and if you do, things will always be good. He called it his 'counter theory.' He said in a woman's brain there is a counter and they count up the good things you say to them and the positive strokes you give them." As far as his work was concerned, Bob didn't want Bonnie to know anything. He had to do a better job of concealing things. And to make matters worse, now a priest was involved.

True to his word, the priest pondered how he could balance his duties to God and the Church without destroying a young family of faith. His initial impulse—that Bob turn himself in to authorities for taking money from the Soviets—would cause pain and humiliation, and harm their innocent children. And both Bonnie and Bob seemed so sincere. This wasn't just a matter of right and wrong; it was how to right the wrong. There must be another way, a better way, to impart a lesson and handle all of this without destroying their family in the process. Father Bucciarelli considered having Bob return the money to the Soviets, but ultimately blessed the following plan: Hanssen would confess his sin, pray for forgiveness, cut off all improper contacts with the Soviets, and donate the money to good works.

Bob told Bonnie he would give away the cash as inconspicuously and anonymously as possible to the charities of Mother Teresa, the righteous nun who lived in India and cared for its poor. Bonnie was relieved. She trusted Bob when he told her he would never do anything like that again, and she tried to put the whole episode out of her mind. It seemed so out of character, and after all, everyone makes mistakes sometimes—that had been the case ever since the Garden of Eden, when Adam and Eve ate of the forbidden fruit, defying God's word. Human beings, far from being perfect, were frail and susceptible to temptation. People sometimes did horrible things. At least in this instance, it appeared to Bonnie that nobody had been harmed. And Bob believed that perhaps the money actually would do some good. "He often said, 'The bad guys, the forces of evil, have lots of money and the forces of good are underfunded,'" according to a friend. Whether that meant feeding the hungry, clothing the naked, providing shelter for the homeless, or taking care of his family, the cash certainly would benefit the world more than if it had remained in the hands of the Communists.

When Bonnie's father the psychologist heard about the situation many years later, however, he said that by merely encouraging prayer and donation of the money to charity, the priest had done his daughter, son-in-law, and the entire family, for that matter, a grave disservice. Though he didn't profess to understand exactly what factors or forces motivated his son-in-law to contact the GRU in the first place, he knew what ought to have been done: send Bob to a psychiatrist or a psychologist to figure out why he sold information to the Soviets and what could be done to prevent this from happening again.

"Clinically, you go back to developmental history and look for things that happened as they were growing up and say, 'Aha! There it is,'" said Bonnie's father, Leroy Wauck. "If Bob was ever told to just pray and pray and pray, that is ridiculous," said Fran Wauck, Bonnie's mother. "Psychologists and psychiatrists were needed."

But instead of talking with a psychologist or psychiatrist, Bob did what came naturally and kept his spying for the GRU a secret. He apologized to Bonnie profusely, telling her she was too good for him, that he was not worthy of being married to such a fine woman and that he would have no further clandestine contacts with the Soviets. Although he didn't say a word about his actions to anyone else, Bob also began telling the very small number of friends he had that he was not deserving of their camaraderie. Reverting back to his childhood days, when he used to retreat to the solitude of his bedroom after his father had left him feeling worthless, Bob turned inward, becoming even quieter and more insular.

By the summer of 1980 the FBI, which knew nothing of Hanssen's espionage for the Soviets, expanded his access to confidential data. But first, he had to read and sign a special nondisclosure agreement covering SENSITIVE COMPARTMENTED INFORMATION, or SCI, a classification level requiring specific additional security clearances:

> I have been advised that direct or indirect unauthorized disclosure, unauthorized retention, or negligent handling of the designated Sensitive Compartmented Information by me could cause irreparable injury to the United States, and be used to advantage by a foreign nation. . . . I pledge that I will never divulge such information, in any form or any manner.
>
> I have been advised that any such unauthorized disclosure by me may constitute violations of United States civil or criminal laws.
>
> I make this agreement without any mental reservation or purpose of evasion.

5

THE PIZZA
CONNECTION

Just as the FBI holds special status in the world of crime fighting, the U.S. Attorneys' Office in the Southern District of New York has prestige in the legal realm. Some of the nation's biggest cases play out in the Southern District's lower Manhattan home, tried by some of the nation's brightest legal minds. The Southern District has long prided itself on its ability to attract so many high-caliber lawyers; attorneys from top-tier law schools typically come to the Southern District long enough to enhance their résumés before heading to a higher-paying job with a private law firm. The prodigious legal talent in the Southern District has enabled the government to win complex, high-profile cases with regularity, and those successes have in turn kept Justice Department brass from cracking down on the staunchly independent office, jokingly referred to as the "Sovereign District."

It was into this heady atmosphere that Louis Freeh thrust himself in 1981 when he returned to New York after his disappointing experience at FBI Headquarters. The thirty-one-year-old Freeh wanted a stimulating new job, and the Southern District provided that opportunity. But the attorneys in the Southern District, many of whom came from privileged backgrounds, did not know what to make of the Rutgers University night school–trained lawyer and FBI agent from Jersey City. Tough young agents from blue-collar families were a common sight at the FBI, but not so at the U.S. Attorneys' Office;

veteran attorney Richard Martin noticed quickly that Freeh "didn't fit the mold." A colleague who knew Freeh told the other attorneys to forget their preconceptions and set aside any prejudices about FBI agents. This Louis Freeh, he said, is a solid guy.

The Southern District in the 1980s was the perfect place for Freeh. The death of J. Edgar Hoover also meant the death of his long-held assertion that there was no such thing as "the Mafia," and after a decade of Mob investigations, the ability of the American law enforcement community to conduct complex investigations against organized crime had advanced by leaps and bounds. La Cosa Nostra was ripe for a major crackdown, but to succeed in breaking the Mafia's self-protective hierarchy, investigators needed freedom to change the rules of engagement for organized crime investigations. The Southern District, where five major Mafia crime families operated, was an ideal proving ground for a new, ambitious model of international crime fighting: the systematic formation of cases against not only Mafia soldiers but also their bosses. The new investigative strategy involved cross-border relationships with police and prosecutors in Italy and elsewhere. Working for years in the FBI's New York office, Freeh had thrived as he employed new and unconventional investigative methods. At the U.S. Attorneys' Office, he would have the liberty to be innovative once again, but now he would be running the prosecution and making use of his intimate knowledge of racketeering statutes to go after the Mob.

Shortly after his swearing-in, Freeh joined Martin, then the deputy chief of the Southern District's Narcotics Division, on a drug case. It didn't take long for the former G-man, who spoke of "lawr enforcement" in a thick North Jersey accent, to impress his new colleagues with a tireless work ethic. "I thought I worked as hard as anyone in the office," Martin said. "Then I started working with Louis, and I realized I was a piker." Freeh worked with Martin and other attorneys, first on drugs, then on Mafia cases, and finally on a landmark case involving drugs *and* the Mafia, as he rose to become a star prosecutor in New York. In an office full of prominent attorneys

headed by the ambitious mayor-to-be Rudolph W. Giuliani, Freeh
was a standout.

In his first major case, Freeh led the effort to drive the Mafia
out of the Fulton Fish Market, a New York institution that had been
dominated by organized crime for generations. The probe headed
by Freeh finally broke the Mob's stranglehold on the market. The
investigative team proved that each truck entering or exiting the
market was forced to pay a "tribute to organized crime"—a duty of
anywhere from $5 to $60 per week—and also showed that the theft
of fish from the trucks was rampant. By October 1982, the investigation had produced more than thirty convictions and guilty pleas from
members of the Mafia and fish wholesalers on charges ranging from
extortion and fraud to theft and labor payoffs.

As he completed his work on the Fulton Fish Market case, Freeh
and a colleague also took on six members of the Bonanno crime family in the climax to a long-running investigation that involved undercover penetration of the New York Mafia. The case, which began
in 1976 when Freeh was only one year into his stint at the FBI's New
York office, involved a fellow G-man from New York, Special Agent
Joseph Pistone, who successfully infiltrated the Bonanno family under the alias "Donnie Brasco." Five years later, Pistone emerged from
his grueling undercover assignment armed with a plethora of damning evidence against the Bonanno clan, and Freeh set about building
criminal cases against the defendants on charges of conspiracy, attempted murder, gambling, hijacking, and drug trafficking. Pistone
had gone deeper into the Mafia than any federal agent—so deep that,
just before the FBI pulled him out of the operation, he had been given
the contract to kill the son of a rival mobster and was being considered for membership in the family.

The arrest of the six Bonanno soldiers and Pistone's penetration stunned the Brooklyn family. According to the rules of La Cosa
Nostra, those who had vouched for Pistone were responsible for his
infiltration. Benjamin "Lefty" Ruggiero, the Bonanno family member who served as Pistone's mentor, reportedly tried to have him

assassinated. Ruggiero had good reason to fear for his own life: "Sonny Black" Napolitano, another of Pistone's contacts, was murdered soon after he posted bail. Given the danger, Freeh petitioned the court, unsuccessfully, to allow Pistone to testify under his FBI alias.

The trial proceeded without further interruptions, and all six men were convicted. Because of Special Agent Pistone's undercover work, Freeh and his law enforcement colleagues gained not only invaluable information about the structure of a Mafia crime family, but also additional confidence that the federal government could execute a drawn-out investigation—they could "let the money walk" with the knowledge that it would lead to more and better convictions. The idea of a slow, methodical investigation that would crescendo with indictments of top-level mobsters was pioneered by the FBI in the 1970s and reinforced by the success of the Bonanno case.

During the Bonanno prosecutions, an FBI agent working on a separate Mafia narcotics investigation brought a set of Bureau wiretap recordings to attorney Richard Martin at the Southern District. When Martin heard what was being said on the tapes, he realized the government had landed on something big. The mobsters implicated on the tapes were top drug traffickers that the Bureau hadn't been able to reach. Here was a chance to bring actual heads of Mafia families in front of a jury. Martin, a seasoned trial attorney, was chosen to lead the prosecution in the courtroom, while Freeh took on the role of lead investigator.

The FBI had been probing members of the five New York Mafia families for some time, and had focused on the Catalano family as part of a large narcotics organization within the United States. In late 1982, Freeh was holed up with FBI agents in a Sheraton hotel in the New York suburb of New Rochelle, working to obtain wiretaps to monitor both the Catalano and the Bonanno crime families. The team had a staggering amount of evidence culled from three years of physical, visual, and electronic surveillance, all of which they laid out in an affidavit. Every application submitted for court-approved surveillance was required to pose a question. In this case, the question dealt with $3.9 million in cash delivered by a reputed mob soldier to Merrill Lynch's Wall Street offices, along with millions more taken to the E.F. Hutton brokerage. The feds knew it was drug money, but the unanswered question was, "Where were the drugs?"

Faced with a mountain of evidence and the threat of extensive organized crime activities, a U.S. District Court judge granted Freeh and the FBI permission to eavesdrop on conversations between members of the Catalano and Bonanno crime families. Beginning in March 1983 and continuing over the course of the next thirteen months, the government listened in on over 100,000 telephone conversations. It was the largest single eavesdropping operation in FBI history. Soon after the eavesdropping commenced, however, Freeh and his fellow prosecutors realized that there was something different about the Mafia organization they were investigating. Conversations picked up by the wiretaps were being conducted in old Sicilian dialects, and many of the people who seemed to be making important decisions were Sicilians themselves, men about whom they knew little.

Freeh went with FBI agent Tom Sheer to report the findings to Rudy Giuliani, who, prior to heading the Southern District, had served as associate attorney general in the Reagan administration. Freeh and Giuliani had visions of a giant international prosecution run from the Southern District; Giuliani would haggle with his contacts in Washington to make sure that the case of a lifetime was not taken apart piece by piece by other ambitious prosecutors. "Rudy was important because he knew how to do these things and had a lot of support and contacts in Washington," Martin said. "When we got into a road block that Louis and I couldn't handle on our own, Rudy would handle it."

Giuliani protected the long-term investigation, but several times Freeh had to pull back overzealous investigators from the brink of a bust, reminding them that any arrest would jeopardize the overall conspiracy probe. That, in the end, was the jewel for Freeh. He wanted to expose the entire conspiracy, wherever it led, from beginning to end. At one point during the investigation, Lew Schiliro, one of

Freeh's FBI classmates from new-agent training at Quantico, heard about a transaction between two of the mobsters under investigation, and was preparing to stop and search one of them to find out what was being passed. As Schiliro said, "Sometimes the only way to find out what's in a bag is to grab it." But Freeh was of a different mind-set and explicitly forbade any action beyond tailing the suspects.

Schiliro grudgingly followed his orders during that transaction, but he still yearned to make a drug bust that would propel the investigation into the next phase. Three weeks later, Schiliro found himself with another opportunity to make an arrest. On August 30, 1983, dozens of FBI agents staked out the Long Island home of Salvatore Mazzurco and saw him take several boxes out of his car just as a man in a gray Chevrolet pulled up. The driver left nearly as quickly as he came, but with a brown paper bag in hand. Sniffing a drug transaction, Schiliro ordered the car stopped. Once the Chevy was safely away from Mazzurco's neighborhood, agents arrested the driver and searched the automobile. The bounty was more than Schiliro expected: $40,000 in cash in the bag and, in the driver's pocket, more than a half-gram of pure light brown heroin.

Schiliro was ready to receive plaudits for exposing such powerful evidence of illegal activity, but when he heard the news Freeh flew into a rage. "Are you guys nuts?" Freeh exclaimed. He chewed out Schiliro for placing the investigation in the open; his former classmate had never seen Freeh so angry. Freeh knew that the contents of any bag or the meaning of any transaction were both pieces of the puzzle that could be ascertained later. The greatest advantage the government had, Freeh believed, was its ability to remain inconspicuous. His theory clashed with the FBI's modus operandi, which centered around "making the bust." When the opportunity arose to throw the book at drug-dealing mobsters, it was difficult for the G-men to resist. Freeh had to reinforce again and again the goal of building a complete conspiracy case. He understood it was like playing high-stakes poker; each time the FBI agents wanted to call and show, Freeh was there to pull back and raise the pot.

With each passing month, wiretaps and other surveillance were bringing in further evidence of a global crime syndicate smuggling drugs into the United States. They learned how the Sicilian Mafia bought tens of millions of dollars of morphine base in Turkey, converted it into heroin in Sicily, and smuggled it into the United States along with cocaine from Latin America. They discovered how the Catalano family of Brooklyn transported the drugs up and down the East Coast and across the country, selling the narcotics out of pizzerias in New York, New Jersey, Illinois, and other states. They learned how the traffickers laundered and transported money out of the country—sometimes physically carrying suitcases full of cash to offshore islands, other times bringing the cash to brokerage houses or depositing it into Swiss bank accounts. They estimated that in the late 1970s and 1980s, the Sicilian Mafia had imported 1,650 pounds of heroin with a street value of $1.7 billion. And they found that at the center of the worldwide operation stood Gaetano Badalamenti.

The United States had never prosecuted a man like Badalamenti. As a boss of the Sicilian mob, Badalamenti was one of the most powerful Mafiosi in the world, and one of its leading drug traffickers. Freeh and Martin understood the global reach of the case and recognized that the prosecution would stall if they restricted it to U.S. borders. So they turned to Giovanni Falcone, a courageous anti-Mafia magistrate in Sicily who was putting together his own case against the entrenched Cosa Nostra across the Atlantic. By working with men such as Falcone, and building a strong law enforcement bond across international boundaries, Freeh and Martin concluded they could take down a substantial part of the Mafia in Italy and the United States.

Prosecutors on both sides of the Atlantic worked day and night to make their case. Soon, law enforcement officials in other countries such as Spain and Switzerland offered their assistance. Long nights gave way to an easy kinship among the prosecutors, who substituted one another for the families they rarely saw. The prosecutors particularly enjoyed Freeh's quick wit, which remained shrouded in public. "We worked like dogs for years, but it was really fun," Martin said. "We had a good time. [Freeh has] got a great sense of humor. That's not something you see at all in the public arena, but working at two A.M. you can have some fun." And Falcone, who was the target of constant Mafia death threats in Sicily, enjoyed his visits to New York, where his relative anonymity enabled him to move about freely. Back in Italy, he rarely ventured outside his home and office. For fifteen years, Falcone and his wife lived in a house with virtually no natural light—sandbag barriers were erected around all the windows—and the couple remained childless, fearing Mafia reprisals directed at their young. So when Falcone announced he was going for a walk in Central Park one particularly dark night, he had to laugh when his American colleagues warned him of the potential danger. "It's not the kind of danger that alarms me," Falcone said.

The break in the case came when Tommaso Buscetta, a longtime Sicilian Mafiosi who had been a prisoner in Brazil since October 1983, agreed to talk to Judge Falcone, making him the highest-ranking Mafia informant ever. After watching two sons and several other family members die at the hands of the Mafia, Buscetta decided to cooperate. In beginning his confession, Buscetta said, "I intend to reveal everything that I had knowledge of regarding that thing which is the Mafia, so that the new generations can live in a more dignified and more humane manner."

Whether Buscetta told all, especially about his involvement with Badalamenti and the drug trade, remains a matter of debate, but his testimony was unquestionably a major coup for U.S. and Italian prosecutors. Buscetta's testimony gave investigators rock-solid evidence of the existence of a global La Cosa Nostra and its involvement in the drug trade. "He explained what we needed to explain—that the business worked because of the rules of the Mafia," Martin said. "And he could show who was a member of what group."

In November 1984, Freeh, Martin, and the rest of the American and Italian authorities were ready to go after Gaetano Badalamenti. The previous April, thirty-six defendants had been arraigned on charges relating to what was known in the United States as "The Pizza Connection." Now, after almost two and a half years of exhaustive work on two continents, Badalamenti was arrested. But Freeh and Martin still worried about how to safely extradite the dangerous criminal to the United States to face trial. Badalamenti wielded considerable power and could engineer a daring escape plot, so Martin decided to fly to Europe to oversee the extradition personally. The prosecutors made sure that no one, not even the Air Force pilots, knew who or what would be flying back with them. Badalamenti was transported on a C-141 military cargo plane with only mesh webbing for seats; because of the heightened secrecy, no special provisions were made. After seeing a picture of Badalamenti in *Stars and Stripes*, the Army newspaper, one of the pilots asked an accompanying guard, "Is—is . . . that him?"

Gaetano Badalamenti was a shell of himself on November 16, 1984, the day of his arraignment in federal court in New York. Rising through the ranks of the Sicilian mob, he had relied on his power to control the will of men through the threat of deadly force. Now, however, Badalamenti could only stand silently as the charges against him were read in the courtroom. Wearing a red sweater, an open-collar shirt, and gray slacks, he bore little resemblance to the larger-than-life Mafia bosses portrayed by Hollywood. Still, the prosecuting attorneys were aware of the enormous influence wielded by the diminutive sixty-one-year-old Sicilian, and the significance of his being brought to trial. After the arraignment, U.S. Attorney Rudy Giuliani said, "I'm not sure that we ever had a drug dealer of the dimension of Badalamenti—ever."

The Pizza Connection trial began on September 30, 1985, and from the beginning it was clear that Freeh's patient investigative strategy had paid off for the prosecution. Mountains of evidence in the form of witness testimony, wiretapped conversations, and surveillance photos passed before the jury. In the courtroom, Freeh and Martin thoroughly detailed the story of the Sicilian drug trade, from morphine base in Turkey to heroin in pizza parlors across America to money in Switzerland. Defense attorneys did not bother to challenge Tommaso Buscetta's testimony as to the structure of the Mafia or the rules by which the Mafia did business. "Once he got off the stand, everyone knew there was a Mafia," Martin said. Other witnesses offered credible testimony about the working relationship between the Sicilian Mafia and the Catalano family of Brooklyn, who acted as the domestic distributors of Sicilian heroin. Judge Pierre Leval allowed Freeh to bring in actors to read the dialogue of defendants in wiretapped telephone conversations. It was a brilliant prosecutorial move. The actors, dubbed "The Pizza Players," were accused of being prejudicial by defense attorneys, especially when some of them attempted to take on *Godfather*-like accents. But their presence and the evidence they put before the jury was extremely effective.

By the time the prosecution rested its case, the defense had been battered and individual defendants were beginning to turn against one another. All the while, the court was abuzz with whispers that Gaetano Badalamenti would testify in his own defense. Not even Freeh and Martin were sure what the little man would do. For a mob boss, especially one of Badalamenti's rank, to subject himself to cross-examination would be extraordinary. Nevertheless, Badalamenti took the witness stand in October 1986. Dressed in a dark suit and a red tie, the spindly Sicilian, with deep-set eyes and a weary expression, settled into the witness box.

"Have you ever become a member of Cosa Nostra?" asked Louis Freeh in his cross-examination, after hearing the witness's almost comical evasiveness under direct questioning from his own lawyer.

"I have never said it. And if I were, I would not say it."

"Do you deny that you are a member of Cosa Nostra?"

"I have already said what I said."

Freeh repeated the question. "Do you deny that you are a member of Cosa Nostra?"

"I have never said it. I have told you. And if I were, I would not tell you."

"Why wouldn't you tell me?"

"I would not tell you," Badalamenti concluded, "because I would respect the oath taken by those gentlemen."

The dance continued for days. In contrast to Martin's hard-charging style, Freeh quietly and methodically laid out the evidence against Badalamenti and then dared him to deny the charges or create an alibi. Astonishingly, Badalamenti did neither. When questioned about Mafia code words for drugs or cash payoffs, he refused to offer an explanation, saying only that the words signified "something that was not drugs." At one point during cross-examination, Badalamenti became incensed at a line of questioning and began a long tirade. Freeh turned away from the witness, sat down in his chair, put his feet up on the prosecutor's table, and waited for Badalamenti to run out of words. When he finally did, Freeh let the silence of the courtroom sink in, then returned to his feet and asked, "Are you finished?"

"It was like taking [Badalamenti's] clothes off in front of the jury," Martin said. Freeh had cut through the bombast and revealed the criminal beneath. No longer was he a man to be feared; instead he had been mocked by a prosecuting attorney in a court of law. Louis Freeh had stripped away Badalamenti's power and taken it as his own.

Badalamenti's poor showing on the stand intensified fears among defendants, and their tension exploded into an all-out Mob war. The body of one of the defendants was found wrapped in a garbage bag in Brooklyn's warehouse district. His assassins had carved an *X* into his scalp and had tried to pull out his tongue with pliers. Another barely survived a hit in Greenwich Village. Defense attorneys, meanwhile, had no alibis to rely on and were faced with a mountain of evidence gathered by the FBI and U.S. attorneys under Freeh. In the end, their only defense was to highlight the sheer enormity and complexity of the evidence and ask jury members whether they could truly understand the case well enough to convict beyond a reasonable doubt. Freeh shrugged off the notion in his closing statement, insisting to the jury, "You have the ability to organize and understand the evidence. . . . The length of this case and all of the evidence will not and should not intimidate you."

The jury was overwhelmed by neither the evidence nor the men who sat before them. On March 2, 1987, after deliberating for only six days after a seventeen-month trial, the jury convicted eighteen of the nineteen Pizza Connection defendants. The Mafia ringleaders in the case, Toto Catalano and Gaetano Badalamenti, were each sentenced to forty-five years in prison. Meanwhile, in Sicily, a massive trial conducted by Freeh's partner Giovanni Falcone was under way. The landmark court case—dubbed the Maxi Trial—would ultimately set the worldwide standard for Mafia prosecutions, convicting hundreds of members from the lowest to the highest ranks of the Sicilian Cosa Nostra.

After the Pizza Connection verdicts were returned, Louis Freeh, Richard Martin, and the rest of the Pizza Connection prosecution team stood beaming as Southern District chief Rudy Giuliani answered questions from the press in his law library. They had taken down a large-scale Mafia operation, and everyone wanted to hear how the legal eagles from the Southern District had closed the massive case. Each time, Freeh repeated the central ideas on which the Pizza Connection and Maxi Trial successes were built —ideas that became his mantra. International partnerships. Cop to cop. Prosecutor to prosecutor. Global crime fighting for global crime.

Five years later and half a world away from the criminal courts of southern Manhattan, the Mafia took its revenge.

Perched on a hillside above a divided highway, just outside the Sicilian capital of Palermo, a group of men waited patiently for a signal. Their mission was nearly complete, with only a single effortless task remaining. They stood around idly, smoking cigarettes to pass the time, and ignoring, with the dispassion of cold-blooded killers, the enormity of what they were about to do. The sound of a ringing cell phone alerted them that the time had come.

On the other end of the line was a spotter, one of several staked out along the highway below. The spotters had been tracking a small motorcade, made up of three armor-plated vehicles racing along the seaside highway, with lights flashing and sirens wailing. The motorcade was coming into view.

Throw the switch, the spotter said. The target is in range.

Seconds later, a massive explosion tore through the armored cars and the vehicle leading the motorcade was hurled hundreds of feet into a grove of olive trees. The bomb, set in a drainage tunnel under the road, was detonated by one of the men on the hill. The blast left a 1,500-foot-long crater in the roadbed. Giovanni Falcone, his wife, and three bodyguards were blown to pieces.

In New York, Freeh was shocked and saddened by the news that his brave crime-fighting partner had fallen victim to the Mob. After they met in 1981 the two had become fast friends. For Freeh, who began his FBI career as a Special Agent on the streets of New York in 1975, it was akin to losing a partner. He vowed to honor Falcone's memory by finding a way to carry on the global fight they had waged against organized crime.

All across Italy, the murder of Judge Falcone reminded people of the Mafia's terrible power to destroy lives and kill dreams. At Falcone's funeral, three days after his death, thousands of Sicilians turned out in the rain to honor their fallen hero and publicly express their outrage over the assassination. During the funeral, people walked right up to senior government ministers and threatened them. "Why couldn't you protect this wonderful man?" one asked. The emotionally charged atmosphere reflected their reverence for Falcone and their desire to regain some measure of control over their homeland.

The Sicilian Mafia wielded pervasive influence, ruling by a culture of fear that permeated the lives of average citizens. There were persistent suspicions, too, about the Mafia's control of politicians, leading people to feel betrayed on all fronts. High-ranking Sicilian officials at the funeral were whisked away from the church amid heavy security, out of fear for their safety in the event of riots. "It did stir up a much greater reaction than I think the Mafia anticipated," Richard Martin said. "They had killed police officers and magistrates before . . . but Falcone had achieved such a reputation and he was seen as an honest guy. And through Falcone's work people thought that for the first time there was the possibility of defeating [the Mob], bringing it out into public and defeating it."

Eventually, eighteen people were charged in the conspiracy to murder Falcone, but it would take five years for Italian authorities to make an arrest in the case. DNA from a discarded cigarette butt found on the hillside overlooking the highway became a key piece of evidence linking one of the suspects to the bombing. Italian investigators made the DNA match thanks to forensic techniques shared by the FBI.

Freeh traveled to Sicily before any arrests had been made in the case, and in the Palatine Chapel in Palermo, amidst images of saints and martyrs, he eulogized his comrade and fiercely denounced La Cosa Nostra.

"Judge Falcone was truly a friend for all seasons, and I will always miss him," Freeh said. "But I have not come to Palermo only to mourn the death of heroes. I am here to praise you for the extraordinary work which you have been doing to eliminate forever the Mafia and its evil allies."

Raising his voice, the square-jawed Freeh continued: "To those men who are sworn falsely to the Mafia…you are not men of honor but cowardly assassins of children, thieves who move in the night, and greedy merchants of drugs, terrorists and bullies. We do not fear you anymore. We do not respect you. We challenge you and will hunt you down to bring you to justice."

Despite his comrade's brutal murder, Freeh exuded confidence and optimism as he spoke of continued Italian-American cooperation battling the Mob. "We will root you out," he said, "from under every rock, from the dark places where you hide."

Yet while Freeh spoke of "rooting out" the Mafia and forming international partnerships, a mole was rummaging about in the highest levels of the Central Intelligence Agency, peddling secrets to the Russians. One of the deadliest terrorist acts in American history would turn out to be home grown. And, eventually, Freeh would discover that a dangerous double agent was on the loose inside FBI headquarters in Washington.

6

BETRAYAL

The birth of a healthy baby girl, Lisa Hanssen, on October 11, 1985, was a moment of supreme joy for Bob. It brought enormous relief, given Bonnie's history of miscarriages, a painful delivery, and their desire for a sixth child. Bob was thrilled to share the good news about the birth of a new baby sister with his children, Jane, Sue, Jack, Mark, and Greg, after returning from the hospital to their home in Vienna, Virginia. They had enjoyed living in the northern Virginia suburbs for four years, since his reassignment to FBI headquarters in Washington. Both Bonnie and Bob liked the relative calm that went along with living at the apex of a cul-de-sac in their two-story brick home at 9531 Whitecedar Court.

But now the Hanssens were being forced to leave, and they were preparing to confront the daunting financial, social, and logistical pressures of relocating for another tour of duty in New York. The strain at times seemed unbearable. While he found his work at headquarters as an analyst of Soviet intelligence compelling, Hanssen was disillusioned with the FBI as an institution and employer, leaving him feeling like an outsider. Bob's lack of respect for the Bureau hit new lows just as the specific details of his upcoming assignment as a supervisor in New York came through. Lacking the money to return to New York and live comfortably with his large family, and without the personality or managerial skills to put himself on the fast track for promotion, Hanssen decided to take action.

This time around, Bob had thought everything through, and he was determined not to be caught by Bonnie or anyone else—especially by what he viewed as the hapless FBI. He chose his words and considered his actions carefully; that way, he could also conceal his identity from the KGB, something that had rarely been attempted. It wasn't just that he had access to a storehouse of secrets that the Soviets wanted. He had used his computer expertise to expand his reach beyond the scope of his own work and into an impressive array of sensitive intelligence in the FBI and other agencies. He sensed, too, that if he initially made clear the value of his information and absolute need for confidentiality, the Soviets would be masterful and confident enough at their own spycraft to resist the urge to tail him. It was like any other relationship—there had to be trust—but it was unlike almost any other relationship, because the risks were high and trust had to be placed blindly. If Hanssen detected a KGB tail, he would cease his activities, cutting off the flow of information. On the other hand, intelligence agents of the *Komitet Gosudarstvenoy Bezopasnosti* were always suspicious of a setup whenever an FBI or CIA agent volunteered to turn over information. But Bob was sure he knew how to assuage their fears.

While Bonnie was in the final weeks of pregnancy and then confined in the hospital giving birth, Bob could think of no better time to get started. He would be living out the kind of fantasy he had dreamed of for years, proving to himself that he was smarter than the FBI, more clever than the Russians, and bold enough to pull this off, without Bonnie or anyone else in the family noticing.

Hanssen had to start somewhere, and through his Soviet intelligence work he knew just the man: Viktor Ivanovich Cherkashin, the number-two-ranking KGB officer in Washington. Cherkashin had an extraordinary ability to keep secrets and protect his sources of information by circumventing the chain of command and going directly to the senior-most levels in Moscow. He had carefully honed his skills as a "handler," especially his ability to understand the psychology of the spies he was running. Though Hanssen didn't know it at the time, earlier in 1985 Cherkashin had begun handling CIA agent Aldrich Ames, who was serving as chief of Soviet counterintelligence and became one of the Agency's most infamous spies. Hanssen also didn't know that his credibility would be established from his initial communication with Cherkashin, in part because he confirmed information about traitorous KGB agents supplied earlier that year by Ames. One thing Hanssen did know for sure was that his skills and smarts might have been overlooked by the FBI, but the KGB would not ignore him.

Selling secrets to the KGB fed his hunger for the thrill of taking big-time risks. As he typed his first letter to Cherkashin, Hanssen knew the consequences would be dire if he got caught, but it was the very prospect of pulling this off without detection that gave him a rush. Being a double agent suddenly transformed him from an unappreciated, overlooked analyst into an important behind-the-scenes actor in a dangerous game, one that he had been preparing to play better than anyone who had come before him.

DEAR MR. CHERKASHIN:

SOON, I WILL SEND A BOX OF DOCUMENTS TO MR. DEGTYAR. THEY ARE FROM CERTAIN OF THE MOST SENSITIVE AND HIGHLY COM-PARTMENTED PROJECTS OF THE U.S. INTEL-LIGENCE COMMUNITY. ALL ARE ORIGINALS TO AID IN VERIFYING THEIR AUTHENTICITY. PLEASE RECOGNIZE FOR OUR LONG-TERM INTERESTS THAT THERE ARE A LIMITED NUMBER OF PERSONS WITH THIS ARRAY OF CLEARANCES. AS A COLLECTION THEY POINT TO ME. I TRUST THAT AN OFFICER OF YOUR EXPERIENCE WILL HANDLE THEM APPROPRI-ATELY. I BELIEVE THEY ARE SUFFICIENT TO JUSTIFY A $100,000 PAYMENT TO ME.

I MUST WARN OF CERTAIN RISKS TO MY
SECURITY OF WHICH YOU MAY NOT BE
AWARE. YOUR SERVICE HAS RECENTLY SUF-
FERED SOME SETBACKS. I WARN THAT MR.
BORIS YUZHIN (LINE PR, SF), MR. SERGEY
MOTORIN, (LINE PR, WASH.) AND MR. VALERIY
MARTYNOV (LINE X, WASH.) HAVE BEEN RE-
CRUITED BY OUR "SPECIAL SERVICES."

DETAILS REGARDING PAYMENT AND
FUTURE CONTACT WILL BE SENT TO YOU
PERSONALLY.... MY IDENTITY AND ACTUAL
POSITION IN THE COMMUNITY MUST BE
LEFT UNSTATED TO ENSURE MY SECURITY. I
AM OPEN TO COMMO [communications] SUG-
GESTIONS BUT WANT NO SPECIALIZED
TRADECRAFT. I WILL ADD 6 (YOU SUBTRACT
6) FROM STATED MONTHS, DAYS AND TIMES
IN BOTH DIRECTIONS OF OUR FUTURE COM-
MUNICATIONS.

Hanssen took care not to sign the letter or leave any external markings on the envelope that would tip FBI agents doing surveillance of Cherkashin. Since he knew that the mail was an inherently risky way of doing business, Hanssen took a series of steps to conceal his communication with Cherkashin and solidify his credentials. Rather than sending it from New York, where he had just begun working, Hanssen mailed the letter from suburban Maryland on a day when he was back in Washington dealing with administrative chores. The envelope was postmarked "Prince George's Co., Md.," not far from the Capital, on October 1, 1985. Instead of sending the letter to Cherkashin himself, Hanssen sent it to the Alexandria, Virginia, home of another KGB operative, Viktor M. Degtyar. Inside the outer envelope, there was a second envelope, which Hanssen marked,

"DO NOT OPEN. TAKE THIS ENVELOPE UNOPENED TO
VICTOR I. CHERKASHIN."

Hanssen knew the FBI might photograph the outer envelope
going to Degtyar's home, but would not open it. To establish his credibility with Cherkashin further, Hanssen, in addition to listing the
three KGB double agents, included a detailed description of a highly
sensitive information-collection technique that was classified as TOP
SECRET. And he further proved his "bona fides" by disclosing the existence and location of a sensitive FBI electronic penetration of Soviet
communications.

The disclosure of the FBI's recruitment of Valery Martynov and
Sergei Motorin, the first known double agents in the KGB's Washington operation, had deadly consequences for the pair. The valuable KGB moles had been compromised earlier in 1985 by Ames, so
the transmission from Hanssen gave the Soviets confirmation of their
identities. Martynov and Motorin subsequently were called back to
the U.S.S.R. under false pretenses, tried in court, and executed for
espionage. Hanssen "contributed to the deaths of people," said Paul
Joyal, former director of security for the Senate Intelligence Committee. "He had blood on his hands." The third agent that Hanssen
compromised, Boris Yuzhin, would be sentenced to fifteen years in a
labor camp.

But Hanssen did not feel guilty about what he had done. Instead,
he viewed the disclosures as fair play in the spy game and knew that
his actions could have lethal consequences if he was caught. In addition, Hanssen reasoned that as long as he regularly confessed his sins
to various priests and sought forgiveness, he would remain in a state
of grace.

After being reassigned in 1981 to a budget unit at FBI headquarters, Hanssen saw many of the Bureau's slipshod operations firsthand.
The FBI's nonsensical bureaucratic practices and outmoded methods made him downright angry. His superior intelligence, education,
and accounting background didn't help matters either, since he
quickly concluded that most of his coworkers were dense by com-

parison. He deplored the way decisions were made based on insufficient data and the way resources were allocated because of Bureau politics rather than goals or performance. He longed for the days of J. Edgar Hoover, when a strong-willed leader headed the FBI and committed agents produced real results.

Dick Alu, a twenty-nine-year FBI veteran who worked with Hanssen in the budget unit in the early 1980s, recalled the intensity of Hanssen's feelings. "Bob is a bright guy," Alu said. "We used to talk. We would talk about management and how the computer system of the FBI was really not up to speed." They would lament how the Bureau remained decades behind the private sector, due to its stubborn reliance on giant mainframe computers that couldn't be easily upgraded and quickly became obsolete. "Bob and I would discuss that and shake our heads in disgust." Alu also recalls Hanssen's total lack of interpersonal skills and his disdain for having to simplify the language he used so that other FBI personnel could understand his sophisticated techno-speak.

"I said, 'If you use technology terms without an explanation, you will go over their heads.' He looked back at me with disgust, that he had to reduce his explanation down to that level," Alu said. "He didn't suffer fools very well. I could see what was running through his head was, 'I am smarter than these guys, I know how to implement certain things and can make the division run more effectively and I have to try to explain this stuff to the hierarchy.' He is probably one of the most intelligent guys I have ever met."

Behind his back, however, FBI agents joked that Hanssen's demeanor and appearance seemed better suited for a funeral home than the Bureau. While he could look at complex problems and incorporate solutions that were unique and effective, he lacked the attitude and personality to sell his ideas. And unlike more gregarious FBI agents, he rarely talked about his family at the office or went out with the boys after work, Alu said. "I would occasionally go out for drinks with the guys at the local bar, and Bob never did that. I don't know if he was even invited. Based on his [personality] and how he interacted, it was obvious he would not have been interested. You're talking about an introvert. Aside from work-related discussions, you just didn't have any."

Yet Hanssen was committed to doing a better job as a parent and husband than his father, Howard, and to breaking the cycle of violence and abuse that had left him emotionally bruised. Hanssen was home for dinner virtually every night by 5:30 P.M., helped with chores around the house in Vienna, and began going to church daily after joining Opus Dei, which delighted Bonnie. He once dejectedly returned a computer he had purchased after Bonnie told him they couldn't afford it; he also returned a motorcycle he had purchased for one of their sons for the same reason. While following Bonnie's dictates at home, he had a sort of laissez-faire approach to parenting, telling his children that he trusted them to do the right thing and steering them toward the Church. In Hanssen's world, what the pope said was gospel and the Divine provided the answers.

Though the FBI and his fellow agents frustrated Hanssen, he liked being involved in intelligence work, and by 1983 he had found his way to the Soviet Analytical Unit as an analyst, supporting counterintelligence operations and investigations involving suspected Soviet spies, as well as providing other support for senior officials in the U.S. intelligence community. Hanssen, in this new role, sensed his preparation and expertise exceeded those around him. He had studied Russian in college, examined the history of Communism for years, and had a healthy respect for Soviet spycraft. After all, the Russians had been spying for centuries, while the United States had only meaningfully undertaken intelligence work for the first time during World War II. As far as Hanssen could tell, the Soviets also had a major advantage in intelligence because theirs was an entire society and governmental system based on deception that bred exceptionally gifted spies and attracted the best and brightest to the KGB and its affiliates. America was another story. Democracies by nature do not put the same premium on the government's ability to effectively carry out—or, for that matter, obstruct—clandestine operations.

Yet when Hanssen secretly launched his carefully crafted contact with the KGB in 1985, espionage was in the air. In what would become known as the "Year of the Spy," the FBI announced three separate arrests in three separate espionage cases involving three different countries in just one week. Over the course of the year, some fourteen officials were arrested for spying against the United States. Soon after Hanssen secretly initiated contact with the KGB and warned of the need for extreme caution to avoid detection, President Ronald Reagan discussed the flurry of espionage arrests in his Saturday radio address. "Some of you may be wondering if the large number of spy arrests means that we're looking harder or whether there are more spies to find," Reagan said. "Well, I think the answer to both questions is 'yes.'"

The Year of the Spy began garnering headlines in the spring, when retired naval officer John Walker, Jr., and his son, petty officer Michael Lance Walker, were indicted for selling naval encryption codes and other secrets to the Soviet Union. Short of cash, Walker had recruited his son, his brother, Arthur James Walker, and another friend in the Navy, Jerry Whitworth, to create the "Walker Spy Ring," an operation the KGB viewed at the time as the most important intelligence operation in its history. The Soviet Union gained access to naval encryption key cards, which enabled them to decipher messages sent to or from the American fleet. The beginning of the end for John Walker came when he tried to recruit his daughter, Laura, who also was in the military. She refused and convinced her mother to go to the FBI. Months later, agents caught Walker depositing documents at a roadside drop site in Maryland.

The flow of American double agents into the public spotlight continued when the FBI arrested Ronald W. Pelton of the National Security Agency, who was accused of selling the KGB information about U.S. eavesdropping systems used worldwide. The Bureau also arrested former CIA officer Edward R. Howard, on charges of selling a litany of secrets to the Soviet Union. Both were exposed by KGB officer Vitaliy Yurchenko, who sought asylum in the United States and provided valuable information about Russian counterintelligence. Three months later, Yurchenko returned to Moscow, claiming he had been drugged by the CIA and forced to defect. The American intelligence community, stunned and dumbfounded by Yurchenko's action, denied his sensational allegations.

As if all of that were not enough, two more high-profile cases arose next, which put Americans on notice that their friends, as well as their enemies, might be spying on them. Jonathan Jay Pollard, a naval intelligence analyst, was arrested just before Thanksgiving for selling classified U.S. military information to Israel, a close ally. One day later, Larry Wu-Tai Chin, a former analyst for the CIA's Foreign Broadcast Information Service, was charged with passing national secrets to China, including classified evaluations of China's "strategic, military, economic, scientific, and technical capabilities and intentions." After being convicted on all counts, Chin committed suicide in his jail cell.

The risks of the spy game were quite clear to Hanssen in 1985. Leaving behind a policy of not prosecuting Americans caught spying for fear that it would lead to damaging disclosures at trial, the new U.S. policy sent an unambiguous message that espionage would no longer be tolerated without severe punishment for double agents caught in the act. "It looks to me like we need more prosecutions because there appears to be an unusual number of Americans spying against this country," said former attorney general Griffin Bell, who played a central role in the shift toward bringing U.S. spies to justice. "We went too long," Bell said, "without using prosecution as a deterrent."

New policies, new laws passed by Congress, and a commitment from the Reagan administration to place a "high priority" on additional espionage prosecutions were all aimed at containing the damage and deterring further betrayals. But for Bob Hanssen, it had precisely the reverse effect. The heightened prospect of detection and the danger of harsher punishment raised the stakes of the game and propelled him forward.

*   *   *

Hanssen knew that to solidify his relationship with the KGB, especially given his anonymity, he had to quickly make good on his promise to deliver a cache of valuable intelligence. He also needed to devise a way for the Soviets to compensate him. Unlike most spies, Hanssen didn't care all that much about the KGB's money and what he could do with it, even with financial pressures that would have overwhelmed most people. If anything, he worried that dealing with large amounts of cash might somehow increase the chance that he would be detected. But he did value the money as an affirmation of his own importance to an intelligence operation. Furthermore, he knew the Soviets well enough to understand that they would suspect some type of sting if he didn't follow through on his initial request for cash with a way for money to change hands. A student of espionage, Hanssen would use his FBI counterintelligence training, as well as the methods he had gleaned from studying successful spies before him, to outmaneuver the Bureau. He was well aware of the recent wave of arrests of American spies and the risks he exposed himself to worried him incessantly, feeding an anxiety about doing anything that might lead to suspicion of his activities.

Hanssen hated using the mail, knowing that it facilitated detection through routine procedures. But until he and the Soviets agreed on a clandestine system of dead drops—an intelligence term for a place where documents can be left by one person and picked up by another without their meeting face-to-face—he had no other choice. At least the move to his new FBI post in New York created opportunities to conceal his identity. In mid-October, he made good on his pledge to Cherkashin. Using the alias "B," Hanssen mailed KGB operative Degtyar a package that contained original documents from the U.S. intelligence community and a significant number of other classified papers. He then followed with a typed letter to Degtyar's home, bearing a New York postmark of October 24, 1985, detailing very specific payment instructions.

DROP LOCATION

Please leave your package for me under the corner
(nearest the street) of the wooden foot bridge located
just west of the entrance to Nottoway Park. (ADC
Northern Virginia Street Map, #14, D3)

PACKAGE PREPARATION

Use a green or brown plastic trash bag and trash to cover
a waterproofed package.

SIGNAL LOCATION

Signal site will be the pictorial "pedestrian-crossing"
signpost just west of the main Nottoway Park entrance
on Old Courthouse Road. (The sign is the one nearest
the bridge just mentioned.)

SIGNALS

My signal to you: One vertical mark of white adhesive
tape meaning I am ready to receive your package.

Your signal to me: One horizontal mark of white adhesive tape meaning drop filled.

My signal to you: One vertical mark of white adhesive
tape meaning I have received your package.

(Remove old tape before leaving signal.)

Hanssen's letter also established times and dates for the signals
and drops, using the plus-or-minus-six formula established in his
earlier communication to Cherkashin. "I will acknowledge amount
with my next package," he typed in conclusion.

In response, the KGB placed $50,000 cash in a package inside a
garbage bag, as directed. They took their parcel to the dead drop site

in Fairfax County, Virginia, which they had code-named "PARK." They also included a note with suggestions outlining various procedures for upcoming secret contacts.

Hanssen knew the PARK site well and considered it beyond suspicion. It was only about sixty paces from the backyard of his former home on Whitecedar Court in Vienna. No high-profile foreign travel involved. No face-to-face meetings. Complete and total anonymity. Easy for the KGB to find, but hard for others to see. It was ingenious in its simplicity.

Surrounded by tall, dense trees and brush, the footbridge, with its walkway of fifty-four individual planks supported by two steel beams anchored in concrete, was well concealed inside Nottoway Park. The only way to see what was happening around the bridge was to approach it directly from either end. A small, muddy brook ran directly underneath; the banks below the footbridge, while not terribly deep or flat, were more than sufficient for hidden packages.

Less than a week after retrieving the money from the dead drop, Hanssen typed a letter to Cherkashin:

Thank you for the 50,000.

I also appreciate your courage and perseverance in the face of generically reported bureaucratic obstacles. I would not have contacted you if it were not reported that you were held in esteem within your organization, an organization I have studied for years. I did expect some communication plan in your response. I viewed the postal delivery as a necessary risk and do not wish to trust again that channel with valuable material. I did this only because I had to so you would take my offer seriously, that there be no misunderstanding as to my long-term value, and to obtain appropriate security for our relationship from the start.

In his letter, Hanssen turned down the contact plans proposed by Cherkashin and the KGB, proposing instead a communications plan based on what he called "a microcomputer 'bulletin board'" at a specific location, with "appropriate encryption." In the meantime, Hanssen suggested making no immediate changes. "Let's use the same site again. Same timing. Same signals." He proposed that the next dead drop take place on September 9. Using the formula outlined in his first letter, the date actually meant March 3, 1986, six months and six days earlier than the stated dead drop date. Hanssen, still worried about getting caught, shared his concerns with Cherkashin in the letter.

> As far as the funds are concerned, I have little need or utility for more than the $100,000. It merely provides a difficulty since I can not spend it, store it or invest it easily without triping "drug money" warning bells. Perhaps some diamonds as security to my children and some good will so that when the time comes, you will accept by senior services as a guest lecturer. Eventually I would appreciate an escape plan. (Nothing lasts forever.)

Then, responding to KGB queries about Motorin and Martynov, the Soviet agents he identified who had been recruited to work as spies for the FBI, Hanssen wrote:

> I can not provide documentary substantiating evidence without arousing suspicion at this time. Never-the-less, it is from my own knowledge as a member of the community effort to capitalize on the information from which I speak. I have seen video tapes of debriefings and physically saw the last, though we were not introduced. The names were provided to me as part of my duties as one of the few who needed to know. You have some avenues of inquiry. Substantial funds were provided in

excess of what could have been skimmed from their agents. The active one has always (in the past) used a concealment device—a bag with bank notes sewn in the base during home leaves.

Finally, Hanssen, whose computer skills afforded him access to secrets across the intelligence community, warned Cherkashin and the KGB of a "new technique" employed by the National Security Agency (NSA) to gather information, which he outlined in considerable detail.

If Hanssen seemed bold in his espionage, he appeared henpecked at home where Bonnie was the boss. She regularly told him what to do, and if he didn't move quickly enough to grill the meat or take out the trash, she told him again and again. He didn't get angry or resentful. Instead, he took her constant nudging in stride, diligently taking care of household chores and other duties, sometimes in unconventional ways. On one fall day, Bob used a vacuum cleaner rather than a rake to remove leaves from around the bushes.

When Bonnie and Bob arrived late at night at their new house at 2861 Mead Street in Westchester County—with their newborn baby and five other children—the place was dark because the previous owners had taken all the lightbulbs with them when they had moved out. To make matters worse, it was immediately clear that the cramped, two-story house near Yorktown High School was a big step down from the home where they had been living in Vienna. Bonnie began shouting at Bob, cursing the move to the smaller house, the transfer to New York, and his handling of the overall situation. Bob may have shrugged it off, but Bonnie's tirade left an indelible imprint on some of their children, who felt sorry for their father.

Underneath it all and hidden from view, Bob actually was the master manipulator, conducting espionage and living out his sexual fantasies, while leaving Bonnie with a false sense of control and maintaining the image of the family with the perfect suburban life.

For his part, Bob took care not to lose focus on his family or on his day job with the FBI, lest anyone suspect that something unusual was afoot. Lacking conventional social and interpersonal skills, he struggled as a supervisor of a foreign counterintelligence squad in New York. He was a good analyst and student of Soviet intelligence, but a supervisor needed the ability to relate well to other agents and motivate them, and that just was not part of his personality.

While he viewed the move to New York primarily as a way to punch a ticket on his FBI career track, spying, on the other hand, left Hanssen fulfilled and energized. Though he professed to hate Communism, he loved the game and relished the idea of leaving the FBI befuddled and the Soviets clueless about his identity. He loved the secrecy, the sense of power and control he felt in his relationship with his handlers. Because of his father's abusive treatment, Hanssen had learned long ago to compartmentalize and conceal.

Bob had never shaken off the effects of the abuse he had received as a child, or the way his father had berated him in front of his children as an adult. It was Bonnie who had forced him to write his father a letter threatening to cut off all contact, including denying him the right to see his grandchildren, if he didn't stop putting Bob down. Finally, the verbal harangues ceased, but the damage had been done. According to Dr. Harvey Rich, founder and past president of the American Psychoanalytic Foundation, Hanssen's suppressed rage against his father—the Chicago cop who had tracked communists—manifested itself in an excessive preoccupation with a fantasy life, effectively leading him to create multiple lives that coexisted separately so that he could survive emotionally. "He had to compartmentalize to cope with it. What one can say is in some people where early childhood trauma is overwhelming and where they are in a helpless position, the child's mind, which is not fully formed, will segment reality and life in different places. If the pain is too great, and there is nowhere to turn, then the mind stays that way and finds it adaptive to keep things separated."

Those who worked with Hanssen at the FBI never suspected he was a spy or had a secret life but they all knew he didn't have what it took to succeed as a supervisor. Roger Patrick Watson, a twenty-nine-year FBI veteran who rose through the ranks to become deputy assistant director, said Hanssen was brighter than the average FBI agent but never felt like part of the Bureau. He said Hanssen had no close friends at work, was "an oddball out," and had nicknames like "The Mortician" and "Dr. Death" because he was a "very dour" sort of person.

Belying the view that Hanssen had no friends at the Bureau, former FBI agent Paul Moore said he had a close relationship with Bob. The two carpooled together and frequently conversed at FBI headquarters, where their offices were near each other. Moore said Hanssen developed the nickname "Digger," as in gravedigger. "He had fairly long, canine teeth so that would give him a vampirelike appearance." Moore, who focused on Chinese counterintelligence issues, also said Hanssen devised solutions to problems more readily than most. "He was a deep thinker. But he wasn't necessarily an original thinker. He would come up with other people's solutions that he could apply to your problem. He was a go-between, a middleman of ideas."

Once, Hanssen proudly told Moore a story about his father. Sometime during his career with the Chicago police department, Howard Hanssen had investigative files in his office that contained politically damaging information about his fellow officers. The matter was handled when the files miraculously went up in flames one day. "Bob respected that," Moore said, adding that despite Howard Hanssen's bad relationship with his son, Bob described him as a man who knew how to make a problem go away by doing "what had to be done."

With an accountant's obsession for detail and precision, the odds of Hanssen making an obvious misstep seemed small, provided he could keep his delusions of grandeur in check. Hanssen's preoccupation with caution was so acute that he was willing to break off contact with the KGB for months. On March 3, 1986, on the predetermined schedule, the KGB left a package for Hanssen at the PARK dead drop. But after the signal site indicated he had not sought to retrieve it, the KGB removed it. Several months later, Hanssen typed and mailed a letter to the KGB's Degtyar.

> I apologize for the delay since our break in communications. I wanted to determine if there was any cause for concern over security. I have only seen one item which has given me pause. When the FBI was first given access to [Soviet defector] Victor Petrovich Gundarev, they asked . . . if Gundarev knew Viktor Cherkashin. I thought this unusual. I had seen no report indicating that Viktor Cherkashin was handling an important agent, and here-to-fore he was looked at with the usual lethargy awarded Line Chiefs. The question came to mind, are they somehow able to monitor funds, i.e., to know that Viktor Cherkashin received a large amount of money for an agent? I am unaware of any such ability, but I might not know that type of source reporting.

Hanssen went on to reveal that the United States knew of a technical flaw in Soviet satellite transmissions and was actively exploiting the vulnerability. It was just the kind of information that undercut work done by the National Security Agency, alerting Moscow not only to which of its communications had been intercepted but also to what changes needed to be made to prevent further breaches. Then Hanssen concluded the letter by casting a new kind of lure.

> If you wish to continue our discussions, please have someone run an advertisement in the Washington Times during the week of 1/12/87 or 1/19/87, for sale, "Dodge Diplomat, 1971, needs engine work, $1,000." Give a phone number and time-of-day in the advertise-

ment where I can call. I will call and leave a phone
number where a recorded message can be left for me in
one hour. I will say, "Hello, my name is Ramon. I am
calling about the car you offered for sale in the Times."
You will respond, "I'm sorry, but the man with the car is
not here, can I get your number." The number will be in
Area Code 212. I will not specify that Area Code on the
line.

Hanssen signed the letter, "Ramon," borrowing the alias of a
successful undercover police officer he had learned about in Chicago.

Based on the previously outlined "minus six" formula, the times
that the advertisement actually was to appear were the week of July
6, 1986, or July 13, 1986. The KGB responded, and from July 14 to
July 18, 1986, the following ad—including the subtle play on the word
"diplomat"—appeared in the *Washington Times*:

DODGE – '71 DIPLOMAT, NEEDS ENGINE
WORK, $1000. Phone (703) 451–9780 (CALL NEXT
Mon., Wed., Fri. 1 p.m.)

The phone number in the ad belonged to a pay phone near Old
Keene Mill Shopping Center in Fairfax County, Virginia. On Monday July 21, "B" called that number and gave the number 628–8047.
The call was received by Aleksandr Kirillovich Fefelov, a KGB officer
who worked in the Soviet embassy. One hour later, Fefelov dialed 212–
628–8047 and told "B" that the KGB had left a package at the PARK
dead drop site. Two weeks later, Hanssen typed and mailed a letter to
Degtyar saying he had not found the package at the dead drop site and
would call the number from the ad again on August 18, 20, or 22. The
KGB, which had placed the package under the wrong corner of the
footbridge by mistake, immediately retrieved it.

On August 18, "B" called 703–451–9780 and spoke with Fefelov
a second time.

B: Tomorrow morning?

FEFELOV: Uh, yeah, and the car is still available for you and as we have agreed last time, I prepared all the papers and I left them on the same table. You didn't find them because I put them in another corner of the table.

B: I see.

FEFELOV: You shouldn't worry, everything is okay. The papers are with me now.

B: Good.

FEFELOV: I believe under these circumstances, mmmm, it's not necessary to make any changes concerning the place and the time. Our company is reliable, and we are ready to give you a substantial discount which will be enclosed in the papers. Now, about the date of our meeting. I suggest that our meeting will be, will take place without delay on February thirteenth, one three, one p.m. Okay? February thirteenth.

B: February second?

FEFELOV: Thirteenth, one three.

B: One three.

FEFELOV: Yes. Thirteenth. One p.m.

B: Let me see if I can do that. Hold on.

FEFELOV: Okay. Yeah.

B: [whispering] Six . . . six . . . That should be fine.

FEFELOV: Okay. We will confirm you, that the papers are waiting for you with the same horizontal tape in the same place as we did it at the first time.

B: Very good.

FEFELOV: You see. After you receive the papers, you will send the letter confirming it and signing it, as usual. Okay?

B: Excellent.

FEFELOV: I hope you remember the address. Is . . . if everything is okay?

B: I believe it should be fine and thank you very much.

FEFELOV: Heh-heh. Not at all. Not at all. Nice job. For both of us. Uh, have a nice evening, sir.

B: *Do svidaniya.*

FEFELOV: Bye-bye.

Based on the "plus six" formula, the dead drop referred to in the conversation was scheduled to occur the next day, August 19, 1986, at 7:00 P.M. This time around, the KGB left the package on the correct corner of the footbridge in Nottoway Park, and Hanssen, in the parlance of espionage, "cleared" the dead drop. Inside the package, he found $10,000 in cash; proposals for two additional dead drop sites to be used by "B" and the KGB; a new accommodation address code-named "NANCY"; and an emergency communications plan for "B" to personally contact KGB officials in Vienna, Austria. The accommodation address was the home of KGB officer Boris M. Malakhov in Alexandria, Virginia, who was replacing Degtyar as the Soviet embassy press secretary. "B" was directed to misspell Malakhov's name as "Malkow."

After all the confusion, Hanssen wrote a short note to Degtyar confirming the success of the dead drop, using the return address "Ramon Garcia, 125 Main Street, Falls Church, VA." He mailed the brief note that same day:

RECEIVED $10,000. RAMON.

7

CONTROL

All his life Bob Hanssen wanted to call the shots. Instead, he felt powerless when his father berated him, when he failed to get promoted, and when the FBI directed him where to work and live. Around the house, Bonnie made the decisions. But in his role as a KGB spy, Hanssen was in a position where he was important, he was in charge. He was, at long last, a man in control.

Though born of his desire to break free from his shackles, Hanssen believed his need for control was critical to avoiding detection. He knew exactly how the FBI tracked down double agents, and knew he could not be too careful. His Soviet handlers sensed this desire for control early in their relationship. Soon after he was reassigned to FBI headquarters to work in the Intelligence Division's Soviet Analytical Unit in the fall of 1987, they proposed meeting face-to-face and made other suggestions. "Ramon" responded emphatically in a letter to a KGB operative, who also served as Soviet press secretary:

Dear Friends:

No, I have decided. It must be on my original terms or not at all. I will not meet abroad or here. I will not maintain lists of sites or modified equipment. I will help you when I can, and in time we will develop methods of efficient communication. Unless a see an abort signal on our post from you by 3/16, I will mail my contact a valuable package timed to arrive on 3/18. I will await your signal and package to be in place before 1:00 p.m. on 3/22 or alternately the following three weeks, same day and time. If my terms are unacceptable then place no signals and withdraw my contract.

sincerely,
Ramon

Using their agreed-upon cipher, the three dates mentioned were September 10, 12, and 16.

Six days after Hanssen mailed the letter, the KGB received a package of TOP SECRET National Security Council documents and other classified papers in the mail. On September 15, the KGB loaded the PARK dead drop site in Nottoway Park with $10,000 in cash. In addition, the KGB proposed dead drop sites in other northern Virginia parks, giving them the code names "AN" and "DEN," and proposed that "B" load the dead drop at PARK or AN on September 26 and that the KGB respond swiftly by loading DEN. Hanssen responded with the following letter, which he included in the package he left in the familiar PARK dead drop site.

My Friends:

Thank you for the $10,000.

I am not a young man, and the commitments on my time prevent using distant drops such as you suggest. I know in this I am moving you out of your set modes of doing business, but my experience tells me the we can be actually more secure in easier modes. [In lieu of a dead drop, Hanssen next proposed an exchange procedure using a parked car.]

Good luck with your work.

If you cannot do this I will clear this once AN on your scheduled date (rather than the other).

Ramon

Hanssen had stuffed the package with other exceedingly valuable secrets, including the "National Intelligence Program for [19]87." Soon thereafter, the KGB deposited $100,000 into an escrow account set up for "B" at a Soviet bank in Moscow. About two months later, after other code-filled communications, Hanssen wrote the following to the KGB about a missed handoff in mid-November 1987:

Unable to locate AN based on your description at night. Recognize that I am dressed in business suit and can not slog around in inch deep mud. I suggest we use once again original site. I will place my urgent material there at next AN times. Replace it with your package. I will select some few sites good for me and pass them to you. Please give new constant conditions of recontact as address to write. Will not put substantive material through it. Only instructions as usual format.

Ramon

Hanssen had far greater range than spies who had come before him. His technical expertise, knowledge of computers, and access to intelligence outside the FBI's realm vastly expanded the universe of valuable secrets he could sell to the Soviets. The package he delivered around Thanksgiving 1987 to PARK, his favorite dead drop site, included COINS-II, the then current, classified version of the United States' "Community Online Intelligence System." Other spies gave up moles or single devices on an ad hoc basis. Hanssen sold entire intelligence systems, as well as information about the debriefing of a defector and a Western spy within the KGB. In return, the Soviets made Hanssen feel extraordinarily important. Soon he was no longer dealing just with senior KGB officials in Washington—his contacts went straight to the top in Moscow, and on a deliciously confidential basis that he cherished. The package he received in exchange for COINS-II included a letter from the KGB director praising him and offering warm regards, confirming the $100,000 deposit for him in a Russian bank at a six to seven percent interest rate, and a request for an array of specific classified information.

To FBI colleagues, unaware of his espionage, Hanssen's transfer from New York as a supervisor to a headquarters post as an analyst was a lateral move reflecting that his Bureau career had stalled. Upward mobility in the FBI into the ranks of middle and senior management carried with it the responsibility initially for overseeing teams and, later, legions of agents. For Hanssen, an analyst by instinct and training, the transfer to headquarters enabled him to do what he did best without continuing day-to-day involvement with others. Without management responsibilities and headaches, it also left him with more time to peruse the electronic and paper files of classified and TOP SECRET information at the FBI, CIA, NSA, and National Security Council for possible sale to Moscow. It also enabled him to sit back in meetings and listen for secrets and clues that a good double agent wouldn't miss. And it made frequent trips to dead drops near his newly purchased house at 9414 Talisman Drive in Vienna, Virginia, simple and easy.

Meanwhile, his FBI colleagues increasingly saw him as a misfit who dressed in dark clothing and always seemed to be hanging around without adding much to the discourse. "Think of somebody in a mortuary talking to a family and they speak in a low tone of voice. That is the way he was. He had a smile but it didn't go beyond that. He would smile and sit there and not say a word," said Ray Mislock, who spent twenty-five years at the FBI and rose to the senior ranks of national security operations and was chief of the Soviet section. "He clearly had a superior attitude about himself but it didn't surface to me in terms of, 'I should be advancing.'"

John Lewis, who ran the national security division at the FBI, said Hanssen seemed to be one of those people who had low self-esteem underneath it all and seemed to be seeking revenge. "He lived in this world of shadows. He recognized he was not sought after. He was there, but kind of wasn't there. . . . He hated so many of the people he worked with; he felt superior but wasn't making it. A lot of people just wrote him off as a technical weenie. He didn't fit the mold. And there is this possibility that this guy committed himself to saying, 'What a bunch of assholes' and 'I'll get my revenge someday somehow.'" Added one former FBI colleague, "He was a mumbler on the back bench. We didn't want to talk in front of him. He was just creepy. You would look up, and he would be lurking in the hallways." Some of that lurking, undoubtedly, was more premeditated than Hanssen's FBI colleagues had any reason to know.

Psychiatrist Kim Gorgens said that after feeling like a loser for so many years, Hanssen finally had discovered something he could do exceptionally well. "Being in the counterintelligence unit must . . . have felt like a sociological experiment on Mars," she said. "That is the feeling I still get of him, this really sorry or pitiable schlep almost. . . . He's never going to be the best lover, the best FBI agent, the best anything you can think of, but he can be the best spy."

Paul Moore now believes that Hanssen was driven by a cold, ruthless desire to be the greatest spy in history. To do that, he gave the Russians the most sensitive and dangerous information possible, the U.S. Continuity of Government Plan, which laid out exactly where and how the president and other top U.S. government officials would operate in the event of a nuclear attack. "That is sick," Moore said. "He's got six kids, he's got a wife, and friends, and he's making it more attractive for the Russians to decapitate U.S. leadership. That increases the chances of war."

Bob Hanssen fully understood the severity of the information he was passing to the Russians, and he knew there was a real possibility of nuclear war between the United States and the Soviet Union. Throughout much of the 1980s, the Soviet government believed that it could prevail in a nuclear confrontation with the United States, Hanssen wrote in a report. At home, he convinced Bonnie that the end of the world was imminent, and that a great firestorm would claim the souls of all sinners.

Family members and friends say Bonnie was paranoid and had delusions that the forces of evil could come to get her at any moment. Hanssen exacerbated these tendencies, manipulating her emotions to cloak his espionage and maintain his dominion. In 1992 he told her that Bill Clinton's victory was financed by gold stolen from Russia. She feared Clinton and saw him as controlled by the devil, especially after he took steps to facilitate government-funded abortions. Hanssen also showed Bonnie maps marked with safe places to go in the event of a nuclear war, fueling her emotions with thoughts of Armageddon. She worried so much that she drank NyQuil, an over-the-counter cold remedy filled with alcohol, to help her sleep. Bonnie tended to see all actions and issues in sharply defined moral terms, and harbored the belief that if you were not with her, you were against her. According to someone who knows Bonnie well and considers her naive, "Bob could not have found a more congenial milieu to carry out his evil deeds. He was like a shark swimming in a sea of minnows."

Although guilt would have overcome most people who prayed daily and went with family to church on Sundays, Hanssen felt little remorse over his espionage. According to family members and others, Catholicism and Opus Dei provided a sense of spiritual cleansing through weekly confession and communal gatherings. In Bob Hanssen's compartmentalized mind, he felt anxiety, to be sure, but not guilt over spying. In his world, there were no gray areas; there was good and there was evil. Hanssen believed that fulfilling his commitments to Opus Dei put him on the path to salvation, allowing him to engage in espionage as an escape. "He saw it as a fun game. It was for the thrill and rush from it," a family member close to Hanssen said.

Contrary to some news reports that the basement of his home on Talisman Drive was used as a war room for espionage, in truth

Hanssen composed many of his letters to the KGB sitting in the den of his modest split-level house while his family was around. "He worked on the computer and wrote his letters to the Russians," said a friend. "He would be sitting by himself, and no one talked to him. Nobody paid attention to him when he was at his computer. Bob hid in plain sight."

Hanssen had an unusual capacity to ignore others too, whether on walks in the neighborhood or on trips overseas. While visiting his friend Jack Hoschouer in Germany, Hanssen sat reading a book when another friend of Jack's stopped by. Hanssen never looked up to say hello or anything else, continuing to read as if no one new had entered the room. Lacking basic social skills, he preferred not to make idle chatter or engage in conversation with strangers.

Hanssen paid careful attention, however, to his KGB friends. In early 1988, he began to include secret computer diskettes in the packages he prepared for them. The disks didn't reduce the flow of hardcopy classified documents and information; they simply augmented it. There was detailed information about a defector; specific information about the communications capabilities of the entire U.S. intelligence community; a TOP SECRET document entitled "The FBI's Double Agent Program," which contained an evaluation of FBI operations for recruiting double agents from foreign intelligence services, including joint operations with other U.S. intelligence agencies globally over the span of a decade; and a set of briefing papers for the CIA director entitled "Stealth Orientation." The KGB, in addition to responding with $70,000 in cash, included a letter of thanks from its chairman, Vladimir Kryuchkov.

Inevitably, supply created its own demand, and the KGB began asking for more. Their work with Robert Philip Hanssen was qualitatively and quantitatively unique. In the cavalcade of East-West espionage, Hanssen had already established himself as the most prolific source of intelligence ever on TOP SECRET U.S. processes, methods, and codes. The exchanges, which almost always took place on Mondays, began occurring at an accelerating rate in the spring of 1988, even as Soviet leader Mikhail Gorbachev and President Reagan pursued a glasnost-driven détente. In that year alone, "B" and his handlers exchanged information or cash at least sixteen times. In one dispatch, the KGB sought information about codes and cryptograms, intelligence support for the Strategic Defense Initiative, submarines, and other classified material. There were no limits. Eventually, the KGB asked Hanssen for "everything that is possible."

He obliged, providing information about KGB agents in New York, as well as intelligence about a KGB double agent known only by his code name. He also sent a steady stream of computer diskettes and a note telling the KGB to use "40-track mode" to reformat one computer diskette to reveal data that Hanssen had concealed. Without using the right codes to decrypt the diskette, it would appear blank. A fifth diskette from "B" included "everything" about a particular KGB officer, information about a defector named Victor Sheymov whom Hanssen had befriended and handled on behalf of the FBI and CIA, and additional data about two other Soviet agent FBI recruitments.

Despite his busy life as an FBI agent, family man, and KGB spy, Hanssen avoided detection through self-discipline in tradecraft and lifestyle. There was no conspicuous consumption. He was enough of a computer expert not to trigger suspicion when he accessed intelligence secrets from databases maintained by the NSA, CIA, FBI, and Defense Intelligence Agency. And it didn't take him long to do the dead drops since they were only minutes from his home.

"He thought out his spying very carefully," a friend of Hanssen's said. "His tradecraft was brilliant. He didn't follow any of the classic rules. Drops are supposed to be widely separated. . . . If you look for espionage, you don't look in the kinds of places he was doing the stuff. Basically, he did everything differently from what they tell you to do [in CIA training]. His theory was, 'People see me walking around near my house, and in my suit; only farmers climbing off a tractor are going to be more noticeable than me walking around my house.' The point of having the dead drops next to his house was he would go to the store and buy a quart of milk and not be gone for long. He was always home."

Though he needed little prodding as he compromised billions of dollars of national security secrets, the Russians shrewdly manipulated Hanssen's emotions with kind notes, cash, and requests for his technical assistance. Said one careful observer, "He grossly underestimated the Russians. I think at first he thought that he was manipulating them. And they were manipulating him almost the whole time. They were playing to his lack of self-esteem." Hanssen's inclination was to blame himself for missed dead drops, even if the Soviets were at fault. In addition, his insecurity and neediness came through in the gratitude he expressed for such basic courtesies as thanking him for his espionage. In a letter he typed and mailed to the KGB with the return address "Chicago" and postmark "WDC 200" (Washington, D.C.), Hanssen wrote:

> I found the site empty. Possibly I had the time wrong. I work from memory. My recollection was for you to fill before 1:00 a.m. I believe Viktor Degtyar was in the church driveway off Rt. 123, but I did not know how he would react to an approach. My schedule was tight to make this at all. Because of my work, I had to synchronize explanations and flights while not leaving a pattern of absence or travel that could later be correlated with communication times. This is difficult and expensive.
>
> I will call the number you gave me on 2/24, 2/26 or 2/28 at 1:00 a.m., EDST. Please plan filled signals. Empty sites bother me. I like to know before I commit myself as I'm sure you do also. Let's not use the original site so early at least until the seasons change. Some type of call-out signal to you when I have a package or when I can receive one would be useful. Also, please be specific about the dates, e.g., 2/24. Scheduling is not

simple for me because of frequent travel and wife. Any ambiguity multiplies the problems.

My security concerns may seem excessive. I believe experience has shown them to be necessary. I am much safer if you know little about me. Neither of us are children about these things. Over time, I can cut your losses rather than become one.

Ramon

P.S. Your "thank you" was deeply appreciated.

8

THE FBI'S BLUNDER

The FBI could have cracked the Hanssen spy case in 1990. While Bob Hanssen was busy selling intelligence secrets to the Soviets, his family accidentally discovered that he was hiding thousands of dollars in cash at home. After learning about the cash and watching Hanssen spend money unusually freely, Mark Wauck, a Chicago-based FBI agent and Bonnie Hanssen's brother, faced a difficult dilemma. Though he was loyal to family, he suspected the cash came from spying and was convinced the matter deserved a full-blown espionage investigation. A sworn officer of the law, Mark Wauck took his FBI oath seriously and felt a legal duty to report what he reasonably suspected. If he didn't and his brother-in-law turned out to be a double agent, his own job would be on the line, and Bonnie could face legal consequences if Bob were caught. If Wauck did nothing, he sensed that treason would be allowed to continue unabated with potentially disastrous consequences.

Wauck told his FBI superiors in Chicago that he had an extremely important matter to bring to their attention. He disclosed that Hanssen had thousands of dollars in cash at home and had been spending too much money for someone on an FBI salary. He told Bureau officials that he suspected his brother-in-law was spying for the Russians. The FBI completely failed to investigate Wauck's allegations about Hanssen, who went on spying for the Russians without scrutiny from law enforcement officials. The Bureau could have halted

Hanssen's damaging disclosures in 1990 by carrying out a standard probe involving physical and electronic surveillance.

Eventually, after Hanssen's arrest in 2001, Wauck revealed his 1990 disclosure to other family members, expressing surprise that the FBI did not act upon the information, and fury at Hanssen for his acts of disloyalty to family and country and for risking everything. Why had the matter been brushed aside inside the Bureau? Could it be that with the collapse of the Berlin Wall and closer ties developing between the FBI and Russian intelligence that there was no appetite for exposing espionage that would embarrass both nations? Had the information he disclosed gotten lost in the FBI's bureaucracy? Or had a friend of Hanssen's killed a probe? Mark Wauck didn't know the answer to these questions, but he had fulfilled his duty as a special agent of the FBI. He knew of suspicious activity, provided the information on a timely basis to the Bureau, and recommended a probe.

Others raised questions about Hanssen's activities or those of other possible Bureau double agents. FBI Agent Tom Kimmel concluded there was a mole within the Bureau in the late 1990s after conducting an internal probe prompted by another spy case. But he couldn't pin down who it was after the FBI's counterintelligence division refused to turn over certain documents. Kimmel lodged a protest with the FBI's top brass, but his probe was stymied.

Separately, Hanssen raised suspicions about himself in the early 1990s after he hacked into a supervisor's computer and showed him that the counterintelligence division's systems were vulnerable. He did it after his observations about the computer system's flaws were ignored, according to Ray Mislock, then chief of the FBI's Soviet counterintelligence section. "He had never come to my office for any reason," Mislock recalled. "He walked in that day and said, 'See, I told you there is a problem. I told you so.'"

Hanssen handed a sheet of paper with sensitive information to Mislock, who had just entered the data into the supposedly secure computer system. Hanssen wasn't punished, even though he had not asked for permission to break into the system. "He was very pleased with himself," Mislock said, adding that at the time he merely thought Hanssen had taken the action "as a personal challenge" and to prove a point. In hindsight, Mislock and others say Hanssen's hacking offered him access to classified information he otherwise would not have been able to get, as well as an excuse in the event anyone traced his computer trail and suspected that he was spying.

Wauck, who had jeopardized his relationships with family members by disclosing his suspicion to the Bureau, remains livid over Hanssen's betrayal. Throughout the decade, he continued working as an FBI agent in Chicago, Bob Hanssen's spying went undetected and uninvestigated, and the Bureau failed to put a halt to the biggest unfolding espionage case in its history. It was a gargantuan blunder. The damage that could have been prevented was enormous, and the FBI's failure would have dire consequences.

9

THE BOSS

After Louis Freeh's tremendous success in the Pizza Connection case and other complex, high-profile matters, Attorney General Dick Thornburgh selected him in 1990 to take over the investigation of a string of mail bombings in the South. In December 1989, Judge Robert Vance of Alabama and NAACP lawyer Robert Robinson of Georgia were killed by separate package bombs that exploded as they were opened. When Freeh went to Atlanta to take over the probe, he found it completely stalled. "Competing law enforcement agencies were fighting over jurisdiction and prime suspects, presenting contradictory evidence to different grand juries," Freeh said. "The friction produced continual press leaks about the high-profile case, threatening the integrity of the investigation. It was a mess, a bureaucratic and operational disaster."

Al Whitaker, Freeh's mentor from his FBI training days at Quantico and the Special Agent-in-Charge of the Birmingham field office, was convinced that the Bureau should focus its investigation on a junk dealer who once owned a typewriter that matched threatening notes sent before the bombs. But Agent Frank Lee of the Bureau of Alcohol, Tobacco and Firearms (ATF) was convinced that the culprit was a Georgia scam artist and convicted felon named Walter Leroy Moody, Jr., who had been convicted eighteen years earlier of possessing a homemade pipe bomb that resembled the ones in this case. The dispute between the investigators was holding up progress.

"The most important day of the case was the day Louis Freeh arrived," said Larry Potts, who was then chief of the FBI's criminal division.

After reviewing the evidence, Freeh ended up siding with ATF agent Lee. Following the first two fatal bombings, officials responding to another suspicious package decided to defuse the bomb rather than safely detonate it. This would give experts the chance to examine an intact bomb for clues. The strategy paid off when a forensic scientist remembered a similar device he had seen years before made by Moody.

Freeh's team employed clever tactics in building a successful case against Moody, a career criminal who had a history of intimidating witnesses. For this particular case, securing the cooperation of Moody's wife and his accomplices in prior crimes was vital. Freeh's team persuaded a grand jury to bring indictments against Moody for perjury and obstruction of justice unrelated to the present bombing case. In putting Moody behind bars without bail, the government was free to develop key witnesses against him without fear of intimidation. After learning that the suspect often talked to himself, Freeh put a secret video camera in Moody's jail cell that made the difference in the case when the inmate muttered to himself on tape: "Kill those damn judges. I shouldn't have done it." In November of 1990, Moody was indicted for murder and other charges based on a prosecutorial strategy devised largely by Freeh. He eventually was convicted on all counts and sentenced to seven life terms plus 400 years.

Two weeks after Moody's indictment, Freeh was nominated by President Bush to be a federal judge in New York. The appointment brought a pay raise and lifetime job security. While working on the Moody case for more than a year, Freeh lived in an Atlanta hotel room, far from his wife and children. He flew home to New York to spend weekends with his family as often as possible, but the long-distance commuting took its toll. Freeh's appointment to the bench would mean he'd have more time to spend with his family. Though his new job may have given him a more conventional schedule, the demands on his time remained immense. When he began working as a federal judge in New York, seven of the 28 seats on the bench were vacant, and sitting judges found themselves with hundreds of cases; on his first day, Judge Freeh inherited 294.

To leave the office in time to spend evenings with his family, Freeh started his day early. He rose at 5 A.M., began his commute from Westchester County on the Metro-North train at 6:05, and was in his office—on the fifth floor of the United States Courthouse in Manhattan's Foley Square—no later than 7:30. Freeh would sneak in a midday three-mile run and eat lunch at his desk while discussing cases with his clerks or poring over training materials.

The young judge had to familiarize himself with the idiosyncrasies of life on the federal bench. He also had to be careful not to forget his new role in the courtroom—something made more difficult by a coincidence on his very first day, when Freeh presided in the same courtroom in which he had spent seventeen months as a prosecutor trying the Pizza Connection case. When the court clerk opened a proceeding for a drug case with the routine question, "Is the government ready?" Freeh almost blurted out, "Yes!"

It wasn't long before Freeh made an error along these lines. Responding to a request by a lawyer for a motion, Judge Freeh steadfastly announced, "The government will grant your application." The puzzled lawyer cautiously asked after a few seconds, "You mean the court?"

"The court, the court," said an embarrassed Freeh.

When faced with setting bail in one case, Freeh admitted having no idea "if it should be ten dollars or ten million dollars." The novice judge called a recess and phoned a more experienced colleague on the bench, who promptly advised him that $25,000 was a reasonable amount.

Although Freeh did not have the opportunity to issue any landmark rulings in his two years on the federal bench, he seemed thoroughly content with the job. "Being a trial judge is the greatest," he said during a 1992 interview. "There's something about the ebb and

flow of human events, ordinary and sublime, all the different hues of
human nature." However, the ebb and flow of human events was about
to carry a Bureau director out the door and bring Louis Freeh back
to the FBI—and into the forefront of American law enforcement.

When the Clinton administration took office in January 1993,
it was presented with a report outlining a number of ethical breaches
by FBI Director William Sessions and his wife, including personal
use of government aircraft and vehicles and misuse of Bureau funds
to build a $10,000 security fence around their home. It was clear that
Sessions could no longer engender the confidence and loyalty of FBI
agents or the American public. While Sessions resisted Attorney
General Janet Reno's requests to step down, Clinton's staff began
developing a list of potential candidates for FBI director. At the top
of the administration's short list was Massachusetts Superior Court
judge Richard G. Stearns, a close friend and confidant of Clinton's
since the two had met as Rhodes scholars at Oxford. However, several people had urged White House counsel Bernard Nussbaum to
consider Freeh, who Nussbaum's sources knew intimately from his
work on the Pizza Connection and waterfront corruption cases.

As the White House scandal dealing with improper handling of
FBI files unfolded, revealing some uncomfortably close ties between
the Bureau and the new administration, pressure mounted to keep
the FBI wholly independent from the White House, and Clinton's
friend Stearns dropped out of the running. Freeh emerged as the
front-runner; he was earnest, dedicated, and seemingly apolitical.
Freeh met secretly with Nussbaum and Attorney General Reno on
April 1, 1993, and both officials emerged from the interview enthusiastic about the candidate. But, according to Senator Al D'Amato of
New York, who had sponsored his nomination to be a federal judge
in 1991, Freeh was wary of Washington.

"Louis Freeh told them, 'I'm not gonna be in a beauty contest,
no way,'" D'Amato said. "'If you resolve your problems with the
present director, Sessions, and if you then decide that you want me,

that's fine. But I'm not going to be in a situation where I'm competing with somebody else.'" Freeh already had an important job with
lifetime tenure and a salary of $129,500. Still, the idea of heading the
Bureau was attractive to a man whose boyhood dream had been to
work as an FBI agent.

Twelve years after turning in his badge and walking out of FBI
headquarters, Freeh was summoned to Washington for an important
meeting at the White House. On the evening of July 16, 1993, the
president met Freeh for the first time. While the rest of the city fought
midsummer Friday traffic on the Capital Beltway, Clinton took his
guest on a leisurely tour of the White House. The pair chatted for
nearly two hours, hardly touching on the FBI as Clinton began to
win over Freeh with his charm and intellect. Freeh found the president genuinely interested in their conversation and in possession of
a reservoir of historical knowledge. Nevertheless, Freeh had some
questions he wanted answered before accepting the nomination.

Freeh emphasized that he "wanted to make sure that the FBI
would be politically independent and have no political interference."
The issue of independence had long been a sticking point for the
Bureau with its congressional overseers and the White House. Although technically part of the Justice Department, the FBI and its
director are meant to be shielded from oft-changing political winds.
Like any other appointee of the executive branch, the FBI director
can be fired by the president. But the director's ten-year term also
means he has the potential to outlast a two-term president and to serve
under presidents from different political parties.

President Clinton promised Freeh that he would preserve the
independence of the Bureau. The president also addressed Freeh's
lingering concerns about how the job would affect his family life.

Freeh told the president, "I'll be a full-time FBI director for you,
but I have four children and there will be times when that might take
precedence over appearances and things like that." Clinton was very
supportive of Freeh's desire to spend time with family, saying that

he, too, cared deeply about family and spending time with his wife and daughter.

"I had some conditions," Freeh recalled. "I was so concerned about doing it over Marilyn's objections—not objections, but she was very anxious about it." He remembers coming very close to withdrawing his name.

"She was crying, she was upset," Freeh said. "So I thought, 'We're not going to do this.' I called Bernie and told him that. Then I told her, and she got mad at me. 'What did you call him for?' We talked about it some more and she said, 'Do it—but what happens if our family starts going to pieces?' And I said, 'I'll quit.'"

On Monday, July 19, Reno finally was given the go-ahead to fire Sessions. Nicknamed "Barnacle Bill" for the way he desperately clung to his job amid the intense pressure for him to step down, Sessions ultimately became the first director in the eighty-year history of the Bureau to be fired. "We cannot have a leadership vacuum at an agency as important to the United States as the FBI," President Clinton said at a news conference following Sessions's dismissal. But the administration knew that the faster they could get news of the firing off the front page, the better. Clinton called Freeh to a Rose Garden ceremony the next day.

On the surface, Freeh and Clinton had much in common. Both were young, extremely bright, and from modest backgrounds. After earning law degrees, they had devoted themselves largely to public service, and were now at the pinnacle of their respective careers. That the two quickly came to admire each other was evident when the president appeared in public with Freeh for the first time to announce his nomination as FBI director. With Freeh's ascension to the helm of the Bureau, they would share the responsibility of ensuring domestic law and order.

"The Federal Bureau of Investigation is the federal government's cutting edge in the fight against crime," Clinton said. "Today I am pleased to nominate a law enforcement legend to be the director of the FBI, Judge Louis Freeh." Calling the forty-three-year-old "experienced, energetic, and independent," the president proclaimed that Freeh was "the best possible person to head the FBI as it faces new challenges and a new century."

The high praise that Clinton gave Freeh was echoed by numerous others, including some of the former prosecutor's courtroom foes. Clinton shared a few such comments in his remarks that day, citing Freeh as "an investigative genius" and a "ramrod-straight and ferocious crusader against the Mob." The president closed by expressing his personal gratitude to Freeh for his willingness to leave a lifetime appointment on the federal bench "for the somewhat less secure work that the rest of us find in the executive branch."

In his own short speech, Freeh introduced his family, outlined the duties of the FBI in fighting crime and terrorism, and touched on his experience collaborating with law enforcement officers at all levels—the latter being an area long in need of improvement according to critics of the Bureau. Freeh stated the traditional mission of the Bureau in plain terms. "Our country must be made safe again, in cities, towns, villages, and the countryside," he said. "The issue is stark: Do we allow criminals to destroy our Constitution and our freedoms, or do we, as a people committed to the rule of law, take effective steps to preserve our most basic civil rights—to be protected against harm, to be free from fear, and to enjoy the full measure of liberty and opportunity in this great nation?" Freeh also mentioned his friend Judge Falcone in commenting that Americans now find themselves in a "global village in terms of law enforcement."

Freeh breezed through his confirmation hearing before the Senate Judiciary Committee, receiving ardent support from senators of both parties. He fielded questions on the independence of the Bureau, budget priorities, the diversity of the FBI workforce, and gun control, but declined to comment on pending legislation, citing his desire to remain independent of politics. Senators were so confident in Freeh's personal and professional integrity that they hardly challenged him on issues of ethics, despite the recent scandals involving Sessions. The president acknowledged that

he was "overwhelmed" at the outpouring of support for Judge
Freeh.

Rudy Giuliani, who had supervised Freeh for five years in the
U.S. Attorneys' Office, called him "the singularly best-suited person
in America to run the FBI." Giuliani also noted: "He is a naturally
gifted leader. He has a great sensitivity toward people, a great understanding of how to motivate people." Former attorney general
William Barr proudly declared, "This is a lawman's lawman." Added
Ivan Fisher, a prominent defense attorney and one of Freeh's adversaries in the Pizza Connection case, "Louis, in a word, is a mensch.
He's a regular person. He doesn't want any perks, any special privi-
leges." Even a felon Freeh had convicted offered his support, writing
in a letter, "Earlier this year you sentenced me to twenty years in
prison. But I want you to know that of the five judges who have sentenced me to prison, you have been by far the fairest, and I endorse
your nomination to be director of the FBI."

Judge Louis Freeh was unanimously confirmed by the Senate
to become the fifth director of the FBI on August 6, 1993. Highlight-
ing his "ordinary guy" persona, Freeh declined the chauffeured lim-
ousine ride to his swearing-in ceremony at FBI headquarters several
weeks later, and instead drove his own Volvo station wagon with his
family piled in the back. FBI Agent Charlie Rooney, an old friend
from the Pizza Connection days, led the way down Pennsylvania
Avenue in his Buick. At the E Street entrance to FBI headquarters,
the agent on duty waved Rooney through, but balked at the family
in the Volvo.

"Don't you have him on your list?" Rooney asked with a smile.
"He's your new boss."

10

THE STRIPPER

Robert Hanssen couldn't take his eyes off the svelte body sway-ing before him on the small stage. As Priscilla Galey took off her business suit, shedding her clothing piece by piece and revealing her pulsating flesh, he was moved in ways he had never felt. He had seen seductive strippers before, and they certainly had their appeal. But there was something in the way she moved, some-thing in the elegant way she danced across the stage on a steamy summer day in 1990 that overwhelmed him. Hanssen had not antici-pated anything like it when he walked into Joanna's on M Street in Washington that day for his standard hamburger, Coke, and lunch-time look. Before leaving the cramped, dimly lit club, with its walls adorned by mirrors and pink neon lights, Hanssen paid the bill, scribbled a handwritten note to Galey, and sent it to her dressing room with $10 attached.

The tip was nothing unusual for Galey, who knew how to empty the wallets of D.C. professionals by slowly removing a business suit, giving them the fantasy of watching one of their office coworkers disrobe. "I'd take off my glasses, let down my hair, set down the brief-case, and go to work. The guys all saw me as that secretary they worked with or that woman they saw walking down the street."

The note from Hanssen, however, was unusual. "He gave me a wonderful compliment, the most beautiful compliment I've had in my life," she said. It was "something to the effect of he never expected to see someone with such grace and beauty in a strip club. It was really beautiful." Galey raced out of the back to find the man who had written the note. She caught up with him just before he headed out the door.

"Excuse me—excuse me, sir. I want to thank you not just for the ten dollars but for the compliment," Galey told him.

"Oh, well, you're welcome," Hanssen replied, sporting a wry smile. "I don't usually come in places like this."

Galey believed him. He seemed rather quiet and out-of-place at Joanna's.

Hanssen told her he worked for the FBI and had been there on official business. Galey had heard all manner of stories and explanations from respectable-looking men who frequented the club, and had no reason to doubt—or accept—this one. The truth was that, despite his love for Bonnie and strong religious convictions, Hanssen relished his lunches at Joanna's downtown as well as at another strip club called The Good Guys on Wisconsin Avenue in Georgetown. After all, he thought of himself as one of the good guys. On more than one occasion, he openly condemned FBI officials who talked about going to see strippers, calling their behavior offensive and unbefitting an agent of the Federal Bureau of Investigation.

Hanssen's affinity for strip joints was just one more secret in a life riddled with contradictions. He could still recall the first time his life-long pal Jack Hoschouer took him to lunch at The Good Guys, where Hanssen found himself aroused while chatting with naked ladies about their chosen profession. The outline of their stories was almost always the same: abused as children, new in town, and broke, this was a temporary job to make some money until something better came along. Hanssen came into this den of iniquity time after time, thoroughly enjoying the conversations he had with the dancers. Though he felt he was doing good by trying to persuade these women to give up their "sordid" profession, he never told Bonnie anything about his visits to the clubs, knowing that she wouldn't approve and would see it as a betrayal of their marital vows and shared commitment to moral rectitude.

Hanssen's visits to strip joints were a secret he shared with Hoschouer, a more intense version of the experiences the pair had enjoyed together over the years. Frequently, when Hoschouer came to visit Hanssen from his military post in Germany, the pair had lunch together at strip bars. They had enjoyed gawking at pretty girls together all the way back to their high school days in Chicago. Once during their college years when they had been walking down a Chicago street, they made eye contact with some good-looking young women and were soon kissing and fondling them in a nearby apartment. More often, they let their imaginations run wild but kept their hands to themselves.

In some respects, not much had changed in the way Hanssen and Hoschouer viewed women since their teen years. Long after they were married men, the duo would do a double take whenever they saw a pretty pair of legs walking down the street, and would talk about what it'd be like to get between them. They reinforced each other's girl-watching habits, turning their escapades into a spectator sport. While others went to the giant Tyson's Corner Mall in northern Virginia to go shopping, walk around, or grab something to eat, Hanssen and Hoschouer went there expressly to pick pretty women out of the crowd and get a good look. Extramarital affairs or one-night stands seemed routine to some of Hanssen's male FBI colleagues who boasted of their philandering and conquests. They never would have imagined that Bob, who openly eschewed such behavior as immoral and who proudly displayed a crucifix on his office wall, secretly shared pornographic Web sites, erotic fantasies, and sexual conquests with his friend Jack.

Priscilla Galey posed a new level of challenge, temptation, and risk for Hanssen. Ordinarily, he would go to strip joints, talk to the women about their lives, try to "save" them, and then move on. But before he left Joanna's on the day they first met, the dancer and the family man exchanged personal information and agreed to see each other again. Hanssen had not fallen for just any stripper. Galey was at the top of her game when they met and she had the credentials to show for it.

A high school dropout, Galey began dancing as a teen after a chaotic early marriage failed and she needed cash. But unlike many of the other women in her line of work, Galey truly loved what she did, proudly winning the crown of Ohio "Stripper of the Year" before moving on to dance at an array of clubs in Boston and Washington and landing at Joanna's. "I loved stripping," she said. "I really did. And I was really good at it."

The thirty-three-year-old Galey found Hanssen both appealing and unnerving when they first met. "I was a little scared of him," she said, recalling how perfectly put together he looked in one of his trademark dark suits, without a hair out of place. She grew more comfortable after spending time with him during heartfelt lunches where he would sit and listen uncritically as she talked about her troubled life. In return, he spoke proudly of his family, emphasizing that he was a loyal, faithful husband and father who had found a better path in life than the one she was traveling. He saw himself as a savior of the "damsel in distress" and desperately wanted to save her from the lifestyle she had adopted; it also made him feel very good that she sensed he was rich and important. He told her at one point that he was the second most powerful man in Washington and had inherited a fortune.

With cash pouring in from his espionage, Hanssen turned his philanthropy toward Priscilla, a woman who, unlike Bonnie, craved money and material things. Soon after their first lunch together, Hanssen sent Galey an envelope containing the money she needed to pay for some dental work.

"I had a tooth up front that was messed up really bad," Galey said. "One day I came into work there was an envelope that [Bob] left for me with a beautiful letter explaining that I owe him nothing, that he wanted nothing, that again he was happily married, and he didn't expect anything out of me. And there was two thousand dollars for my dental work."

As he had done with other strippers he'd met, Hanssen also began proselytizing. "He would just tell me things, you know, that I did need to change my life," Galey recalled. "And it always revolved around being closer to God."

At their second lunch, Hanssen stunned Galey by giving her a piece of jewelry. "It was a beautiful sapphire, diamond necklace," Galey said. "I thought he was just extremely rich or extremely generous. He said he had a large inheritance and he would really like for me to have this. . . . It was beautiful." Bonnie Hanssen's closet was filled with secondhand clothes from thrift shops, and her idea of a good birthday present was a new vacuum cleaner. In Galey, he had found a fun use for the fruits of his espionage, and it made him happy to see Galey so taken with his generosity. Hanssen was living out his dream of being a secret agent able to shower gifts on anyone at anytime.

Priscilla Galey and Bob Hanssen did more than eat lunch together. He took her to the National Gallery of Art to see paintings that embodied religious themes, and they took long walks together near the White House. (Once, on the way to the White House, Hanssen purchased a pair of blue pumps for Galey to wear in place of her spiked heels so she wouldn't stand out in the crowd.) He took her to nicer restaurants than she was accustomed to and private law enforcement eating clubs, often telling her that he enjoyed her companionship.

Hanssen also regularly visited Galey at Joanna's, coming to watch her perform while eating lunch. One day, he even took his friend Hoschouer to meet her outside the club. The relationship also meant enough to him that he asked her what her dreams were and sought to fulfill them, something no one had ever done for him. After he told Galey of an upcoming trip to Hong Kong—where he was inspecting one of the FBI's new legal attaché offices—she expressed a strong interest in having him bring her some kind of souvenir from Asia. Instead, he immediately helped her get a passport and bought her an airline ticket. From her perspective, the strange thing was that they flew back and forth to Hong Kong in late 1990 on separate planes and registered in separate hotel rooms. Galey strolled around the city, shopped, and enjoyed the electric atmosphere, and at times wondered whether Hanssen secretly was watching her movements. At night, they shared fancy dinners; Hanssen loved the way heads turned in restaurants when he walked in with a beautiful woman by his side.

Something seemed odd to Galey, but Hanssen refused to tell her what he was doing each day. "I could tell you," he said lightheartedly, "but I'd have to kill you."

Hanssen and Galey enjoyed each other during the two-and-a-half-week trip, including growing closer through a more intimate sexual relationship. Hanssen has told several people that he had sex with Galey once on the trip after she had made repeated passes at him, but he downplayed its significance. Members of Hanssen's family believe that after his arrest Galey was trying to protect them by suggesting the two never had sex.

Galey asked Hanssen to dance one night after dinner. They enjoyed going to piano bars and listening to music together. One evening, the pair requested "As Time Goes By," the famous song from *Casablanca* that contains the line, "A kiss is still a kiss, a sigh is just a sigh," which he told her was one of his favorites.

Galey began to view Hanssen as a savior, someone who had mysteriously entered her life, showered her with gifts and attention, and listened intently to her discuss the difficulties she faced. She had never had a relationship that was so fulfilling. She told him she struggled with paying the rent and meeting other expenses. As Hanssen began giving her hundred-dollar bills, her worries began to dissipate.

"I thought the man was an angel. I really had nothing to think but great, wonderful thoughts," Galey said.

As if all of that were not enough, Hanssen put Galey into orbit during lunch at a Mexican restaurant in the late summer of 1991, after their trip to Hong Kong. Galey fondly remembers it as "the lunch that changed my life."

"I have three little surprises for you," Hanssen said.

"Well, what is it?" Galey replied. "What is it? What is it?"

Hanssen handed Galey an envelope containing $1,000 in cash, an American Express card, and keys to a used Mercedes. He told her the American Express card was hers to keep provided she used it only to pay for gas or servicing the car. Galey was ecstatic; she had never had her own American Express card, and she had dreamed of driving a Mercedes. In return, Hanssen said he wanted her to quit her job at the strip club, attend church regularly, and promise not to live with a man before she married him.

"When you drive up in a Mercedes, they are not going to ask you if you went to college, they're not going to ask you anything," Hanssen told Galey. "They are going to treat you right."

Immediately after lunch, Galey got into the Mercedes and just drove and drove, feeling that this was the happiest day of her life. For the next few weeks, Galey stared outside her apartment window to be sure that nothing happened to the car. She also told Hanssen that at this stage, it would take more effort on her part, rather than his, for her to overhaul her lifestyle. "In order to change, I've got to learn how to do things I know nothing about, like learn to use a computer," Galey told him. "I need a new job." Soon thereafter, Hanssen gave Galey a computer to learn how to use and, as she put it, "the stepping stones I needed to change."

Though he was actively spying during the eighteen months while his relationship with Galey grew, she knew nothing about it. Asking him during one of their discussions if he had ever done anything wrong, Hanssen replied "Yes. I changed some test scores in college."

In addition to the other risks he took with Galey, Hanssen brought her to the FBI Academy in Quantico where he gave her an extensive personal tour. He also invited her to attend Mass at St. Catherine's, so she could see Bob with Bonnie and their children and gain a greater appreciation for religion. Galey, who drove to the church separately, observed from outside as Hanssen entered with his family. But she couldn't bring herself to enter the church. "I made it as far as sitting there and watching them go on, and I just sort of declined," Galey said.

The fantasy that Galey was living, with Hanssen as her guardian angel, ran into an ugly reality when she left the Washington area and returned to visit her home in Columbus, Ohio, for the Christmas holidays in 1991. She had planned to return to Washington and possibly go to Europe, where Hanssen allegedly had a job waiting for her. But back in the old neighborhood, her life began to fall apart. Among other things, she used her American Express card to buy cigarettes and other items, including Easter dresses for her nieces. Though Hanssen had told her to use the card only for car-related expenses, she thought he would appreciate the importance of Easter dresses, given his religious convictions.

Galey was wrong. When the American Express bill arrived, Hanssen was livid that she had not followed his orders precisely. Hanssen flew to Ohio, retrieved the credit card, and ended their relationship just as abruptly as it had begun more than a year earlier.

After that, Galey's life went into a tailspin. She became a crack addict and pawned everything of value Hanssen had given to her. The necklace, the Mercedes, the laptop computer—all were sold to support her habit. Even the dental work didn't last, as Galey lost her upper teeth. She made money working the streets as a prostitute, and eventually, after Galey was arrested for drug dealing in 1993, her mother attempted to get help from Hanssen. He declined to intervene. Galey served a year in jail and never heard from Hanssen again.

Now living in Columbus, Ohio, with her mother and young son in a crime-filled neighborhood, Galey looks back on her relationship with Hanssen and is amazed that she has nothing left to show for it. She believes that Hanssen may have been testing her to see if he could use her in connection with his work as a double agent, perhaps unwittingly have her deliver packages to certain places. But it seems his motives were more straightforward. Having been an abused son who felt a sense of helplessness, he was now in the business of trying to save someone else's soul. In exchange for that, he demanded total control and self-discipline. It was more than Galey could handle and, in the end, her tale is one of sorrow.

"He always pulled at my heartstrings," Galey said. "He thought I could do much better with my life." By abandoning her, Hanssen, who tried to bring religion into her life, left Galey worse off than if they never had met. "He has taken away," she said, "any faith I ever had."

11

THE UNWITTING
PORN STAR

Bob took delight in having sex with Bonnie as a reinforcement of his manhood. He also relished the fantasy of having other men watch him in action. He derived pleasure from thinking about how he could turn the saintly Bonnie into a ravishing woman in bed—and shared those thoughts and more with his friend Jack Hoschouer through fifty to sixty e-mails a day. He looked up to Jack, whom he viewed as a real man because he had served in Vietnam and had far greater sexual experience. He fantasized about what it would be like for Jack to have sex with Bonnie. Jack was married without children, and Bob told him it would bring him great joy if he fathered a child with Bonnie. These were fantasies, since both men knew that Bonnie didn't feel comfortable around Jack, didn't like his extended visits to their home, and would never entertain the possibility of such ideas in the first place. They remained, instead, part of the ongoing exchange of ideas and pornography across the Atlantic between two old high school friends who never really left the adolescent phase of their infatuation with sex.

Since Bonnie would not have allowed herself to be swapped between friends, Bob invited Jack on numerous occasions to do the next best thing: secretly watch husband and wife make love. Without Bonnie's knowledge, Bob asked Jack to watch them from a deck outside their bedroom. Later, Bob installed a secret video camera in the bedroom of their northern Virginia home so Jack could watch them on a monitor in another part of the house via closed-circuit video. Jack hadn't asked to watch Bob and Bonnie in bed; it was always at Bob's invitation. Bob wanted to show Jack what a fantastic lover he was and what an incredible woman Bonnie became between the sheets.

Jack continued to watch them have sex when he visited from the mid to late 1980s and into the 1990s. Bob relished talking with Jack about the experiences afterward. It was a major turn-on for Bob, who later wrote that he "loved having men's tongues dangle out looking at his wife." It was also part of the James Bond image Hanssen imagined for himself, with a beautiful woman who made him the envy of all lucky enough to catch a glimpse. In those moments of fantasy, Bob also became the perfect double agent: too clever to be detected, too upright to be suspected.

In the following story Bob wrote and posted on an Internet bulletin board where people shared tales of sex, he fantasized about the early days of his marriage in Chicago. Many, but not all, of the details in the story were taken from Bonnie and Bob's life together. Ever the risk-taker, Hanssen claimed authorship for the story and used their real names.

From: Robert P. Hanssen (hanssen@nova.org)
Subject: Bonnie (wife, exhib, true)
Newsgroups: alt.sex.stories

It was only around four in the afternoon, and Bonnie still had plenty of time as she walked over and perched on the high wooden stool. She sat, freshly showered and still naked, in the warm light of the summer Chicago sun which streamed through her apartment's large bedroom window to her left. Refreshed from her shower after teaching second grade at the parish school, it was time to fix her hair. This was her habit, her little ritual after a shower, a time to herself to unwind and feel feminine, a time to feel the air on her skin and fix herself all pretty for Bob.

People said she was the best lay teacher at Saint Anne's. She was even better than some of the dedicated nuns teaching there. But Bonnie was no nun. Bonnie wasn't the type to be locked up away from men.

Bonnie looked gorgeous. But unlike some beautiful women, she saw only the "flaws." Happy today in her own modest little newly-wed's apartment, a relatively inexpensive one because it was next to the "El" tracks, she was primping for Bob. She'd gotten married to Bob just last fall, and they'd moved to their first place together, a one-bedroom apartment on Winthrop Avenue on Chicago's north side. Bonnie looked in her mirror at her naked figure. She didn't like what she saw exactly. To her way of thinking she was too buxom, and she thought her hips too wide for her narrow waist and she was so "high waisted" compared to most girls. Still, it seemed to work for men. Men called it being leggy. All it meant for Bonnie is that she could only wear petite sizes that never had quite enough room for her breasts, and she was always looking like she was about to pop out of her sundresses. Of course men never seemed to object to that look.

Bonnie ran a wide untangling comb through her long brown hair, thinking men had no taste. She wanted to be pencil skinny like those models in the women's fashion magazines. She looked more like those slutty buxom girls in "Playboy" magazine. But then she supposed men did go for that. After all the fraternity poll at college had voted her best legs on campus. She felt she had good legs.

At college, she'd found from experience that she loathed fraternities types generally. All they wanted to do was party and drink so they could feel-up girls and try to get in their pants. Bonnie detested it. Bob hadn't been at all like the fraternity types. She'd met him during the summer at the hospital where they'd both worked. She'd been attracted to him from the first because of the way he'd treated the patients and he to her, it turned out for the same reason.

Bonnie loved the afternoon sunlight. She was getting ready to
go to dinner with her husband. Today was his birthday, and she
wanted to look especially nice. Bob was a dental student. He'd
scored in the top two percent on his national Dental Boards,
and Bonnie was proud of him. She was going to show him a good
time. Bonnie knew that a good time meant letting Bob show her
off. Bob loved having men's tongues dangle out looking at his
wife.

Bob was a leg man, Bonnie knew that, and Bonnie knew she had
legs that could handle that. She'd learned shopping with him
that no dress was too short. So, tonight Bonnie intended to do
something she'd never allowed herself before, to push the limit
in that direction—to please him. She'd hunted for and found a
secret weapon—a dress, a special one for a special occasion.
She'd found it in a store down on Rush Street. Bonnie was quite
innocent and naïve in many ways really, and had no idea it was
a store catering to strippers.

The dress Bonnie'd gotten was short. Well, you'd have to say
it was indecently short. It was made of a stretchy lycra mix and
was jet black. She thought, when she'd bought it, that she'd have
to be a bit careful, for it tended to ride up and there wasn't much
up remaining upon which to ride, that is, below her crotch.
When she'd tried it on though, she knew Bob would love it.

Bonnie was playing with her hair, trying it different ways. She
tried it up, she tried it down, and was about to settle for up when
she noticed an odd movement out on the elevated train tracks
across the alley from her bedroom window. She looked out the
window quickly. "My God!" she thought. There were five workers standing leaning on their shovels looking at her. In a panic,
she bounded from her stool across the bed to try to grab the
shade and pull it down. Because the bed stood only a foot below the window and along the wall, this move necessitated her
standing stark naked on the bed to reach up for the shade pull.
She was there in full view of her suddenly bemused audience.
Bonnie grasped the shade and pulled it down, with short-lived

relief. The shade didn't catch and flapped up again. She sprung back a second time, her cute little bush finally exposed, and tried again. She yanked it down again and again it flapped open. Worse, this time instead the cord tied itself around the shade roller. Bonnie went up for it again. Bonnie's face was flushed. The men were looking right at her and she was totally naked. It seemed like forever while Bonnie stood in that window trying to untie it, but she got it. This time, a little calmer from the delay, she laughed at the smiles of her audience and closed it slowly and deliberately like putting the curtain for them on a good show, and had even given them a little wave goodbye.

Then Bonnie collapsed panting from the excitement on her bed. Her heart was pounding. She felt galvanized as if by electricity from the experience. She realized she felt something else too. She felt aroused. "If only Bob were here," she thought, I'd show him even a better time than the workers on those tracks.

It was a while, but Bonnie collected herself. Bonnie peeked out the shade. One of the men saw her and pointed her out, and she jumped back. She thought to herself, "Well that's it. I'll have to cover up." She went to her drawer and picked out a sheer black bra and delicate panties.

Bonnie pointedly didn't even look out the window when she opened the shade and resumed her perch on the stool. "Let them eat cake," she thought.

She tried on her dress about a half an hour later and decided that the bra would not do under it. She'd just slid the dress off again when she glanced out and seen that she still had an audience. It was then that she slid the bra off, stripping herself of her bra in full view of the window knowing they were watching, before wiggling into the dress again. Bonnie was starting to enjoy this.

In her heels, Bonnie bent over to look at herself from the rear. She told herself she would have to remember not to bend over like that, but then removed her panties too. Bob was going to get his money's worth tonight. Bonnie slipped her blazer over her tight dress. There was about a half inch of tight dress below the blazer. She still had good legs especially in the heels.

She looked again in the mirror and was pleased with the image. It spoke expensive-flashy not cheap-flashy. Using Bob's criteria she looked just right.

Bonnie glanced out the window. Her audience had departed. But God she was turned on. Luckily Bob would be here any minute.

Bonnie Hanssen didn't know that her husband had written and posted his fantasies on the Internet, just as she was unaware that Jack Hoschouer had watched her having sex with Bob. The sexual desires and actions ascribed to Bonnie in the story reflected Hanssen's active fantasy life, rather than Bonnie's emotions or activities. Hanssen wrote about her innocence with reference to shopping in a sex shop and says she "hardly even knew about strippers." In reality, Bonnie believed nudity had its place in the bedrooms of married couples and nowhere else. Living in Chicago in the 1960s, Bonnie was dismayed by the sexuality in mainstream culture and appalled by the behavior of some of her neighbors. Once, when some "hippies" failed to heed her warnings to stop parking in her outdoor space, she put sand and a hose in their car and turned on the water. Then, she waited on her apartment balcony for them to discover the mess. "It only goes downhill from here," she shouted, brandishing Bob's gun.

Often at the supermarket, Bonnie would turn issues of *Cosmopolitan* magazine around so that the covers would not be visible and she once walked into a Victoria's Secret store and berated a clerk for displaying pictures of women in lingerie in the storefront windows. "I enjoy this intimate apparel myself," she would later say, "but I don't think it should be on public display."

Her husband had other ideas. Notwithstanding all of his "soul-saving" conversations with anonymous strippers, Hanssen sometimes behaved crudely and primitively around other women. On two separate occasions, he snuck up and touched the exposed breasts of one of Bonnie's sisters while she was breast-feeding a baby, sending her racing out of the room and asking never to be left alone with him again. Another time, after a female subordinate at the FBI left a late-afternoon meeting even though he had ordered her to stay, Hanssen chased her down the hall and grabbed her by the arm. Both were disciplined, the woman for insubordination and Bob for acting inappropriately.

He hated that the FBI employed women as agents, deeming them inferior, weak, and incapable of holding their own. In addition, Hanssen abhorred the idea that homosexuals worked at the Bureau, and some family members described him as homophobic. In an e-mail called "Depressing Things," Hanssen described his disgust at driving through the capital city and spotting a senior FBI official at a gay and lesbian rally. Hanssen, who rarely exercised and had little experience in locker rooms, also was extremely uncomfortable undressing in front of other men. On the rare occasions when he went to the gym, he wore a bathing suit into the communal showers. Several psychologists and psychiatrists who have had experience with patients exhibiting similar behavior have suggested that Hanssen repressed his own homosexual feelings through shared experiences with pornography and in other ways.

When Hanssen once visited Hoschouer in Germany, the pair went sight-seeing in Frankfurt and walked into a "House of Colors," where prostitutes lined the halls waiting to be plucked and led into nearby rooms for sex with their customers. Hanssen and Hoschouer looked over the selection, before Bob picked a leggy woman and invited her into one of the bedrooms. He proceeded to begin proselytizing, but didn't seem to be making much progress and gave up. Bob and Jack left the whorehouse soon after to resume their sight seeing. But Bob had become fixated on the woman they had met and fantasized about the possibility of having sex with her at the same time as his friend Jack. "Let's go back," Bob said. They returned to find Bob's woman standing and waiting in the same place as before. This time, after the trio entered the bedroom, everyone disrobed and Bob lived out one of his grandest sexual fantasies.

With their needs fulfilled, Bob and Jack got dressed, left the "House of Colors," and continued sight seeing. Though he would not get the chance to visit Jack in Germany again, Bob thought about the trip often, recharging his longing to share his wife with his best friend. Again and again, he replayed the experiences they shared until the line between fantasy and reality disappeared. In Bob's mind, the woman who had made them both erect was his beautiful Bonnie.

In January 1999, Hanssen posted the following story about himself, his wife Bonnie, and his friend Jack Hoschouer on an adult Internet site. While many of the details reflect Hanssen's fantasies, the broad outline of this first-person narrative, entitled "The 'Unwitting?' Porn Star" by Hanssen, is consistent with testimony given by Hoschouer to FBI agents, prosecutors, and a federal grand jury.

> For years, I have sent nude pictures of Bonnie, my wife, to my close friend Jack. It began back in the Vietnam War years. Jack was over there and I was safe here at home. I'd tried to join the Navy as a dental student, but couldn't see well enough—too nearsighted, even though I was corrected with lenses to 20:20. That same problem kept me out of the draft. I felt bad. Here Jack was making all these sacrifices for my country and there was so little I could do to support him. Well, Bonnie was just 21 then and we'd just married. Jack had been my best man, and Bonnie was very pretty in those days, still is of course though she is older now. She was only 5'4" but shaped 34–23–36 with long brown hair and big brown doe eyes. Gorgeous would not be an overstatement. Pretty as she was, she made an excellent subject for photography. She tolerated posing nude for her husband too. Actually, she claimed to tolerate it, but when she

got going posing nude she was like a spaniel to water. She put her soul into it, and the resulting pictures were electrifying.

Now, my hobby was always photography and Jack's was too. Even in our little apartment while I was in school, I had set up the bathroom with a board I could put on the tub to hold the enlarger above the trays and the waterbath below. It worked well, and I had this great supply of knockout pictures of Bonnie. Unfortunately, I had no one to whom I could appropriately show them. She wasn't about to let me show them either, artistic though they were! So one day, I sent a few off to Jack in one of my regular letters—he loved it. He got to see a whole side of Bonnie he'd never knew existed. Technically, I guess you could say he got to see all sides, crevices, and cracks of Bonnie, but that might be a bit crude. (Bonnie did a lot of posing with her legs spread. It turned her on. Bonnie was a great one for generating photos of "artistically posed girl with wet and gaping pussy." They all went to Jack.)

As I said, Jack was a photo enthusiast too, and eventually I ended up sending him negatives, and he was doing his own enlargements of them with the advanced photo-club enlargement equipment they had for recreation over there. He'd send large blow-ups back to augment my supply. We had a ball with it, and it kept his mind off the war and on home. Bonnie never wondered where I got the big prints. She isn't very scientific so didn't realize such prints don't come out of 8x10 trays. She just accepted it.

When I finally bought a house, I went to work and built a darkroom down in the basement and stored all of Bonnie's photos there. Bonnie was having problems getting pregnant then so there were no kids around to get into things like that. In the end, Jack came back from the war with a Bronze Star and other decorations to make a career as a military officer, visiting often when blowing through town enroute to some military assignment. Bonnie enjoyed him greatly and was as proud as I was of the risks he'd undertaken for his country. He's survived where others hadn't.

Bonnie even posed for Jack occasionally, including some in a tight
sweater that sizzled, but never nude, probably because Jack could
never get up the guts to ask her. She did offer, on her own however, to let him come to our house any time he wanted to use the
darkroom, knowing her pictures where stored there. This was at
a time when Jack briefly had a place locally. I think, as she later
maintained, that she simply forgot they were there, but you never
know with Bonnie. When I found out she'd let him use the darkroom, I thought the time was ripe to let her know that Jack had
seen the nudes of her. I wanted her to know he'd already seen
her so she'd have nothing to be shy about in case she was ever
tempted to pose for him, and this way I could blame it on her. So
when she told me about it, I said, "Oh Bonnie, all your pictures
where down there, and Jack told me he saw them." I added, "and
thought they were great." She was greatly embarrassed, said she'd
forgotten and all, but I was never completely convinced.

Jack had often dreamed of photographing Bonnie himself or of
just seeing her nude in person. One never knows about the photography. It may come to pass, but we could do something about
the seeing. That could be arranged. We initially made some
forays in this regard where Jack watched Bonnie shower
through the glass shower-stall door. I would talk to her as she
showered, and he would look through the bathroom doorway
from the darkened bedroom behind me. This was fun but not
totally satisfying.

Our schemes progressed in this regard to the point of letting
Jack see Bonnie and I having sex. The first time we did this Jack
was visiting for a week. It was a warm fall. Each night, I'd leave
the shade up a bit and leave our bedroom window open about
six inches so Jack could come up and stand on a pre-positioned
chair on our deck and look in while I had sex with her at night.
That worked like a charm. He could see her walking around
the room naked and I'd position her in different ways on the
bed while fucking her so he'd get a good look of my cock going
in and out or of her tits bouncing. By pure chance, to his good
fortune, she even bent over right in front of the window once
when he was there, and he got a good view of her pussy from

about a foot away. It was great. I was dying watching. Our house backs on the woods so there was really little risk to him in doing this, but it still got old because of the chill and risk. It was then that technology came to the rescue.

At a security show, we bought subminiature video cameras designed for surveillance purposes. We bought two. One was no more than a little one-inch by one-quarter inch box with a low light CCD sensor that looks through a pinhole. The other was slightly larger; a high quality but very small lensed camera. We also bought video transmitter/receiver combinations, which could relay the signals from the cameras in place in our bedroom down to our den. After some experimentation (while Bonnie was out of town for a few days,) we set up a great system. Jack could sit in our den when he visited and see everything up in the bedroom. This proved no end of fun during his visits. Often now he'll stay five or six days doing things like research on his Ph.D. thesis at the various libraries here. On recent trips, in the mornings he sits and watches Bonnie on the large screen TV in our den as she gets showered and dressed. (Bonnie still fixes her hair while nude each morning.) At night, he watches the nightly sex scene or, once, Bonnie modeling her Victoria-Secret white nylons, sheer bra and heels for me before we fucked. That really got us all going.

This whole business has been no end of fun. He can even tape the sessions on our VCR. Bonnie may be the only teacher at the elite girl's school where she works who is also a porn star! Of course, she doesn't know it. Well at least we think she doesn't know it. I do notice that when Jack visits she wants sex every night. Perhaps it is just that I'm always ready for it when he's here as you can imagine. Of course, Jack flatters her a lot too. He's still hoping some day for THE BIG modeling session, and women love to be flattered.

Anyway, Jack and I have our fun. Bonnie looks great. Jack and I love seeing her tits slapping together as she takes cock hard. She is now size 36 on top and she's kept her waist and hips trim. She's still a beautiful woman.

How do you explain a husband providing closed-circuit video of his wife naked so his best friend can watch them have sex? "I just loved showing her off," Hanssen said in another Internet posting. Hanssen had deep feelings of inadequacy and sought reaffirmation of his masculinity by sharing his sexual encounters with his best friend. As he did in other aspects of his life, Hanssen also blended fantasy and reality in this tale.

While Bonnie did allow Bob to take some nude photographs early in their marriage, she never knew the pictures were shared with Jack. As a devout Catholic and part-time teacher of religion and morality at Oakcrest, Bonnie simply was not the posing type. As recently as 1999, however, Bob Hanssen snuck up on his wife while she was dressing or getting out of the shower and took photos, telling her that there was no film in the camera. (On at least one occasion, Bob took photographs of Bonnie using Polaroid film and showed her the photos. He told her he was taking the pictures to prove to her that she was thin since Bonnie complained of being fat whenever she ate ice cream.) Federal authorities discovered nude photographs of Bonnie on Hoschouer's computer hard drive, and he acknowledged receiving them from Bob.

Hanssen rationalized the notion of sharing Bonnie in the flesh with Jack as an act of patriotism to aid a friend and war hero he admired. But he also knew what he contemplated was wrong. His yearning to share photographs with Jack led him to think of the act as one of goodness, not evil, and of revelation rather than revulsion. He also introduced Jack, who was married, to an adult Web site called "myhotwife.com," which they visited and discussed via e-mail. In Hanssen's mind, with its many strands that never pulled together to stop him from living out destructive fantasies, there are loose wires rather than completed circuits.

"It is the behavior of a person who is not integrated," said psychiatrist Dr. Stephen Hersh. "You end up with a loosely woven piece of cloth."

As he sent Hoschouer photos of Bonnie over the years, Hanssen maintained that she was a "secret exhibitionist." In reality, she was a woman constantly manipulated and duped by her husband. Hoschouer told federal authorities that one day in the 1970s, while he was serving in Vietnam, he received a brown envelope from Bob with naked pictures of Bonnie. Hoschouer immediately sent Bob a letter saying he must have sent the pictures mistakenly. But the next day, Hoschouer received a letter from Bob asking him whether the pictures had lifted his spirits. After Hoschouer asked him to stop mailing the photos, Hanssen took breaks but still sporadically transmitted more naked photographs of Bonnie. Confirming aspects of Hanssen's Web posting, Hoschouer told federal law enforcement authorities that without Bonnie's knowledge and at Bob's invitation, he watched the couple having sex during some of his visits to their home, adding that what he had done was shameful and wrong.

The troubled Hanssen found solace and insight in literature. In one of his favorite books, *The Man Who Was Thursday* by G. K. Chesterton, he strongly identified with the main character, Gabriel Syme, a poet-turned-policeman-turned-spy who shared many of his unusual character traits. Hanssen read the book often and shared it with his family; two of the Hanssens' children are studying Chesterton as part of advanced degree programs. Good, thoughtful, clever, and courageous, Syme, like Hanssen, saw the beauty of order, describing things like train timetables as poetic. Hanssen also could relate to Syme's cunning as a spy and to the description that "he was less meek than he looked."

Chesterton wrote that "Syme, indeed, was one of those men who are open to all the more nameless psychological influences in a degree a little dangerous to mental health. Utterly devoid of fear in physical dangers, he was a great deal too sensitive to the smell of spiritual evil." Like Hanssen, Syme's character radiated conflicts. Another character ridiculed Syme's assertion that he was a poet of law and respectability. "You say you are a poet of law; I say you are a contradiction in terms." From his life among strippers, pornography, and spying to his days as an FBI agent, respected father, and member of Opus Dei, Hanssen too was a paradox. And just as Hanssen kept much to himself since the days of his childhood abuse, Syme also "endured these thunders with a certain submissive solemnity."

After the poet Syme joined the police force, his primary missions became saving the world from the evil of anarchy and avoiding discovery, goals that resonated powerfully with Hanssen. As someone who spoke about the need for good works and proselytized about his religion, Hanssen attempted to save the world by reaching out to its troubled souls. In addition, he cleverly and carefully sought to avoid detection in the secret part of his life that energized him—spying for the Russians. But both Hanssen and his literary alter ego were consumed with the issue of sanity. In a letter to the Russians, Hanssen describes himself either as "insanely brave or quite insane," while Chesterton writes that Syme was "quiet, courteous, rather gentle" with "a spot on his mind that was not sane."

In describing Sunday, the larger-than-life figure in Chesterton's novel who represented the awesome forces of Nature, Gabriel Syme might as well have been talking about the need people feel to understand the conflicting sides of double agent Bob Hanssen: "Bad is so bad we cannot think good but an accident. Good is so good that we feel certain that evil can be explained."

12

FRIENDS

Dear Friend:

Time is flying. As a poet said: "What's our life,
                                 If full of care
                                 You have no time
                                 To stop and stare?"

You've managed to slow down the speed of Your running life to send us a message. And we appreciate it.

We hope You're O'K and Your family is fine too. We
are sure You're doing great at Your job. As before, we'll
keep staying alert to respond to any call from You
whenever you need it.

We acknowledge receiving one disk through CHARLIE.
One disk of mystery and intrigue. Thank you.

Not much a business letter this time. Just formalities. We
consider Site-9 cancelled. And we are sure you remember: our next contact is due at ELLIS.

Frankly, we are looking forward to JUNE. Every new
season brings new expectations.

Enclosed in our today's package please find $10,000.

Thank You for Your friendship and help.

We attach some information requests. We hope You'll
be able to assist us on them.

Take care and good luck.

Sincerely,
Your friends.

The Russians understood that friends were lacking in Hanssen's
life and aimed to fill that void. Sharing a poem, expressing appreciation for gestures large and small, wishing his family well, warmly
greeting the man they had never met. In every way possible, the
Russians sought to make Hanssen feel as though their mysterious,
invisible relationship of dead drops, signal sites, and cold-blooded
espionage was the genuine article, a true friendship.

After a lifetime of secrets, Hanssen felt he finally had a reliable
partner and a sympathetic ear in the KGB. As a boy, he had never
told his mother or anyone else what troubled him. As an adolescent
and teenager, he had made one lasting friend through school, Jack
Hoschouer, who was best man at his wedding. Though they lived far
apart, Jack was the sole person he could rely on over the years to share
some good times and keep certain secrets. But Hanssen, who hadn't
told his closest friend about the espionage, had urged the KGB to
recruit Jack as a spy. (They didn't.) Bob told Bonnie little about his
counterintelligence work for the FBI—he didn't dare to utter a word
to her about the KGB after the incident in 1980. He had not developed
many friends at the FBI, and even at church he typically would rush
out to get the car when Mass ended rather than linger a few minutes
to greet his fellow parishioners.

And so it seemed a bit unusual to those who worked with him
to see what a seemingly close relationship Hanssen had developed
with Soviet defector Victor Sheymov, who, along with his wife and
daughter, slipped out of Moscow in 1980 with help from the CIA.

Sheymov, who operated out of KGB headquarters in Lubyanka Moscow Center, had been among the elite, regarded as a star of Soviet intelligence. If anyone knew the inner workings of the KGB, it was Sheymov, who had been head of security for coded communications worldwide and one of a handful of people who had knowledge of the entire system, including the KGB's ultrasecret Eighth Chief Directorate, which ran its global communications and eavesdropping systems. Hanssen, with the FBI's blessing, became Sheymov's confidant after he defected. Hanssen recognized there was much he could learn about the inner workings of Moscow and the KGB from Sheymov.

"The KGB is a most sophisticated, deviously intelligent organization, and far more dangerous than the brutal thugs often presented to the public," Sheymov has written. "The massively multi-layered complexity of the KGB is mind-boggling. Few people, even within the KGB, know enough to comprehend it.

"Despite the general perception of Soviet incompetence, it should be remembered that the Soviets drew on a culture that produced a long succession of great mathematicians and chess players. The fact is that whenever the Soviets established a major priority, they usually achieved extraordinary results. Soviet space, nuclear, laser, and eavesdropping technologies are just a few examples. The operation of the KGB made full use of them. The KGB is probably the most deliberately and carefully created large organization in the world. . . . Still a million strong, it has no real budget and cost is no object. It is a classic example of management by objective."

Just what kind of friend was Hanssen to Sheymov? To hear his fellow FBI agents and others tell it, a very sincere one. This was as close as Hanssen would get to making a new friend, or so it seemed. Sheymov, who initially had been handled by CIA officials, turned to Hanssen after he grew disenchanted with the way things were going. Former FBI national security chief Ray Mislock, who first met Hanssen during a debriefing of Sheymov, said Hanssen was a diligent gatekeeper and protective of the defector: "Sheymov became more enamored of his FBI handlers and it cemented his relationship with Hanssen. Hanssen went out of his way to help this guy and became his primary handler in the Bureau. It went beyond that. He became his friend. I know that Hanssen had Sheymov to his house and introduced him to his family and went way beyond what would be normal in terms of facilitating this guy's resettlement. Most people who end up doing these kinds of things form a relationship, but it never goes beyond a certain professional limit. It went way beyond a professional and became a personal relationship."

But Sheymov didn't know that his friend Bob Hanssen imagined he had even better friends at the KGB. Hanssen disclosed secrets about Sheymov's defection, and his thoughts, movements and whereabouts. "On one hand," Mislock mused, "you can genuinely befriend somebody beyond what is required in your job, bring him into your home and family, and help them adjust. And at the same time, you are selling them down the river." The risk to Sheymov from Hanssen's disclosures was immense. As the KGB tracked his movements, Sheymov, living under the alias "Dick Shepard," was in imminent danger.

Hanssen's growing loyalty to his Soviet "friends" ultimately overwhelmed the tremendous distaste he had for some U.S. officials, including Felix Bloch, a senior State Department official who had met with the Russians in Europe and for years been suspected of committing espionage. When asked about the Bloch probe during press briefings in the summer of 1989, President George Bush expressed grave concern about the potential damage: "I ran the Central Intelligence Agency and the entire intelligence community for a year, and you are always concerned about people who are willing to betray their country. It is most serious. I've known about this matter for some time, and the minute I heard about it, I was aggrieved because it is a very tragic thing, should these allegations be true." Bloch, for his part, claimed he didn't know that the man he was photographed dining with in Paris worked for the KGB, adding that the suitcase he passed along to him underneath the table had stamps from his stamp collection, not intelligence secrets. The sensational Bloch probe, which captured the public's imagination with stories of his multiyear relationship with a high-priced prostitute who said they engaged in sadomasochistic sex, was stymied once Hanssen tipped off the Soviets.

According to a phone call taped by the FBI, Bloch, the number two official in the U.S. embassy in Vienna, was told that Pierre, the surreptitious name for his KGB contact, "cannot see you in the near future" because "he is sick" and that a "contagious disease is suspected . . . I am worried about you. You have to take care of yourself." Bloch, who understood the cryptic message, was never prosecuted and denied engaging in espionage. He later was fired by the State Department for reportedly making false statements to the FBI. To avoid the media glare, he moved to North Carolina, where he first got a job bagging groceries and, more recently, began driving a bus. But he again attracted attention after being arrested for petty shoplifting.

In a letter to his KGB friends, Hanssen wrote that he alerted them to the FBI's Bloch probe because Bloch was a "friend" of the KGB:

> Bloch was such a shnook. . . . I almost hated protecting
> him, but then he was your friend, and there was your
> illegal I wanted to protect. If our guy sent to Paris had
> balls or brains both would have been dead meat. Fortu-
> nately for you he had neither. He was your good luck of
> the draw. He was the kind who progressed by always
> checking with those above and tying them to his mis-
> takes. The French said, "Should we take them down?"
> He went all wet. He'd never made a decision before,
> why start then. It was that close. His kindred spirits
> promoted him. Things are the same the world over, eh?

Tipping the Russians to the classified FBI probe of Bloch was only one of many valuable jewels Hanssen passed to his KGB friends during the late 1980s and into 1991, a period of regular exchanges of an unparalleled amount of sensitive information through dead drop sites in suburban Virginia. Many of them took place near Hanssen's house on Talisman Drive, a split-level structure with a dark brown exterior, a small front yard, and dueling antennas—one for television reception, the other for ham radio. Despite the continuing flow of tens of thousands of dollars from the KGB to Hanssen, there were no dramatic changes at the house, in the aging cars he drove or in any other visible aspect of family life. Hanssen was determined not to make the same mistakes as other spies before him by spending the funds conspicuously.

The Soviets, for their part, got a bargain. The KGB had paid more for less many times before, and they surely would have anted up in this instance if Hanssen had requested it. But, as his former FBI colleague David Major said, "He didn't do it for the gain. He did it for the game." In exchange for their encouraging letters that gave Hanssen a sense of kinship, importance, and adventure, the KGB received a steady stream of TOP SECRET intelligence and classified military secrets that went well beyond anything an FBI double agent ever had given up before.

The most costly single breach involved Hanssen's disclosure of a surveillance tunnel beneath the gated Soviet diplomatic compound on Wisconsin Avenue that stood on a hilltop overlooking the Georgetown section of Washington, D.C. Devised by the National Security Agency and monitored by FBI agents in a nearby house where the signals were transmitted, the tunnel used sophisticated laser technology for electronic eavesdropping. It had taken careful planning and shrewd maneuvering to install the secret tunnel and it was estimated to have cost the government hundreds of millions of dollars. It was later described in government documents as "a highly sensitive United States technical operation classified at the TOP SECRET/SCI level." Hanssen's betrayal enabled the Soviets to avoid the trap and instead feed disinformation back to the United States.

Among the various CIA documents Hanssen planted at the dead drop in Nottoway Park in 1988 was a remarkable 530-page packet of materials that included a classified CIA description of America's nuclear program and a CIA Counterintelligence Staff Study titled, "The Soviet Counterintelligence Offensive: KGB Recruitment Operations against CIA," which bore the CAVEATS NOFORN, NOCONTRACT, and ORCON. The warnings indicated that it was not releasable to foreigners or government contractors under any conditions. There also was an FBI review of Soviet recruitments and defectors labeled TOP SECRET that contained the following warning:

IN VIEW OF THE EXTREME SENSITIVITY OF THIS DOCUMENT, THE UTMOST CAUTION MUST BE EX-ERCISED IN ITS HANDLING. THE CONTENTS IN-CLUDE A COMPREHENSIVE REVIEW OF SENSITIVE SOURCE ALLEGATIONS AND INVESTIGATIONS OF PENETRATIONS OF THE FBI BY THE SOVIET INTEL-LIGENCE SERVICES, THE DISCLOSURE OF WHICH WOULD COMPROMISE HIGHLY SENSITIVE COUN-TERINTELLIGENCE OPERATIONS AND METHODS.

In return, Hanssen received $25,000 in cash and a letter asking for specific information about surveillance systems, the agent network in New York, illegal intelligence, and several FBI recruitment operations. To speed things along, the KGB also proposed the use of two new nearby dead drops, where Hanssen could leave material by 9:00 P.M. and the KGB could remove it and replace it with cash and any instructions by 10:00 P.M. Increasingly, Hanssen passed infor-mation on diskettes. After he left the seventh diskette, which con-tained technical information about surveillance systems as well as operational details about FBI counterespionage operations in New York, the KGB deposited another $50,000 in his special Moscow bank account. The eighth diskette, focusing on specific Russian recruitment targets of the FBI, allowed the KGB to adjust its tactics to foil American operations.

Within days, the KGB responded gratefully, leaving a package at the new BOB dead drop site containing a diamond, as requested by Hanssen, and a letter with praise and thanks from KGB Chairman, Vladimir Kryuchkov. The fall 1988 letter delved into communications procedures, security measures, and passports, and sought specific information about U.S. missile technology and FBI programs.

As the winter holidays approached in 1988, Hanssen geared up for a major data dump. On the day after Christmas, he transferred 356 pages of documents, a diskette containing classified information, and a stunning report with the title, "Soviet Armed Forces and Capabilities for Conducting Strategic Nuclear War Until the End of the 1990s." Earlier in the year, Hanssen had provided a TOP SECRET analysis of Soviet intelligence collection against U.S. nuclear weapons capabilities that focused on early warning systems and other means of defense or retaliation against large-scale attack. Coupled with this latest document, the Soviets had the blueprints of U.S. planning and intelligence in the event of nuclear war. The KGB reciprocated with a second diamond, $10,000 in cash, and a broad request for more classified information. By providing the Soviets with advance intelligence that they could use to prevent a potential American counterstrike, Hanssen's disclosures heightened the prospect of nuclear war.

Although Hanssen's clandestine relationship with the KGB had begun with him volunteering what information to provide, increasingly he took orders from the Soviets. As time went on, they doled out assignments, he sought the information, and they compensated him, all without ever meeting face-to-face. Though he did the KGB's bidding, Hanssen believed that he ultimately remained the boss and the Russians his supplicant, as he requested the return of certain papers, denied some requests, and put a premium on his personal security.

The pattern of exchanges continued in the winter of 1989. Hanssen and the KGB used alphabetized code names—AN, BOB, CHARLIE, DORIS, ELLIS, FLO, and GRACE—to identify the growing number of dead drop sites. By March, Hanssen had given the Soviets a twelfth computer diskette and a growing collection of sensitive documents. These included a TOP SECRET briefing paper for the CIA director that contained a "Warning Notice" about the confidentiality of the intelligence sources or methods vital to U.S. National Security. The sensitive document, which he asked the Soviets to return, contained specific technical information about the highly advanced "Measurement and Signature Intelligence Program," a sophisticated communications technology enabling the United States to track and intercept an array of communications. At the CHARLIE dead drop where the exchange occurred, the KGB left a third diamond for Hanssen, as well as $18,000 and a letter requesting new dead drop sites and suggestions for how to increase operational security. The KGB also inquired about Hanssen's precautions for the diamonds; he told them he would say the gems came from his grandmother.

By this point, senior KGB officials were awash in U.S. intelligence, with information flowing simultaneously from the FBI's Hanssen and the CIA spy Aldrich Ames. Simultaneously, the biggest spy in CIA history and the biggest spy in FBI history were answering Soviet questions about sensitive intelligence matters without knowledge of each other. The KGB officers involved in handling Hanssen were honored with the highly coveted Order of the Red Banner, the Order of the Red Star, and the Medal for Excellent Service.

After determining that the diamonds the KGB had left for him were flawed, Hanssen returned two of the diamonds they had given him and requested cash instead. At the same time, Hanssen delivered a thirteenth diskette and eighty pages of material that included the "National Intelligence Program [19]90–91," a thorough description of the U.S. intelligence budget. He also suggested that the Russians make deposits for him in a Swiss bank account, the kind of transaction that would make Hanssen feel dashing and important. The KGB returned the document that Hanssen had requested and promised additional payments would be forthcoming in their next exchange.

Documents, diskettes, and money continued to change hands as 1989 progressed. The Russians turned down Hanssen's request for a Swiss account and proposed a new dead drop site called ELLIS, with a highly visible signal site on the sign at the entrance to Foxstone Park. Whenever the KGB loaded a dead drop and Hanssen did not indicate on the signal site that he had retrieved the package, the Russians removed it themselves to prevent someone else from discovering it. On Halloween, the KGB left $55,000 for Hanssen at the ELLIS site along with a diskette with a new "accommodation address" for him to mail instructions. They also left instructions for how Hanssen ought to advise the KGB as to which materials could go straight to Moscow and which needed to be opened in Washington, and they conveyed good wishes from the KGB chairman along with significant requests for information about a U.S. intelligence program targeting Moscow.

In 1989, Christmas took on an entirely new dimension for Bob Hanssen as he did business with the KGB, delivering his seventeenth diskette and a number of documents including a briefing paper prepared for the director of the CIA entitled, "The Soviet System in Crisis: Prospects for the Next Two Years." The diskette included praise from "B" for the KGB's efficiency, up-to-date information about several ongoing FBI operations to recruit Soviet intelligence officers, the identities of several new FBI sources, and information about four defectors. The KGB left $38,000—payment for the October dead drops, the returned diamonds, and a Christmas bonus. The exchange occurred in Idylwood Park beside a wooden footbridge, with five-foot-high steel guardrails, that spans a ravine of jagged rocks. The ground beside the footbridge provided excellent cover; dense brush, leaves, and vines left packages barely visible.

Why would Hanssen do a dead drop with the KGB on Christmas? According to someone who knows him well and has celebrated Christmas at the Hanssen household, the answer is that, with all the chatter and commotion, "nobody would have been watching."

As Hanssen's friendship with the KGB grew, exchanges of intelligence for cash were conducted at CHARLIE, then DORIS, then ELLIS, FLO, and GRACE. The dead drop site in Eakin Community Park, CHARLIE, contains a wooden footbridge supported by concrete slabs, which provide ample space for a concealed package. The path leading to the bridge has a magical feel from the natural archway created by parallel rows of trees. In this tranquil setting far inside the park, the rapid flow of information continued unabated: the names of Soviet nationals, a KGB mole, a Soviet illegal, and two KGB defectors all serving as FBI-CIA sources, in addition to hundreds of pages of documents.

The KGB, careful not to blow Hanssen's cover, sought guidance on how to utilize certain classified program information:

Dear Friend:

We attach some information requests which we ask Your kind assistance for. We are very cautious about using Your info and materials so that none of our actions in no way causes no harm to Your security. With this on our mind we are asking that sensitive materials and information (especially hot and demanding some actions) be accompanied by some sort of Your comments or some guidance on how we may or may not use it with regard to Your security.

We wish You good luck and enclose $35,000.
Thank you.

Sincerely,
Your friends.

In the summer of 1990, Hanssen received a new assignment from the FBI—he was placed on an inspection team to review Bureau offices in the United States and around the world. His new position would require travel. While Hanssen worried that his FBI field office inspection duty would make espionage more difficult and sporadic, his handlers at the KGB, taking a long-run view, didn't see it as a problem. And they continued to play to Hanssen's ego, always capitalizing the "Y" in "You," "Yours," or any other direct reference to their pen pal.

Dear Friend:

Congratulations on Your promotion. We wish You all the very best in Your life and career.

We appreciate Your sympathy for some difficulties our people face—Your friendship and understanding are very important to us. Of course You are right, no system is perfect and we do understand this.

Speaking about the systems. We don't see any problem for the system of our future communications in regard to this new circumstances of Yours. Though we can't but regret that our contacts may be not so regular as before, like You said.

We believe our current commo plan—though neither perfect—covers ruther flexibly your needs: You may have a contact with us anytime You want after staying away as long as You have to. So, do Your new job, make Your trips, take Your time. The commo plan we have will still be working. We'll keep covering the active call out signal site no matter how long it's needed. And we'll be in a ready-to-go mode to come over to the drop next in turn whenever You are ready: that is when You are back home and decide to communicate. All You'll have to do is put Your call out signal, just as now. And You have two addresses to use to recontact us only if the signal sites for some reason don't work or can't be used. . . . But in any case be sure: You may have a contact anytime because the active call out site is always covered according to the schedule no matter how long you've been away . . .

Thank You and good luck.

Sincerely,
Your friends.

As the Soviet Union disintegrated during the course of 1991, the risk of working as a spy for Russia increased tremendously. Hanssen, in a rare slip that hinted at his geographic roots, suggested to his friends via diskette that the Soviet Union "could benefit" from a thorough study of Mayor Richard J. Daley, the political mastermind who lorded over Chicago for many years. To assuage Hanssen's concerns about the political upheaval in Moscow and to massage his ego, the KGB left a package that included the following message of camaraderie:

We intend to work on the scenario so wisely suggested by You. And the magical history tour to Chicago was mysteriously well timed. . . . There have been many important developments in our country lately. So many that we'd like to reassure You once again. Like we said: we've done all in order that none of those events ever affects Your security and our ability to maintain the operation with you. And of course there can be no doubt of our commitment to Your friendship and cooperation which are too important for us to loose.

Sincerely,
Your friends

13

INDEPENDENCE DAY

O n July 4, 1994, inside the packed hall of the Russian Interior Ministry of Police, Louis Freeh peered out from the lectern with a keen sense of delight. Surrounded by one-time archenemies of the United States, including some former KGB operatives whose zeal for espionage had outlived the collapse of the Soviet Union several years earlier, he prepared to take a giant step on a holiday that meant a great deal to him. Freeh celebrated the occasion by issuing a proclamation of his own that outlined his view of the Bureau's place in the new world order. That he found himself on foreign soil didn't disturb him—he needed to bring his case directly to the Russians, and he relished the symbolic significance of marking this day in an extraordinary way.

To Freeh, the ability to form cop-to-cop relationships between FBI agents and Russia's national police was essential, given the increasingly global nature of Russian organized crime syndicates and cyber-criminals. So the FBI director prevailed upon the Russians to allow him to do something that would have been unfathomable before the collapse of the Berlin Wall—open the first ever FBI office in Russia on the Fourth of July.

In forming his global vision for America's premier domestic law enforcement agency, Freeh followed a logic similar to that of Willie Sutton, who when asked why he robbed banks replied, "That's where the money was." Computer hackers were now committing international bank fraud from their homes. Terrorists holed up in remote mountain compounds were issuing orders via cell phone to their operatives in major Western cities. Hate groups were recruiting new members and plotting attacks via the Internet. And the largest criminal organizations were becoming well represented worldwide.

With crime becoming increasingly global, the FBI director concluded that an international deployment of agents was needed. In his vision, the Bureau would team up with its foreign counterparts around the world, shoving politics aside through cop-to-cop relationships. In decades past, FBI agents chased criminals across state lines, bridging the divide that prevented state police from venturing beyond their borders. Conceptually, the new challenge was no different—the Bureau would put into place a global structure built on law enforcement relationships paralleling the international nature of crime and terrorism.

The idea had been on Freeh's mind ever since he was appointed FBI director. "One of our top priorities and concerns is going to be our ability to work more closely with foreign police agencies," he said on his first day at the helm of the Bureau. "They have the intelligence bases that we don't have with respect to some of these emerging [terrorist] groups, and I think working closer with them is going to aid us greatly in preventing these events."

Now, as he turned toward the sea of faces in Moscow, the challenge before him was a different one: persuading a group of Russian police that he was sincere and would make good on his promises, and that the FBI, which had its own history of going beyond defined legal boundaries at home, was not looking for a beachhead to do the same thing abroad. If he was to gain the Russians' trust and cooperation on police matters, Freeh would need a persuasive way to make clear that fuzzy line between foreign police work and intelligence gathering. If he could get the Russians on board, other nations certainly would follow. Though he had testified before Congress many times, briefed White House officials, and visited a number of countries in Eastern Europe en route to Moscow, this was the single most important speech he had delivered to date as FBI director. The risk was considerable: If he fell flat, his vision of the FBI as a global crime-fighting machine would not be realized.

"It is my privilege to speak with you on the Fourth of July, a day of enormous significance and pride for me and all Americans," Freeh began. "Two hundred and eighteen years ago today, the United States declared its independence as a democratic nation. With the emergence of the Russian Federation just a few years ago and the great strides since then in Russian-American relations, we can honestly say that our two nations have more in common than ever before. Most especially, we share a belief in the importance of democratic ideals, human rights, and the rule of law."

Despite Freeh's words, these lofty ideals hardly had been embraced in the Kremlin or by the Russian people since the collapse of the Soviet machine. Now they were besieged and overwhelmed by everything from shortages in food supplies to the rise of corruption and criminality filling the void left by the demise of the state-run economy. Before losing his audience, Freeh switched gears, moving toward common ground that resonated with the Russian officials.

"Please understand, I have not come to Russia to point an accusatory finger," Freeh said. "The United States has had an entrenched organized crime problem for many decades. I ask only that we work together, learn from each other and combine our efforts to address the emerging threat from organized crime groups. We hope that Russia can avoid the types of mistakes that American law enforcement made in responding to the gangsterism that swept through the United States in the 1920s and 1930s . . . as well as during the 1940s and 1950s. Neither you nor we can afford a repetition of the dreadful law enforcement errors that were made over many decades in America."

The FBI, he explained from firsthand experience, had made catastrophic mistakes by waiting too long to recognize the mammoth problems posed by the Mafia, allowing gangsters to corrupt industries and public officials for decades, and leaving the Bureau trailing hopelessly behind. Now, the same kinds of organized crime groups operating in Moscow and parts of eastern Europe were doing business in the United States. This created the need for international cooperation and sharing of information before the situation spiraled completely out of control, as it had in the United States before intense legal efforts were made to begin to dismantle the Mob.

"Just a few months ago," Freeh said, "President [Boris] Yeltsin bluntly stated that 'Organized crime is trying to take the country by the throat.' He is right. As you well know, violent crimes, such as murders, extortions, kidnappings and robberies, have siphoned off vast amounts of wealth from your economy, often in conjunction with criminals from the United States." The number of reported kidnappings in Moscow had skyrocketed to 118 in the first half of 1994, a tremendous increase over the 16 reported during the same period in 1993. And the global community now faced a new kind of nuclear menace: "One criminal threat looms larger than the others: the theft or diversion of radioactive materials in Russia and eastern Europe." The most frightening prospect, Freeh said, was that these groups would sell the stolen materials to the highest bidder, without regard for the consequences. "We cannot afford to wait until there is a successful diversion of a significant amount of nuclear material before we develop and implement an international law enforcement plan of action to address this grave threat. The time to develop such a plan of action is now, before that dreadful incident occurs."

What was needed, Freeh declared, was a permanent FBI office in Moscow, working directly with Russian police and intelligence. In the eyes of Bob Hanssen and others who viewed Freeh as naive, however, the Soviets had not just been the enemy but the embodiment of evil itself—a dangerous rival that sought to replace democracy with communism through infiltration and deceit. The one remaining certainty following the Cold War was that under no circumstances were the Russians to be trusted.

But a new era had dawned, Freeh argued, requiring a radical departure from this perspective. The United States and Russia shared common enemies now, multinational crime families and terrorists, and the battle against them could be waged effectively only through direct cooperation.

Interpol, the international police organization set up to combat cross-border crime, was no match for criminals operating across nations and oceans in a world with advanced communications and travel. Though Interpol served an important purpose as a central clearinghouse to be sure, neither the FBI nor the Russians had any intention of sharing critical case-sensitive information with an international body that could not be relied upon to maintain confidentiality. Freeh's vision was to cut out the middleman. FBI agents in the United States would transmit requests for information to Bureau officials based in Moscow, who would in turn ask the Russians for help combating kidnapping, money laundering, and a variety of other crimes. Tips could be shared and Russian requests for information about criminals in the United States channeled through FBI agents based in Moscow. The FBI also could offer high-level training to Russian police so they could learn more about U.S. law enforcement practices and policies. "J. Edgar Hoover," the *New York Times* reported, "must have rolled in his grave."

"Over the centuries, the foreign troops have invaded Russia in the hopes of claiming your land as their own," Freeh continued. "The enemy today is somewhat different, yet extremely dangerous. It is an enemy within."

In closing, the FBI director shared the words of the Russian poet Anna Akhmatova: "We know what lies in the balance at this moment, and what is happening right now. The hour for courage strikes upon our clocks."

The Russians, who for centuries had been suspicious of outsiders, nodded in approval. Freeh had won the day, winning over some of the rank and file, and setting new, powerful forces in motion as he signed a landmark cooperation agreement with Russian Interior Minister Viktor Yerin. "The genie is out of the bottle," one American politician said.

Without passing any law, without seeking the permission of other branches of the federal government operating overseas, and without looking back for a moment, Freeh had begun to carry out his dream. Before he was finished, the globe-trotting Freeh would station FBI agents permanently in dozens of countries and create an international law enforcement academy in Budapest, Hungary, to offer training and promote global networking. Numerous heads of state and law enforcement officials from around the world began scheduling visits with the FBI director when they came to Washington. He would, by sheer force of will and personality, establish a global crime-fighting network, a change that did not go unnoticed by senior Clinton administration officials.

"Let me state clearly here and now: We are in a new phase of foreign policy," said Assistant Secretary of State Richard Holbrooke. "The CIA and Defense Department issues that have predominated during the Cold War have receded. The FBI is moving to the forefront of this new foreign policy."

Not everyone was as enamored by what they saw as a brazen power grab by Freeh, particularly given the array of crimes on U.S. soil—including murder, drug trafficking, and financial fraud—that were going unsolved by the FBI. They argued the FBI would dilute its impact through a global approach and pointed out that the FBI did not need to duplicate the efforts of the CIA or the Drug Enforcement Administration abroad. "I just did not feel, and still do not feel, the FBI, whose charter is to be our domestic and paramount federal law enforcement agency, has any business spreading themselves so thin all over the world," said former House Appropriations Committee chairman Bob Livingston, a Louisiana Republican who sought to slow the FBI's overseas expansion by withholding funding for new offices abroad. "I would feel better off if they were doing their job better here." Former secretary of state Alexander Haig argued, "To pervert the mission of the FBI to become an external, international law enforcement agency is wrongheaded and merely another contributor to enlarging the bureaucracy, which is already bloated beyond recognition."

The expansion posed moral issues, too. FBI agents operating on foreign soil would be forced, at times, to look the other way when valuable evidence was gathered through torture and other practices that would be prohibited in America. "They do not ask, 'How did you question them?' They will just ask, 'Is it good information?'" said Otwin Marenin, a criminal justice professor at Washington State University who has studied the FBI's overseas practices. "You learn how to live with that part even though you wouldn't do it yourself."

To make all of this work, Freeh not only would have to persuade the Russians and other foreign powers, but also would have to prevail in turf battles in Washington. After all, it had been a long-held axiom that the FBI operated domestically and the CIA globally. Freeh pressed on, arguing that with drugs, terrorism, and cyber-crime spreading around the globe, the Bureau actually would do a more effective job of protecting Americans at home by having a permanent presence abroad. He was also determined to do away with the notion of the FBI's ceremonial postings in London and Paris, the "wine and cheese circuit," in his bid to turn the Bureau into a global law-enforcing juggernaut.

"The world," Freeh stated passionately and often, "has become a very small and dangerous place."

FBI agents stationed around the world, known in Bureau parlance as "legats," a nickname for legal attachés, had widely varying experiences depending on where they were based and who they worked alongside. Some CIA station chiefs resented their presence and viewed them as competitors in the race for intelligence. That rivalry between them had historical roots. After World War II, FBI agents posted temporarily in South America boasted that they would drive the Bureau's cars into the water rather than turn them over to the CIA.

Gaining the cooperation of the Russians would take time as well. There was a big difference between Freeh declaring that a common enemy of Americans and Russians existed among criminals, and getting the Russians and others working in the trenches to overcome years of ingrained suspicion of the FBI. "It started out with a little suspicion because the FBI also works counterintelligence," said Bill Kinane, one of the Bureau agents tapped to open the FBI legat office in Moscow in 1994. "In the beginning, on both sides, as enthusiastic as we both were to work together, there was still a mind-set of looking pretty closely to see if this was genuine."

"It was tough. It was the biggest challenge I ever had in my Bureau career," said another former FBI agent involved in opening the Moscow branch. "The Bureau was, and still is, known to Russians as '*Spetz Sluzhba,*' or special services. That is how they look at the Bureau and the CIA. They look at us as having an intelligence mission."

But over time, Kinane said, as both sides began to see the fruits of their labors, many of the barriers began to come down. Trust between the parties grew as Russian criminals hiding in the United States were nabbed, a kidnap victim was returned to safety, and a smuggling ring in San Francisco that sought to steal some $200 million in Russian diamonds was busted. "[While] working with the Russians on issues of law enforcement we had a mutual enemy in terrorists or criminals," said Kinane. "We were not playing chess with them."

A key moment in the development of the new U.S.–Russian partnership was the arrest and conviction in the mid-1990s of a kingpin known as the "Russian Godfather," who was thwarted in his efforts to carve up parts of the United States for Russian organized crime and convicted on extortion charges. "They were helpful to us in trying to get witnesses," an FBI agent said. "That case was a real watershed in the relationship. It demonstrated to the Russians we were serious people and were not afraid of going after someone who in their minds was one of their top mafioso types." Successful joint efforts at combating cyber-crime also helped solidify the relationship. Freeh often cited a 1994 case involving Russian teens in St. Petersburg who had managed to hack their way into Citibank's computers, stealing roughly $10 million before a joint task force cracked the case.

For the FBI agents themselves, working in Moscow carried with it an occupational hazard: vodka flowing like tap water. "Their main way of partying is drinking vodka," Kinane said. "I realized early on I wouldn't survive this job unless I controlled this situation. Whenever I got into a social situation, I invited them to a restaurant where I could sip a beer. Vodka is cheap there. You can buy a bottle for a buck. So they were very, very generous with it. I realized early on that Russian cops are tremendously strong guys but they drink and smoke a lot and don't do too much jogging. If they get their hands on you, it is all over. I was such a novelty, constantly being invited to these excursions. I had to figure out a way to be sociable and not kill myself."

After setting the global crime-fighting initiative in motion, Kinane stayed in close contact with Freeh, who displayed a strong interest in the Bureau's new relationship with Russia. "I've had a lot of face time with him," Kinane said. "This [was] his pet program."

14

RESPECTING
THE RUSSIANS

Bob Hanssen's admiration for the Soviet Union and the KGB went beyond spycraft, extending to the broader modes of operation adopted by Moscow in the post–Cold War era of the late 1980s and early 1990s. Confident that he understood the Russian psyche, Hanssen thought that most U.S. government officials naively believed too much of what the Russians had to say without recognizing the artifice behind the message and the messenger. At the heart of cleverly masked misrepresentations from Moscow in the 1980s were a series of covert "Active Measures" aimed at achieving the goal of Communist dominance through nonmilitary means. These Active Measures included the use of forgeries, propaganda, and false news reports to strengthen the Soviet Union and tarnish the West. Hanssen had no illusions about Russia: The era of good feelings and warm words Moscow embraced publicly after the fall of the Berlin Wall actually was a sophisticated, tactical shift filled with deep-seated deception.

Hanssen identified key elements of the Active Measures campaign: the notion that boycotting grain and other sales to the Russian market would exacerbate unemployment; the rumor that Washington and Moscow were on the verge of a secret agreement that would exclude western Europe; the generation of fears that widespread famine and global instability would result without a big increase in Western aid to Russia during the long winter; the use of forged and leaked letters to show close ties between the United States and South Africa in the late 1980s; and the notion that AIDS was invented in a U.S. laboratory.

As a double agent, Hanssen had seen Russian operations at work firsthand. He knew what kind of intelligence his KGB contacts wanted and had received, and he knew that the nature of the information was neither defensive nor benign. While most people celebrated the new conciliatory lexicon of glasnost and perestroika, Hanssen said he wanted the U.S. government to remain vigilant against the Communists and adopt his hero Gen. George S. Patton's approach: "Let's punch 'em in the nose and kick 'em in the balls."

For Hanssen, looking at Russian propaganda operatives at their best was a bit like glancing in the mirror. Both he and they operated at extraordinary levels of subterfuge. The Russians' systematic manipulation of public opinion, engineered through misrepresentations, falsified documents, and the intentional spreading of rumors and lies, was aimed at bolstering Moscow's standing on the world stage and undercutting the United States'. Hanssen could see right through the facade, and he had contempt for the FBI, the CIA, the State Department, and legions of other U.S. officials who lacked his clairvoyance. If the Russians' ultimate goal was the global triumph of Communism, they would have to prey upon the trusting instincts of Americans and other Westerners; in place of the "politics of force," they would need to make do with "the force of politics." Given the deficiencies in the Russian military, there were very few alternatives.

"It was often very, very difficult for Westerners to comprehend this fundamentally different Soviet approach to international relations and, as a result, the centrality to the Soviets of Active Measures operations was gravely underappreciated in the West," Hanssen explained in a briefing paper he developed for Congress while he spied for the KGB and worked Russian intelligence for the FBI.

Hanssen detected, with a degree of admiration, the disinformation that comprised the prototypical Active Measures—measures that frequently succeeded in influencing unsuspecting, gullible foreigners and their governments. That he had come to appreciate the shrewd Soviet style was a testament to its cunning.

"The Soviet Communist Party created what was, in all likelihood, the most formidable political influence machine in the modern world," Hanssen wrote in his monograph. "Although the Soviets had the disadvantage of 'selling' an enormously unpopular 'product,' they evolved a great deal of manipulative and deceptive techniques to try to compensate for this disadvantage. A close examination of how they sought to influence foreign publics and governments by orchestrating and spreading carefully selected information, disinformation and a variety of crude, sophisticated, derogatory, conciliatory, and alarmist arguments and slogans contains important lessons for the future."

Former KGB Major General Oleg Kalugin said the Soviet Union relied heavily on Active Measures, including covert manipulation of the Western press, to spread damaging social and political information about the United States without any concern for its accuracy. Confirming Hanssen's analysis, he described the U.S. media and the American public as prime targets for manipulation. The Soviets also engendered anti-American feelings by planting "sinister" stories in other parts of the world. KGB agents were at ease with the use of these techniques, given the deception they had grown up with, where the truth about Mother Russia and its place in the world community reflected the views of the political elite rather than reality. "Russia is not what it purports to be," Kalugin said. Kalugin had done undercover work himself while posing as a Russian journalist, attending Columbia University as a Fulbright scholar and then working as a Radio Moscow correspondent at the United Nations. "We converted the free flow of information from [the United States] into our own propaganda," said Kalugin, who is now affiliated with the Centre for Counterintelligence and Security Studies in Virginia.

Hanssen described numerous examples of effective manipulation of Americans and other Westerners through Active Measures. In late 1988, the Russians sought to create a false image of the new

KGB as benign, a ploy that within a short period led to an official visit by KGB officials to FBI headquarters in Washington, something that only a few years earlier—or even later—would have been unthinkable. In addition, the Soviets, attempting to garner support for keeping the country together, capitalized on Western fears by disseminating "alarmist" messages about the potentially disastrous consequences of the spread of nuclear weapons in the event the U.S.S.R. crumbled. But Hanssen identified the "new political thinking" as the most pervasive type of Active Measure, a strategy that generated appealing conciliatory slogans. While they may have improved Russia's image temporarily, the tactics ultimately failed as Communist governments across Eastern Europe collapsed by 1990 and free elections failed to produce support for the new Communist Party.

Hanssen displayed a special interest in covert operations coordinated by Service A of the KGB's First Chief Directorate—the unit that handled foreign intelligence operations. It had a clear mission: to use covert media placement, state-controlled media, forgeries of official documents, agents of influence, and other mechanisms to introduce slogans and language in business, religion, and government of target countries to sway public opinion. "The Soviet Active Measures apparatus dwarfed, by a factor of perhaps 20 or 30 to 1, the U.S. governmental apparatus set up to analyze and counter its activities," according to Hanssen. The Russians had more than 200 KGB and military intelligence operatives in the United States by the mid-1980s, a number that dwindled significantly after the fall of the Berlin Wall before spiking up again to around 200 in the late 1990s. The greatest number of intelligence agents were based in New York, with the next largest contingent in Washington, comprising about fifty agents.

As an example of covert Soviet Active Measures, Hanssen highlighted Jacob Holdt, a Danish photographer and author whose book, *American Pictures,* depicted poverty and racism in the United States through hundreds of photographs of impoverished blacks. KGB agents actually recruited Holdt as an operative, and then implemented a covert campaign to boost circulation of the book in Europe, widely disseminating the negative images of America.

As part of Active Measures, Russian intelligence agents would move seamlessly from the KGB, and its successor agency, the *Sluzhba Vneshy Razvedki Rossii* or SVR, to jobs as correspondents for the Russian media. News deemed to be of value to enemies was suppressed by Moscow. At the same time, the Russians placed operatives in their embassies to work as press attachés, enabling them to glean information from Western journalists.

In a society where the whole is valued as greater than the sum of its parts, powerful institutions such as the KGB demanded greater loyalty from individuals than did the FBI, the CIA, or the NSA. This facilitated Active Measures and counterintelligence that relied upon the use of attractive Russian women. In the 1980s, the KGB infiltrated the American embassy in Moscow through the use of female agents who seduced U.S. foreign service workers and Marine guards.

In one instance, a gorgeous twenty-four-year-old Soviet worker employed at the U.S. embassy was invited to an embassy ball and zeroed in on a young Marine guard. They soon left the party and enjoyed a night of drinking and sex. When confronted later by his commander, who had noticed him missing, the Marine replied, "Yes, sir. Best piece of ass I ever had, sir." While this Marine was transferred out of Moscow, others were ensnared in KGB "honey traps" and compromised into becoming double agents. Rather than viewing these operations in ethical terms, Hanssen viewed them as a sign of the Russians' greater dedication to winning the counterintelligence war.

From 1988 to 1991—as the Soviets moved away from dependence on military force and Active Measures took on added importance—Hanssen felt those who believed spying ended with the Cold War misunderstood Moscow completely. "The resources devoted to Active Measures increased substantially during this period, contrary to the popular perception that these types of activities had virtually disappeared," Hanssen wrote. "From the Soviet viewpoint, this was entirely natural. If reliance on military power was to be lessened, political methods for making Soviet influence felt in the world had to be bolstered."

Hanssen was in a unique position to know and understand Active Measures. As an FBI agent, a Russian counterintelligence expert, a KGB operative, a student of literature and history, a master of deception, and an astute manipulator, Hanssen was convinced the Soviets were learning more from him about spycraft than he was from them. He often insisted, for example, on using a single dead drop site for delivery and retrieval of both intelligence and payment, rather than multiple sites, which the Russians traditionally favored. Hanssen's approach involved fewer steps, theoretically diminishing the risk of detection.

With feet in both camps, Hanssen—immersed in the sources and methods of both the FBI and the KGB—was performing the ultimate deception by devising a monograph, for distribution on Capitol Hill, that surely would find its way to Moscow. But no one on either side would know that he wrote it, that these were his ideas, that he had gone out on a limb once more. The cover and protection of the United States Information Agency, under whose banner the report he was crafting would be submitted to Congress, would give him the shield he needed to enjoy his unique status as analyst, participant, observer, and double agent.

Hanssen's analysis also highlighted the stunning view held by the Soviets, prior to the end of the Cold War, that a nuclear war actually could be fought and won. Official changes in posture were enunciated by Gorbachev in his 1987 book, *Perestroika: New Thinking for Our Country and the World*, in which he made it clear that nuclear war was not an instrument to achieve goals and could result only in destruction. Straightforward as this might seem to Westerners, Gorbachev characterized this as a "truly revolutionary" shift for Russian leaders, a point Hanssen emphasized by quoting a senior adviser to Gorbachev who, as late as 1989, stated that "Even comparatively recently, we believed it was possible to survive and even win a nuclear war." Meanwhile, the Russians had sought over time to deceive the world by claiming to spend only a small amount on defense. Hanssen claimed Russian defense expenditures were double U.S. estimates by 1991. But his report failed to emphasize that tremendous Soviet military spending destabilized the economy and crippled the country.

Not content merely to analyze failed Russian operations, Hanssen had by 1992 identified what remained of the Active Measures campaign. "Although the Soviet Active Measures and disinformation colossus that sought for decades to undermine the Free World with a variety of hostile and manipulative campaigns has disintegrated," he concluded, "sizable fragments of the old system have survived and continue to operate. Some are sponsored by the Russian government and others apparently by disaffected Communist hard-liners who wish to exert as much power as they can."

Steeped in knowledge of the Kremlin, Victor Sheymov, the former KGB officer who defected and had been handled, debriefed, and befriended by Hanssen, refined the concept in his own words.

"Intelligence ends with the first shot fired. Real intelligence much more resembles a fascinating chess game, much complicated by the fact that the figures and their positions are not known to the players.... The common notion that Communism is dead badly needs clarification. The important point here is the definition of Communism. It cannot be viewed simply as a political movement. Communism is not an ideology, it is also a mentality, a mind-set that is still alive and well.

"Too many participants of the so-called 'Cold War'—which sometimes took rather hot turns—are still living. My point here is that for some time to come the West will be dealing with those who were brought up within the communist system and are still driven by a communist mentality. Therefore, it is imperative to understand those people, who for at least three generations were raised in an atmosphere of hatred to the West."

15

DOUBLE TROUBLE

The news from Moscow on the morning of August 19, 1991, had the world on edge. Tanks and armored personnel carriers were rumbling into the Soviet capital as part of a coup d'état by hard-line Communists to prevent the breakup of the U.S.S.R. Leaders of the revolt arrested President Mikhail Gorbachev at his vacation home and imposed a nationwide state of emergency. Thousands of people were gathering outside Russia's parliament building in a show of support for the Gorbachev government and its democratic reforms. The uprising was being led by military leaders as well as KGB chief Vladimir Kryuchkov, who were making a serious threat to take power by force and bloodshed. The wave of political upheaval that began with the fall of the Berlin Wall in 1989 had finally crested in Russia. The only question remaining was what lay ahead.

In Washington, Bob Hanssen had mixed emotions about the coup and its implications. In the course of his spying, Hanssen had developed a polite, if impersonal, relationship with KGB director Kryuchkov, who had extended salutations and praise for Hanssen's espionage work and even made some specific information requests to his prized FBI mole. Yet Hanssen said he despised the communist system that Kryuchkov was trying desperately to restore. Hanssen knew that if the coup failed, his prediction of communism's self-destruction would be vindicated. On the other hand, the dismantling of the KGB and other Soviet agencies could pose a grave danger to his security as a spy.

Hanssen wasn't the only one in the U.S. intelligence community with conflicting interests in the events unfolding in Moscow. Aldrich "Rick" Ames, a career CIA officer working in the agency's Soviet/East European division, had been spying for the KGB since 1985 and was also worried about his security. Despite the political upheaval in Russia, KGB's Washington station was still open for business.

With this in mind, Bob Hanssen tuned out the coverage of the chaos on Moscow's streets and completed a scheduled dead drop with the KGB in the quiet and solitude of Lewinsville Park. Hanssen passed a cache of classified intelligence documents and a computer diskette, receiving $20,000 in return. Just two days later, however, the KGB-backed coup ended in failure and Kryuchkov and the other leaders of the uprising were arrested. Angry protesters gathered in the square outside the Lubyanka headquarters of the KGB and toppled the statue of "Iron Felix" Dzerzhinksy, the notorious founder of the Soviet secret police. The Soviet parliament's subsequent decision to appoint an outspoken critic to take over the agency was a harbinger of the future; the new chief reportedly accepted the post only on the condition that he be allowed to dismantle the KGB.

Hanssen would fill two more dead drops in late 1991 before breaking off contact in December and confessing his spying during an FBI inspection trip to Indianapolis. "He went to that priest as a crutch to help him quit," said Washington attorney Plato Cacheris, who would represent both Hanssen and Ames. Aside from the turmoil in Russia, Hanssen was spooked by other events, including a KGB delegation's visit to FBI headquarters and rumors that a KGB archivist had defected to the West with a massive collection of case files. In addition, it was around that time that Priscilla Galey went home to Columbus, Ohio, and got hooked on crack cocaine. The stripper's association with Hanssen became an even greater wild card—if the Bureau ever learned of the affair, Hanssen's lavish gifts to Galey would surely trigger an investigation. Hanssen had already learned of a counterintelligence probe being conducted around the corner from his FBI office out of a room dubbed the "Black Vault." It was obvious that the Bureau had uncovered a mole within the U.S. intelligence community, but the target of the probe remained a tightly guarded secret.

The espionage under investigation in the "Black Vault" had been going on for six years, ever since Rick Ames started spying shortly after returning to the United States from a CIA tour in Mexico City. While abroad, Ames had fallen madly in love with a Colombian embassy worker named Maria del Rosario Casas Dupuy, whom he met through diplomatic circles. Struggling to complete a divorce and support a lavish lifestyle for his new love on a government salary, Ames was in a financial bind. In addition, his drinking problem was getting worse, making the agent prone to erratic behavior. Despite all the difficulties, he was desperate to find a way to make the relationship succeed. "If I failed in loving Rosario," he said, "only a kind of living death or suicide remained for me." Exasperated, Ames decided to take drastic measures.

From the outset, Ames lacked Hanssen's skilled spycraft. In addition to his drinking and womanizing, his spending of KGB monies was conspicuous. When his KGB contact failed to show up at a meeting where he was to make his first espionage pitch, Rick downed a couple of drinks and marched directly to the Soviet embassy to make his first delivery, even though he knew the FBI maintained constant surveillance of the building. Several weeks later, he again flouted American authorities by returning to the embassy, this time to drop off a package of highly sensitive information, a move that would become known as "the big dump."

Ames's initial flurry of spying came under the direction of Viktor Cherkashin, the KGB's seasoned counterintelligence chief and the most respected handler in the agency's Washington station. Ames became one half of Cherkashin's jackpot in 1985; six months later, Bob Hanssen requested that the skilled KGB officer handle his case file as well. Cherkashin's work on the two cases, in contrast to other aspects of the Soviet spy agency, was masterful, allowing the two moles to continue their work for years. "When it came to handling human assets in the field, he was real good," said Yuri Shvets, a former senior KGB official who worked closely with Cherkashin. "In the Soviet bureaucracy of the time, no one wanted to take responsibility. Cherkashin was the guy who assumed responsibility and made decisions." Among top KGB officials in Washington, Cherkashin alone had the moxie to allow Hanssen to spy for Russia anonymously. "It goes against all the rules of the KGB intelligence tradecraft," Shvets said. "It was only Cherkashin who had the position, authority, and courage to assume responsibility for such an act."

An old-school Soviet spy, Cherkashin believed that the fewer people one had to trust, the better. After Ames's "big dump," he bypassed the chain of command, flying to Moscow to personally deliver the sensitive information directly to the KGB chief. Similarly, when Hanssen sent his initial package of classified documents to Cherkashin, the KGB operative ensured that only a precious few in Washington and Moscow even knew of its existence.

Cherkashin ultimately was awarded the prestigious Order of Lenin for his deft counterintelligence work. Despite being held in high regard by his superiors, Cherkashin viewed the KGB leadership as overly politicized and reckless. Typically, an intelligence agency that learns of a rash of traitors takes great care to protect the source of its information, proceeding slowly to weed out moles or feeding disinformation to the turncoats, turning them into "triple agents." But in the mid-1980s, increased pressure was being placed on the KGB; the newly empowered Gorbachev was extremely dissatisfied with the agency's political reporting from abroad. According to "The Mitrokhin Archive"—the collection of case files brought to the West by the KGB archivist-turned-defector—the new Soviet leader "would have gained a more accurate insight into American policy by reading the *New York Times* or the *Washington Post* than by relying on reports from [his] own residencies."

Whispers around Moscow were that Kryuchkov's job as head of KGB foreign counterintelligence was in danger. Ames's dump was the big score that he needed to regain political capital at home. Ames and his KGB handler give different accounts of exactly what information was passed along in their first two exchanges, but there was no ambiguity about what happened next. In the weeks following Ames's big dump, no less than twelve double agents that the United States had recruited in Soviet intelligence agencies were rounded up, recalled to Moscow, and convicted of espionage. At least ten were shot. (One other agent was saved from a similar fate: Oleg Gordievsky, who had been covertly working as a spy for the British intelligence service, MI6, was dramatically rescued from a busy Moscow street and spirited back to the West.) The cumulative damage to the CIA's Soviet program was immense, and Ames's betrayals were tantamount to mass murder.

Kryuchkov ordered swift action to bring all known double agents to Moscow. But the hasty recall of so many spies put American intelligence officials on alert. Ames immediately recognized as much when the KGB warned him of the impending arrests. "Jesus Christ!" Ames exclaimed. "You're going to get me arrested. Why not just put up a big neon sign over the agency with the word *mole* written on it?"

FBI and CIA officials gathered to assess the damage. They concluded that the losses were due to a human penetration, and that previously identified moles such as Edward Lee Howard did not have access to all the names that were compromised. But in the immediate aftermath of the Soviet recall, that was all they discovered. Independent investigations at the FBI and the CIA turned up no suspects, and interest in the matter faded fast. The Bureau was already investigating about a dozen espionage cases in 1985, the "Year of the Spy," and the CIA was busy trying to quell an unrelated scandal. Senior FBI officials were never informed of the full extent of the intelligence losses suffered by the CIA or the Bureau, and Ames would continue his espionage unfettered.

While on a tour of duty in Italy from May 1986 to July 1989, Ames settled into a new routine of spying. As the station chief of the "enemy targets" branch in Rome, he had wide access to information from the CIA, the State Department, and the National Security Agency, including details about the safe houses where U.S. agents met to debrief defectors. He passed this information along to the KGB, which photographed Russian agents meeting with U.S. officials.

Unlike Hanssen, Ames did not remain anonymous to his KGB handlers or refuse their entreaties to meet outside the United States. He often met with his handlers, and traveled to Vienna, Bogotá, and Caracas to deliver information. To conceal the substantial payoffs he was receiving for spying, Ames set up a crude money-laundering scheme that funneled cash through Swiss bank accounts. He took care to keep most of his bank deposits in the United States below the $10,000 limit reported to the IRS, but he showed no discretion in making extravagant purchases. In Rome, Rick and Rosario spent lavishly on clothes, gifts, and travel. After returning to Washington, Rick bought a $50,000 Jaguar and a $500,000 house without a mortgage. His new lifestyle, along with his heavy drinking, caught the attention of some at CIA headquarters. "You ought to have smelled his breath," one CIA employee said, adding, "Then he goes off to Rome and comes back and buys this big house and car and is wearing thousand-dollar suits. Where the hell is he getting all the money?"

Rick, who received $2.3 million for his espionage from the Russians, had always maintained that the source of his sudden wealth was a large inheritance left for Rosario by her mother. But CIA officials determined that was a lie as early as November 1989. While it would take more than a year for the FBI and CIA to begin a joint probe of Ames once they began, it did not take investigators long to correlate large bank deposits to meetings he had attended with the KGB. They also discovered FBI videotapes documenting Ames's visits to the Soviet embassy and recovered a Post-It note from his trash that detailed signals for a dead drop.

The Bureau's criminal investigation of Ames, code-named NIGHTMOVER, reached its climax on the morning of February 21, 1994, when FBI agents arrested Rick and Rosario Ames for conspiracy to commit espionage. The decision to charge Rosario was almost overturned by the assistant attorney general, who thought that the couple's young son should not be deprived of both parents. But the FBI and the prosecuting attorneys knew that Rosario, who supported and encouraged her husband's spying, could be used as leverage to coerce Rick to plead guilty and debrief intelligence officials about what he had compromised. FBI Director Louis Freeh fought to prosecute both husband and wife; the decision to do so likely saved the case from a protracted court battle. Freeh knew that Ames could not bear to see his wife sent to prison for the rest of her life. After his arraignment, Rick had spoken briefly to an FBI agent, saying, to the dismay of his attorneys, "Hey, I'm really looking forward to cooperating fully with you guys and your investigation. I want to do anything I can to help my wife." Ames cut a deal and pleaded guilty to espionage charges on April 28. After months of debriefings, he was sentenced to life in prison without parole in exchange for his cooperation. In return, Rosario was given a reduced sentence of five years.

In the fallout from the Ames case, CIA Director James Woolsey was pressured into stepping down. In response to the executions that Ames's espionage triggered, Congress reinstated the federal death penalty in cases where the information compromised leads to the deaths of agents working on behalf of the United States. Federal legislators also granted more powers of search and seizure to the Foreign Intelligence Surveillance Court, a panel at the Justice Department that secretly reviews surveillance requests in national security cases.

Freeh's FBI, meanwhile, basked in the praise awarded it after its investigation and arrest of the deadliest mole in CIA history. Though the Bureau had for years overlooked blatant missteps by Ames, the FBI was given credit for ultimately capturing him, especially since he was not working within their own ranks. In the aftermath of the Ames case, Louis Freeh pushed for increased Bureau authority over counterintelligence to the scorn of many CIA officials who felt that he was kicking the agency while it was down. Even as Freeh pushed for a greater role in the intelligence field, the FBI boss continued to oppose polygraph tests for his own operational employees, even though similar measures already were in place at the CIA. The tests were not flawless, as Ames himself proved by successfully beating two polygraphs given after he had begun selling secrets, but many counterintelligence and law enforcement officials agree that polygraphs serve as a deterrent to espionage.

Despite the tensions, Louis Freeh touted the successful resolution of the Ames case on Capitol Hill and elsewhere as an example of enhanced cooperation between the FBI and CIA on counterintelligence matters. "Ironically, the relationship we have forged now is better and more effective than the one existing at the height of the Cold War," Freeh would write in his 1998 *Report to the American People.*

In public, the FBI exuded supreme confidence in its ability to protect confidential sources. Behind the scenes, however, investigators were getting a far different picture of the state of the U.S. intelligence community from Ames. He spoke freely and with little prompting about his betrayals of Soviet double agents Polyakov, Martynov, and Motorin—all of whom were also given up by Hanssen and then executed—as well as many other Russian moles. As the debriefings progressed, Ames recalled other agents whom he had identified, as well as compromises of vital U.S. intelligence operations. In all, he related specific details of more than thirty major breaches, and admitted that there were yet more he could not remember.

Despite the magnitude of Ames's betrayal, the government's debriefing team quickly surmised that he had no knowledge of many significant U.S. programs that had been compromised. There was only one conclusion that could be drawn: the Americans still had another mole lurking. Ames said as much in an interview, offering with a smirk that while he worked alone and did not know specifically of any moles himself, that didn't mean that other spies weren't around.

Months after the Ames debriefing, Tom Kozel called his boyhood friend Bob Hanssen at FBI headquarters to ask a favor. Kozel had attended Taft High School and Knox College with Hanssen, but over time the pair had lost touch. That day, Kozel, a biology professor at a small college in Georgia, was calling on behalf of one of his students, who was interested in pursuing a career in forensics. Though he didn't know much about the FBI's summer internship program, Hanssen was happy to hear from his old pal and promised to do what he could to help. For the next two hours, they reminisced, catching up on the major events of their lives. Tom had never pegged Bob as a future G-man when they were growing up, but it seemed that his friend enjoyed his job and had found true fulfillment, as Hanssen said, "working for God and country." Kozel was extremely impressed when Hanssen told him that he had questioned the deadliest spy in CIA history, Aldrich Ames.

"He really liked the idea that he was one of the principal debriefers on Aldrich Ames," Kozel said. "I said, 'Wow, that's really cool. You have a much more interesting job than I do.' And he thought about it a bit and said, 'Yeah, I really do have an interesting job.'"

Two dangerous double agents in one room. One roaming free, the other in shackles. The victor interrogating the vanquished. Hanssen knew that this was the stuff of great spy novels, but according to his superiors at the Bureau it wasn't true. His exaggeration of his role in the Ames case was another example of Hanssen's desire for a central place in FBI counterintelligence operations and his frustration that those doors remained closed to him. Paul Moore, a long-time friend and coworker of Hanssen, said that while Hanssen may have read Bureau documents about the Ames debriefings and been as well versed as the agents conducting the interrogations, he was not involved himself. If he could not achieve the kind of success and adventure that he wanted in real life, Bob Hanssen could still do so in his imagination.

While Louis Freeh appreciated the windfall of increased FBI funding and authority from Congress resulting from the Ames case, he remained uneasy and had a deep sense of foreboding. "Any moles who are still in place must be unmasked," Freeh said, knowing that another Russian mole was on the loose at the highest levels of U.S. intelligence. But Freeh and his colleagues didn't know who it was or where to look.

Ray Mislock, the FBI's former national security chief, recalled the director remaining focused and determined: "Louis was aware there was more work to be done."

16

THE CASE
AGENT

Standing near the remains of the Alfred P. Murrah federal building in Oklahoma City, FBI Director Louis Freeh surveyed the damage from one of the worst terrorist attacks in American history. Only days earlier, a bomb blast at 9:02 A.M. had killed 168 people and injured hundreds more as they began their workday. From the moment Freeh learned of the explosion on April 19, 1995—two years to the day after the FBI's deadly raid on the Branch Davidian compound in Waco, Texas—he involved himself in every aspect of the OKBOM probe. Outraged and energized, Freeh shifted into high gear, pursuing the culprits like a supercop. By redeploying thousands of detectives at a moment's notice and dispatching special FBI units to the scene, he had unleashed the full investigative resources of the Bureau, arresting the prime suspect within two days, pursuing other leads, and providing a measure of hope and order to a nation shaken by a grisly act.

Now, as the FBI director stood amid the debris, he thought of the nineteen children who had been safely dropped off at day care before perishing in the explosion. He wished the FBI had prevented the blast in the first place, but there had been no warning signs. Freeh knew he couldn't bring any of the victims back to life, but he was determined to honor their memories by ensuring that justice was done.

"*Hostes humani generis.* Enemies of mankind," Freeh translated from the Latin, as the cameras rolled. "You cannot slaughter innocent men, women, and America's kids and get away with it. We will not rest or have peace until this crime against humanity is adjudged and punished."

Though Freeh lacked formal training in managing a sprawling network of thousands of agents, he knew how to roll up his sleeves and work a big case. He sent a veteran FBI official to Oklahoma City to oversee the day-to-day OKBOM investigation. He also mobilized all fifty-six FBI field offices to follow up on the thousands of tips and clues pouring in on a special hotline. Freeh's instincts took over as he made dozens of daily decisions about the conduct of the investigation, helped senior Justice Department officials craft legal strategy, and remembered to check in at home to find out how his wife and children were holding up in the aftermath of the frightening attack. He put the Bureau's Rapid Start Team to work logging every piece of relevant information and analyzing the data on laptop computers. He sent a highly specialized forensics team to Oklahoma City to assist local authorities in identifying the victims, and unleashed the Evidence Response Team to comb the site. Lest there be any doubt among city, state, and federal officials, President Clinton made certain that everyone involved understood that Louis Freeh was in charge.

"To assure the strongest response to this situation, I have deployed a crisis management team, under the leadership of the FBI," the president said. "We are sending the world's finest investigators to solve these murders."

Freeh knew that the FBI was at its best in a crisis, and he talked tough from the start. "We will search you and find you," he said. "There is no place on earth where you will be safe from the most powerful forces of justice." The director made it clear that he and other senior FBI personnel, along with thousands of agents and forensics experts working the case, were on a mission. Instead of regular shifts, they began putting in as many hours as possible each day until they needed a few hours of rest. It was during times like these that Freeh, director of an agency with a multibillion-dollar budget and thousands of employees, earned the nickname "the presidentially appointed case agent." Rather than planning for the long-term or staying abreast of developing cases and issues, Freeh became completely and totally involved in the details of the Oklahoma City bombing and a handful of other high-profile cases on his watch.

Given the plethora of federal, state, and local authorities descending on the crime scene, it was imperative that Clinton establish a clear chain of command. At the federal level alone, the probe involved the FBI, the Justice Department, the Bureau of Alcohol, Tobacco and Firearms (ATF), the Secret Service, the Federal Emergency Management Agency, and the military. "It is significant that the president identified the FBI as in charge and it's good he did it early," said former FBI director William Webster. The bipartisan support Freeh received on Capitol Hill while overseeing the massive FBI probe brought the nation together, as did the unusually high level of cooperation among federal, state, and local law enforcement. "Director Freeh, I join with everyone else in recognizing the great skill and professionalism with which you and your agency have moved," said Senator Joseph Biden of Delaware. "It does make a difference when the public and the Congress and both political parties start off with the same basic premise, and that is that they have absolute faith in the man or woman in charge of the enterprise."

The first suspect in custody, Timothy McVeigh, was stopped by a state trooper near Perry, Oklahoma, ninety minutes after the bombing and arrested for speeding, driving without a license plate, and carrying a concealed weapon. Though neither the trooper nor the local sheriff knew that McVeigh had anything to do with the bombing, he was not immediately released on bail. Meanwhile, the FBI issued a composite drawing of McVeigh and sought help from the public without knowing he was sitting in a prison cell waiting to see a judge. Many early news reports and investigative theories focused on the possibility that Islamic extremists were behind the attack; much of this speculation stemmed from the World Trade Center bombing two years earlier. But white supremacists and others also were on the FBI's radar screen, and Freeh personally called Reno and Clinton to warn them not to make statements about the possibility that the attack was the work of foreigners or any particular religious group.

The cooperation of law enforcement authorities, and a bit of serendipity, prevented McVeigh from being released and fleeing after posting bail on the traffic charges. His hearing was postponed a day due to another case. Meanwhile, an ATF agent entered McVeigh's name into an FBI criminal database after he was identified as a leading suspect in the massive probe under way. After the agent noted that the sheriff in Noble County, Oklahoma, recently had plugged McVeigh's name into the same system, he contacted the sheriff, learned that McVeigh was in custody, and ordered him held there until federal agents arrived.

McVeigh's choice of the federal building in Oklahoma City had been deliberate. The facility had minimal security and included offices of the Drug Enforcement Administration, the Secret Service, and the ATF, in addition to other federal employees. McVeigh, a Gulf War veteran, had been outraged by the FBI's assault on the Branch Davidian compound near Waco, Texas, two years earlier and vowed to seek revenge. A devotee of white supremacist, antigovernment propaganda, he had told a friend several days in advance of the attack that "something big is going to happen," and told his sister it would happen on April 19. McVeigh, who had visited Waco during the nearly two-month standoff between federal officials and the Branch Davidians, had never forgotten watching the compound burn to the ground and seeing ATF agents hoist their flag. In a letter to the *Lockport Union-Sun and Journal*, an upstate New York newspaper, McVeigh had asked, "Is a civil war imminent? Do we have to shed blood to reform the system? I hope it doesn't come to that. But it might."

McVeigh had a troubled past. He had grown frustrated after failing to make it into the Green Berets in the Army; after falling under the influence of the antigovernment brothers Terry and James Nichols, he developed extremist views and sought to avenge Waco.

He detonated the homemade, 5,000-pound bomb of agricultural fertilizer, ammonium nitrate, and diesel fuel in a Ryder truck he had rented under his own name. When he stayed at nearby motels in the nights just before the explosion, he also used his own name rather than an alias.

"I am a prisoner of war," McVeigh said after being arrested, refusing to cooperate beyond giving his name, rank, and serial number.

The FBI amassed substantial evidence linking McVeigh to the bombing and had enough information to name two of his close associates, the Nichols brothers, with conspiracy connected to bomb-building. Freeh's deep involvement in the details of the case was crucial in keeping both brothers in custody. Top Justice Department and FBI officials had concluded that they had strong enough evidence to hold only one of the brothers. But Freeh, in a late-afternoon meeting inside the FBI's command center, persuaded the others by listing the facts on a yellow legal pad that formed the basis for charges against both. By the following day, the FBI had amassed even more information on the pair, proving Freeh correct. Senior Justice officials said they listened closely to Freeh on legal matters in the Oklahoma City case—even though such issues were not his responsibility—because he had successfully directed complex investigations and prosecutions and had experience as a federal judge.

Freeh and the FBI showed strong leadership following the tragic explosion. The Bureau processed more than 1 billion documents, 43,500 leads, 28,000 interviews, and 7,000 pounds of evidence, and indicted McVeigh four months after the explosion. All that was left was for prosecutors to win the overwhelming case at trial. "This will rank as one of the FBI's most outstanding triumphs," predicted George Terwilliger, a counterterrorism expert and former senior Justice Department official.

The message was clear—the FBI had what it took to redeploy armies of agents, track criminals, and get its man, a mantra repeated over and over by senior Bureau officials. With the political wind at his back, the FBI director successfully lobbied the Clinton administration and Congress for additional funding for the Bureau and greater authority to monitor domestic terrorist groups, including authority to infiltrate and investigate those organizations that financed terrorism. He also sought new legal authority for the FBI, to be automatically designated the lead agency in all future terrorist matters. "Somebody ought to be in charge when the bomb goes off," Freeh told Congress. "We think that should be the FBI."

The afterglow of the successful OKBOM probe didn't last, however, and Freeh began encountering political problems, some that he inherited and others that he created. The Larry Potts affair was the catalyst for Freeh's retreat from public view in August 1995. Potts had headed the criminal division during a deadly shoot-out with a group of white separatists in Ruby Ridge, Idaho, in August 1992, one year before Freeh took the helm. From his office in Washington, Potts oversaw the standoff as the "Feds" were called in following an initial gun battle that left two dead. With the FBI in charge, sharpshooters surrounded the house where Randy Weaver and his family were holed up. Contrary to typical Bureau procedures, the sharpshooters had been given orders that they "could and should" fire on any armed adult male who left the house.

When Weaver and two others emerged with weapons, an FBI sniper shot and wounded Weaver and one of his friends. The trio retreated, but an agent fired another shot that killed Weaver's wife, Vicki, as she stood in the doorway of their house holding a ten-month-old baby. Inside the Bureau, the overriding question became: Who issued the "shoot-on-sight" order? The field commander insisted that Potts had issued the command, while Potts denied it. Freeh sided with Potts, his longtime friend, issuing him a mild rebuke while suspending and demoting the field commander.

The internal controversy likely would have ended there but Freeh, acting on bad advice and his own poor judgment, soon thereafter promoted Potts to deputy director, the number two position in the FBI. The promotion made Potts's rebuke look like a sham, raising long-standing questions about the disparate treatment of top officials and frontline employees when it came to discipline. A political uproar ensued amid fresh allegations of a Ruby Ridge cover-up. An FBI agent acknowledged destroying documents that might have implicated Potts in issuing the deadly force orders, and it was clear Freeh had fumbled the ball. Under political fire to take action or risk his own standing in Washington, Freeh's self-protective instincts carried the day. He suspended and demoted Potts, defusing the political controversy by coldly cutting off a friend who left the Bureau and went to work for a private investigative firm.

The Potts debacle made Freeh look like a political novice, and afterward, his willingness to conduct interviews with the media waned as he cloistered himself with his inner circle. Over the first several years of his term, Freeh regularly ate lunch in the headquarters cafeteria and jogged with virtually every class of recruits at Quantico before swearing them in, always emphasizing the importance of his "bright line" ethics policy. But now the director spent more and more hours on the road or in his seventh-floor office suite, which agents referred to as "the bunker." When Freeh came into the top spot at the FBI, he had won praise for streamlining the headquarters staff and taking the time to meet privately with agents in the field to hear their comments and complaints. Wearing baggy suits and scuffed shoes, he came across as a regular guy. But he soon surrounded himself with old friends he could trust, creating a cadre of elite advisers. He brought in associates from his Pizza Connection days, naming Bob Bucknam the FBI's first chief of staff, choosing Howard Shapiro—his right-hand man in the Moody mail-bombing case in Atlanta—as general counsel, and promoting a handful of others who quickly became known throughout the Bureau as the "Friends of Louis." The heavyset Bucknam, resented by many and derisively referred to as "the round man," played gatekeeper to the director. "Louis just disappeared," a former high-ranking FBI official close to Freeh said.

In the aftermath of the Ruby Ridge fiasco—which, like Waco, became a rallying cry of antigovernment groups—Freeh revamped FBI methods for dealing with crisis situations that called for a more nuanced approach and did not necessarily involve menacing black-clad SWAT teams. He noted, for example, that while the FBI had its highly trained Hostage Rescue Team at Waco and Ruby Ridge, there hadn't been any hostages to rescue. Under the new guidelines, the FBI's first line of response became nonconfrontational negotiators, working under the joint direction of the Hostage Rescue Team and the behavioral sciences unit.

The new procedures proved successful in the summer of 1996, after an eighty-one-day standoff with the Montana Freemen, an armed antigovernment group wanted on bank fraud charges. The standoff ended peacefully, validating Freeh's new approach. But it did not wipe away the stain of the Potts affair and the allegations of cover-up, which proved "very, very painful" for Freeh, according to a colleague.

Things would get worse for Freeh and the FBI before they got better. With its mistaken public identification of security guard Richard Jewell as the culprit in the 1996 Atlanta Olympic Park bombing case, the Bureau soon had a major public relations and investigative debacle on its hands. Jewell's name had been leaked to the press, ruining his reputation, and FBI agents had sought to question him under the false pretense that he was helping them make a training video on how to interrogate witnesses. After hearing about the way the probe was being handled, Freeh, again involving himself in the details of a high-profile case, called Atlanta and directed agents to read Jewell his Miranda rights before he was questioned further. "I will be on the phone and will take charge of cases as I have whenever I think it's appropriate for the leader of the FBI to have that presence," Freeh said, acknowledging that it was a bit unusual to have the director micromanaging individual cases. But the gilt-edged reputation the FBI had earned with Oklahoma City lost some of its luster, as Jewell ended up being released without any charges filed. Jewell's name was smeared, and members of Congress blamed the Bureau for media leaks.

"Senior management at the FBI puts too much emphasis on its image and budget and not enough on its product," said Senator

Charles Grassley of Iowa. "Beyond the veneer is an ugly culture of arrogance that uses intimidation, disinformation, and empire-building to get what it wants. . . . Civil liberties and the protection of every American are at stake when the FBI does not meet the very highest standards."

Freeh's troubles didn't end there. The extraordinary success of the Oklahoma City bombing investigation was called into question by a blistering April 1997 Inspector General's report saying that the FBI lab had produced substandard work, exaggerated findings, reached conclusions to assist prosecutors, and mishandled evidence. The probe had been prompted by allegations lodged by whistle-blower Frederic Whitehurst, who said the FBI lab had even fabricated evidence. "I'll tell you this, Mr. Director. We're facing a serious problem, a problem of management and integrity," Rep. Harold Rogers of Kentucky told Freeh in a congressional hearing. If the damaging allegations could be proven in the court, the Bureau risked undermining the prosecution of Timothy McVeigh and turning its greatest success into a spectacular failure. Freeh acknowledged the lab's shortfalls and vowed to fix the problems by recruiting an outside expert to professionalize the lab's operations and seek proper accreditation. And the Inspector General gave the Bureau some breathing room when it did not support Whitehurst's claim that evidence was fabricated out of thin air. Still, Freeh seemed off balance. "I think Freeh is a fish out of water, being pulled in fifteen different directions at once," a former FBI agent said.

The broader problem, according to Justice Department Inspector General Michael Bromwich, was that lofty public expectations of the Bureau were impossible to fulfill. "I think all of us have a view of the FBI and the FBI lab as just places where good work is done, and we tend to have a Superman cape around the FBI," he said. "That's not realistic. The FBI is an institution made of human beings who are as fallible as the rest of us."

While there was some suggestion that the evidence was not handled as professionally as possible in the OKBOM case, a court ruled the lab did nothing to contaminate crucial evidence in the probe. In the spring of 1997, the government prevailed by convicting McVeigh and Terry Nichols. Prosecutors later won the right to impose the death penalty on McVeigh. It was, in the end, a moment of justice, tremendous relief, and vindication for the families of victims as well as for the Federal Bureau of Investigation in the largest probe it had ever undertaken.

"I think Director Freeh did a great job," said Senator Orrin Hatch of Utah.

Around the same time, the Bureau also found a traitor in its midst. After the FBI received a tip that its counterintelligence agent Earl Pitts had been a spy, the thirteen-year veteran was arrested after he fell prey to a successful Bureau undercover operation. In July 1997, Pitts, only the second FBI agent ever arrested for espionage, was sentenced to twenty-seven years in prison for crimes including selling Moscow a classified manual called "Counterintelligence: Identifying Foreign Agents." He received $129,000 in cash and another $100,000 supposedly set aside for him in an overseas account. The intelligence Pitts sold the Russians from 1987 to 1992 was classified below the TOP SECRET level; otherwise he would have faced life in prison. "This case shows that spies can be anywhere, and the FBI is determined to find them even if they are on our own rolls," Freeh said. "It is profoundly disturbing that an FBI Special Agent would be a spy for a foreign government. But I am proud that the FBI pursued this case so vigorously, letting the chips fall where they may."

Increasingly, though, Freeh began paying attention to which way the chips might fall. His hard-fought victory in the Oklahoma City bombing case and the momentous yet painful events that followed changed him in fundamental ways. He not only analyzed issues based on what was best for the Bureau or the nation but also considered more carefully than before the way that his decisions would play in the corridors of power. Louis Freeh, the self-described policeman, had finally gone to Washington.

17

CLASHING WITH CLINTON

No two men in Washington came to respect each other less and despise each other more by the end of the 1990s than Louis Freeh and Bill Clinton. Their antipathy and lack of trust affected everything from the conduct of foreign policy to decisions about national security. At issue were fundamental questions: Was the White House entitled to briefings on matters that could affect foreign policy if divulging the information might compromise an investigation that may lead to the Oval Office? Was the FBI a loyal part of the administration or a force separate from it?

If Clinton seethed at his impotence in controlling the FBI, Freeh thought the president's philandering and loose fund-raising practices brought dishonor to the White House. As time went on, the feud became personal. Clinton came to believe Freeh acted self-righteously while running a highly politicized agency, accountable to no one, that became overtly antagonistic toward him. Freeh was deeply suspicious of Clinton and viewed him as unfit to serve as president.

When Clinton nominated Freeh, he had won the judge's allegiance, calling him "a legend" in law enforcement and "my kind of guy." But for men accustomed to trusting their instincts, this was a case of first impressions being spectacularly wrong. "They had conflicting mutual expectations and inaccurate mutual perceptions," said former deputy attorney general Jamie Gorelick. But even as intense animosity quickly came to define their relationship, the battle took place largely behind the scenes. "I think Clinton felt there was some type of vendetta," said former FBI deputy director Robert M. "Bear" Bryant. "Freeh doesn't respect him, but I don't think he hates him."

Even before probes of Clintons' fund-raising practices strained ties between them, their relationship soured over the FBI's aggressive investigation of the Whitewater land deal. The probe led to the appointment of an independent counsel soon after the president took office. After Republicans took control of Congress in 1994, Freeh became more responsive to them than to his own bosses in the administration. To make matters worse, Freeh further showed his distrust of Clinton by turning in his White House pass, saying he wanted to sign in and out as a visitor each time he came to the West Wing. The self-protective Freeh saw it as a way to guard against allegations of impropriety; Clinton took it as an insult.

One Clinton aide said the relationship "went nuclear" in the summer of 1996, after disclosures that a mid-level White House aide had improperly collected hundreds of FBI files at the White House. Clinton administration officials blamed a bureaucratic error for what came to be known as "Filegate." Freeh threw kerosene on the raging political fire by issuing a statement that "The FBI and I were victimized" by the White House. Clinton was livid over Freeh's self-serving statement, especially since the Bureau had willingly turned over the files.

"Louis Freeh is a goddamn fucking asshole," Clinton reportedly said behind closed doors.

Freeh's absolute commitment to cases he deemed important, as well as his lack of respect for Clinton, were dramatically displayed throughout the Khobar Towers case, a probe into the bombing of a U.S. military barracks in Saudi Arabia. On the evening of June 25, 1996, two men in an explosive-laden tanker truck pulled up beside the perimeter fence of the Khobar Towers barracks, jumped into a waiting car, and sped away. Sentries stationed on the rooftop noticed the suspicious behavior and attempted to rouse the American airmen sleeping in their quarters, but they could not evacuate the high-rise building quickly enough. The truck bomb exploded a few minutes later, killing nineteen people, injuring hundreds more, and decimating the giant building. Freeh, in New Jersey visiting relatives when he received word of the blast, immediately dispatched a team of agents to Saudi Arabia and soon traveled there himself. He viewed the carnage that the bomb had wrought, spoke with the families of the dead, and vowed to bring the guilty to justice.

Homicide detectives often say that every time they get a case, it is as if a fog descends upon them. They cannot think of anything else. Louis Freeh pursued Khobar Towers like a man trying to lift a fog. His dedication to the investigation is a testament to his integrity and his belief in truth and justice; but it is just as much a testament to the complete breakdown in communication and trust between the FBI and the White House. Freeh also demonstrated his willingness to venture beyond the FBI director's authority to carry out his mission, even it meant making foreign policy himself.

Tensions between the FBI and the White House, and between Freeh and Clinton, mounted as investigations into misconduct by administration officials pushed on. By 1997 FBI agents were assisting investigations by four separate independent counsels, and Freeh was recommending a fifth, to examine Democratic fund-raising improprieties related to the 1996 elections. In May 1997 the relationship between the Clinton administration and the FBI hit a new low. A number of senior administration officials had come under investigation for possible campaign-finance violations, including the acceptance of donations from the Chinese government. Attorney General Janet Reno assigned a task force led by Justice Department prosecutor Charles LaBella to investigate. LaBella concluded that the Justice Department had a conflict of interest, and could not investigate an administration of which it was a part. Freeh agreed and wrote a strongly worded twenty-two-page memo to Reno recommending that an independent counsel be assigned to the probe. Reno rejected Freeh's arguments, but soon the memo was leaked to the press. White

House officials were convinced that the FBI director, seeking to curry favor with congressional Republicans, was behind the leak.

FBI officials, meanwhile, were livid over the campaign-finance flap and wanted the president booted out of office. The scandal also created operational problems for the Bureau. Central to the whole matter was the dilemma created by the Chinese angle: How could the FBI fulfill its duty to brief the White House on national security matters regarding China without compromising the integrity of a possible criminal investigation?

Clinton grew more furious later that year when he and National Security Adviser Sandy Berger read in the newspaper that the FBI was probing suspicions that China may have been using hidden political contributions to buy influence and conduct espionage in Washington. It became clear that Freeh had briefed members of Congress, but not the White House, on the China probe.

Jim Steinberg, Berger's deputy, said the problem of insufficient information sharing had grown due to the FBI's increased involvement globally in law enforcement. While the FBI followed its tradition of maintaining confidentiality in a law enforcement probe, Steinberg said the administration was dealing with China on numerous issues and ought to have been informed. For the FBI to keep such a probe secret, he concluded, required "an overwhelmingly compelling reason."

During a telephone call between Freeh and his senior deputies over whether to brief Secretary of State Madeleine Albright on the investigation before an upcoming trip to China, Bryant minced no words in talking about the president. *The New Yorker* reported that Bryant adamantly opposed the sharing of information that could be relayed to the president, saying, "Why should we brief him? He's a crook. He's no better than a bank robber. Would we tell a bank robber about our investigation?" Freeh also took a hard-line stance, releasing minimal information to the administration. On December 4, 1997, White House spokesman Mike McCurry, when asked whether the president still had confidence in the FBI director, said, "I think

the president thinks that the FBI is the world's greatest law enforcement agency, and I think the president has great confidence that Louis
Freeh is leading that agency—as best he can."

McCurry's attack on the FBI director, and the leaked campaign-
finance memo, brought the war between Freeh and Clinton into
public view. Freeh fired a salvo of his own, writing a personal letter
of thanks to Clinton nemesis Kenneth Starr, sent the day after Starr
resigned his independent counsel post in 1999. The director hailed
Starr's "persistence and uncompromising personal and professional
integrity." The director's carefully aimed shot across Clinton's bow
was "vintage Freeh," said Jonathan Turley of George Washington
University, who added that the director "may be one of the best political operatives in the city." Freeh had concluded he stood the best
chance of getting maximum funding and support for the FBI by getting closer to congressional Republicans. After Clinton had resented
Freeh's public criticism of the administration for a proposed cut in
the FBI's budget a few years earlier, Freeh found that a supportive
Congress could get the job done for him, no matter what became of
his relationship with Clinton.

But if the director was looking for complete and total refuge
during the middle years of his tenure, he wouldn't find it on Capitol
Hill. While the FBI did receive plaudits and greater authority following its capture of CIA spy Aldrich Ames, its timely apprehension
of Timothy McVeigh after the Oklahoma City bombing, and its bare-
knuckles approach to Clinton, the Bureau also came under heavy fire
for what seemed like one bungled operation after another. A wave of
controversies—from mishandling of evidence in the FBI crime lab,
to the Bureau's probe of the downing of TWA Flight 800, to the
embarrassment following the Atlanta Olympic Park bombing investigation—put the director on the defensive. To maintain the support
of his employees, Freeh had to defend the FBI before Congress, sometimes for rather indefensible failures. Yet Freeh also had to appear
contrite enough to appease the committee members who held the all-
important appropriations purse strings. On more than one occasion,

this balancing act put Freeh in the position of looking up from the witness table at a panel of congressmen, swallowing his pride, and flatly admitting, "Yes, we did wrong." Along the way, he mastered the art of lobbying Congress by meeting with members one-on-one, sharing sensitive information about probes prior to hearings, and developing close personal ties.

This approach didn't mollify everyone, however. In one of the most stinging rebukes that Freeh received, House Appropriations Committee chairman Bob Livingston, a Louisiana Republican, said in a 1997 hearing, "I've always had tremendous faith in the credibility and integrity of the FBI, and I still have faith in the rank-and-file FBI agents. But I think the leadership of the FBI has brought the entire organization into question. And you are the leader."

Freeh's blunt response surprised Livingston. "I don't pass the buck to anybody in my organization. I am the director, and, as you said, I'm the leadership. And if I'm not doing a good job in this regard, then they ought to get a new FBI director."

Disarming, heartfelt, self-protective, sanctimonious, shrewd—Freeh could be all of these at once, as his appearances on the Hill illustrated. His manner of testifying before Congress was effective because it was hard to define where his genuine personal convictions ended and where his political machinations began.

"I am not a politician, I am a policeman," Freeh said often.

Yet few navigated the political course so deftly or played one side against the other so adeptly. Freeh had no party apparatus to bolster him and few natural allies in Washington. However, his position did offer the advantage of the long-standing tradition of Bureau independence fostered by J. Edgar Hoover. Freeh said his goal as FBI director was to maintain his integrity and political independence. "After twenty-one years of only working in the government," Freeh said, integrity "is basically the only asset that I have."

Most of the time, the director prevailed in these political battles. Despite his chronic shyness, Freeh had always been effective in one-on-one dealings, and he was ballsy. As an FBI agent, Louis Freeh

charmed his way into an unlikely friendship with a fearsome gang-
ster during an undercover operation. He convinced Mob bosses to
rat on their associates. And as a prosecutor, he openly socialized in
the courtroom with defendants and their lawyers, making friends in
some cases even as he worked to lock them away. If Freeh was in-
timidated by the Mafiosi he was trying to bust, he never showed it.
As FBI director, he sought to build a global crime-fighting network
through personal relationships and trust. Now, he was forging those
same bonds with influential congressmen, the gatekeepers to budget
largesse.

Slowly, GOP committee chairmen, charmed by Freeh's straight-
talking style, and impressed by his rebukes of Clinton, began to accept the Bureau's top cop as their own. They did not mind that a mea
culpa from the FBI director would often be accompanied by requests
for more money and more authority to fix problems and prevent
future ones. Freeh had mastered this classic Washington political
maneuver. At one point, even as he was apologizing before Congress
about long-standing mismanagement in the FBI crime lab, construc-
tion moved ahead on a new state-of-the-art lab facility. Over time,
Freeh became legendary for his apparent immunity to criticism and
tough questioning.

Freeh's political savvy protected the FBI on the Hill, but back
at headquarters the Bureau's blunders continued, often overshad-
owing landmark successes in important operations. The FBI's work
leading up to the millennium kept Americans safe at a time when
large-scale festivities had been planned in cities around the country.
But while the Bureau could have been garnering praise for preventing attacks and bloodshed, both the president and the public instead
were focused squarely on the charges of misconduct and racial profiling in the case against Wen Ho Lee.

Lee, a mathematician at the Los Alamos nuclear testing facility, had been under FBI suspicion of espionage for China since the
early 1990s, when he was seen warmly embracing a Chinese nuclear
weapons designer. The possible breach was made all the more dan-

gerous by the fact that Lee's work in X Division at Los Alamos had given him access to America's most sensitive nuclear secrets.

Though not widely discussed, the FBI's arsenal includes "confrontational interviews" permitting agents to tell subjects that they failed polygraph exams that they had passed, misleading them about pertinent facts, and using other tactics to coerce them to confess. Now the FBI, frustrated with his evasiveness and occasional false statements, was about to get confrontational with Wen Ho Lee.

"Do you know who the Rosenbergs are?" an FBI agent asked Lee during an interrogation on March 9, 1999.

"The Rosenbergs are the only people that never cooperated with the federal government in an espionage case. You know what happened to them? They electrocuted them, Wen Ho."

"Yeah, I heard," Lee replied.

"Wen Ho, you're in trouble. You are in big trouble," the FBI agent asserted later.

"I know," Lee said. "But I tell you one thing. I'm the victim. I am innocent."

During his time in X Division, Lee repeatedly engaged in behavior that raised the suspicions of his superiors. He downloaded hundreds of thousands of pages of classified material onto portable computer tapes, offered to help a fellow weapons researcher who was under investigation for espionage, failed to report all contacts with Chinese scientists whom he met on travels abroad, and attempted to gain access to the secure Los Alamos computer network from a hotel room in Taiwan while attending a conference. When the CIA learned in 1996 that the Chinese possessed blueprints and detailed information about the W-88—a miniaturized thermonuclear warhead considered the most advanced U.S. atomic weapon—Department of Energy investigators quickly assembled a list of suspects who might be responsible for the compromise. Lee was at the top of that list, and the FBI formally opened an investigation in May 1996.

From the outset, however, the FBI's probe was beset with problems. The Bureau never pursued the other suspects identified in the

Department of Energy inquiry, yet in the two years they focused on Lee, investigators were unable to find hard evidence that implicated him. In fact, they assembled so little evidence in support of espionage charges that they were unable to convince the Justice Department in 1997 that they had probable cause for a search warrant. The FBI's subsequent efforts to enhance the warrant application, which Freeh later admitted "could and should have been more aggressive," also proved unsuccessful.

Freeh and the FBI were under immense political pressure from congressional Republicans to explain how China had gained access to sensitive data about U.S. weapons technology. Polygraphs yielded some inconclusive and deceptive answers, and in accompanying interviews Lee admitted to having helped Chinese weapons scientists solve a mathematical problem, though he repeated his denials about having shared classified information.

The search of Lee's office and a subsequent raid on his home revealed that, over the course of six years, the scientist had abused his security clearance by downloading a hefty amount of classified information—more than 400,000 pages—onto his nonsecure computer and portable magnetic tapes. Seven of the ten tapes that Lee created were missing. While Lee's attorneys maintained that he destroyed the tapes, the FBI found no evidence supporting that claim.

Louis Freeh called the tape downloads Wen Ho Lee's "own secret, portable, personal trove of this nation's nuclear weapons secrets." Freeh pressed Attorney General Reno and the Justice Department prosecutors to indict Lee on charges of mishandling classified data, even though they had no proof of the far more serious charge of passing any secrets to China or any other country. On December 10, in the federal courthouse in Albuquerque, New Mexico, the government issued a fifty-nine-count indictment of Lee. Several of the counts carried a maximum sentence of life in prison.

At Lee's detention hearing, an expert from Los Alamos testified that the information on the tapes represented fifty years of nuclear weapons development by the U.S. that could "change the global strategic balance" if they got into the wrong hands, and recommended that Lee be held without bail until trial. FBI Agent Robert Messemer provided testimony about Lee's alleged actions, arguing that he was a high security risk who could not be trusted. The presiding judge, James A. Parker, agreed with the prosecution's argument that releasing Lee would be a risk to national security as long as the location of the portable computer tapes was unknown. Ironically, the prosecution's victory in the bail hearing would turn out to give Freeh's FBI another black eye.

In subsequent court hearings, a weapons expert testified for the defense that the secrets Lee allegedly downloaded were not "the crown jewels" of America's nuclear arsenal, as was first implied. And Messemer, the lead agent on the case, admitted to giving false testimony at the bail hearing. Meanwhile, press reports said Lee was kept in solitary confinement in a cell with a constantly burning lightbulb, was shackled during his daily hour of exercise time, and had extremely limited visitation rights.

While conducting the Lee investigation, the FBI was also hard at work rooting out terrorists planning to wreak havoc on millennium celebrations. U.S. border agents in Washington state stopped an Algerian man attempting to bring a carful of powerful explosives and other bomb-making equipment into the United States in mid-December; he later admitted in court that he was going to bomb Los Angeles International Airport. The Bureau, with help from its overseas counterparts, also uncovered a terrorist plot to blow up tourist sites frequented by Americans in Jordan. FBI agents immediately made several arrests and began looking for additional clues linking the plots to other possible terrorists, including Osama bin Laden, the Saudi fugitive hiding in Afghanistan.

Inside the FBI's command center, there was a locked room devoted solely to bin Laden, with a poster describing him as "the face of evil." Ever since he was charged with directing the deadly terrorist attacks on U.S. embassies in Kenya and Tanzania a few years earlier, the FBI has maintained a twenty-four-hour "bin Laden" watch.

Freeh gathered with Reno and Berger to monitor the situation from the FBI's high-octane Strategic Information and Operations Center on December 31, 1999. One day earlier, FBI agents had rounded up and imprisoned dozens of suspects across the United States, worried less about successful prosecution than about keeping them off the streets when the ball dropped in Times Square. Tensions were high throughout the day, but as midnight on the East Coast came and went peacefully, the FBI agents and technicians manning the Bureau's command center popped open bottles of champagne and toasted the New Year. The FBI's success in preventing millennial violence was a monumental achievement. Freeh's increased emphasis on counterterrorism, and his goal of preventing attacks from occurring rather than catching terrorists after they struck, had helped to keep peace on a landmark day.

However, the Bureau's investigation into Wen Ho Lee was not faring nearly so well. As time went on, Judge Parker began to express doubts about the strength of the government's case. Fearing that the government ran the risk of never finding out what happened to the missing tapes if the case went to trial, Louis Freeh met with senior Justice and Energy Department officials in early September 2000 to discuss options for a plea bargain. Freeh worried that the government's case appeared weak and also wanted to avoid embarrassing disclosures in court, including internal FBI memos that were critical of Messemer. Five days later, Reno, Freeh, and prosecutors in New Mexico unanimously blessed a plea bargain that set Lee free in exchange for a guilty plea to a single felony count that did not mention espionage.

In a harsh tone rarely heard from the bench, Judge Parker lashed out at the government's handling of the Lee case and apologized to the scientist for his "demeaning, unnecessarily punitive" detention. The judge said that he had been "led astray by the executive branch of government." Parker blamed the "top decision makers" in the executive branch—a clear reference to Freeh and Reno—for causing embarrassment "by the way this case began and was handled." The

judge stated that FBI investigators "have embarrassed our entire nation and each of us who is a citizen of it."

President Clinton took pleasure in harshly criticizing Freeh, his
archenemy at the FBI. An administration official characterized an
internal report on the investigation as "a top to bottom criticism of
the FBI's handling of the Wen Ho Lee case." As charges of misconduct and racial profiling flew in the press, Clinton himself said, "The
whole thing was quite troubling to me. I think it's very difficult to
reconcile the two positions, that one day he's a terrible risk to the
national security and the next day they're making a plea agreement
for an offense far more modest that what had been alleged." The
president also chastised law enforcement officials for holding Lee in
prison for nearly a year without bail, saying his confinement ought
to be "disturbing" to the American people. "It just can't be justified,"
the president said. "I always had reservations about the claims that
were made denying him bail."

Still, the badly limping Khobar Towers probe ultimately became the most glaring example of the ongoing distrust and animosity between Clinton and Freeh. In it, one could trace the nerves
running between the White House and the FBI, as well as the thin
line that Freeh walked between his moralistic and his Machiavel-
lian sides. Perhaps because of these reasons, the Khobar Towers case
was largely shielded from public view. Even within the Bureau, it
was a highly compartmented matter; Dale Watson, head of the FBI's
counterterrorism division, said, "It's a killing offense around here
to talk about it."

Freeh faced new challenges that spanned not only policing, but
also diplomacy, human rights, and politics in the Khobar case. While
domestically Freeh was exchanging blows with the Clinton administration over a host of other matters, he was pondering tough, soul-
searching dilemmas in Khobar about how to cooperate with a country
that tortured prisoners and rounded up suspects in a seemingly in-
discriminate fashion. He had to exert relentless energy to keep the
Clinton administration moving the case forward, and he would even-

tually take the extraordinary step of asking a former president to intervene on his behalf. He struggled to find the right words to say to the families of the bombing victims who wanted to know if the attackers would be brought to justice. And he played a delicate game of political chess with his Saudi contacts to ensure their continued assistance, even as he hoped to bring indictments against apparently complicit Iranian government officials that risked provoking a military conflict in the region.

From the outset, the FBI investigators ran into roadblocks put up by the Saudis, who were less than forthcoming with critical pieces of evidence. Freeh called on cabinet officials, including the secretaries of state and defense, to urge cooperation from their Saudi contacts. According to Sandy Berger, President Clinton himself got involved, personally writing to King Fahd and meeting with Fahd's half brother, Crown Prince Abdullah, to elicit support for the FBI's involvement in the investigation. Despite promises from high-ranking officials, however, little progress was made and Freeh was growing impatient; he didn't feel the White House was making the case a priority. He recalled the maddening bureaucratic obstacles he faced as an agent in New York; now he was the FBI director, and the same sorts of obstacles still existed.

Irrepressible, Freeh worked to secure his own allies in the Saudi government to push for help in the investigation. First on his list was Prince Bandar bin Sultan, the Saudi ambassador to the United States and a nephew of King Fahd. Bandar was well known as an extravagant fixture on the Washington social scene, but he also wielded real influence on the Saudi government and served as a useful go-between for Freeh. In mid-1997, however, the Clinton administration began to make overtures to the more moderate secular government gaining power in Iran, and the Saudis sensed that America had abandoned interest in Khobar. Furthermore, in 1998 the White House became preoccupied with the Monica Lewinsky scandal.

Running out of options, and allies, the FBI director made a bold and unprecedented plea for help behind Clinton's back. Freeh solicited former president George Bush, who still enjoyed high popularity among Saudis for leading efforts against Iraq in the Gulf War, to make a personal appeal to the Saudi royal family. President Clinton never knew about his predecessor's involvement in the case; the relationship between Clinton and Freeh had fully deteriorated by then. In fact, Freeh and Clinton never met alone after the FBI director's views on the China fund-raising allegations had surfaced.

Freeh's political ploy worked, as Bush's intervention with the royal family brought about a breakthrough. At a meeting with Crown Prince Abdullah, Freeh secured a compromise that would enable FBI agents to participate indirectly in Saudi interrogations of suspects, the breakthrough that Freeh had been seeking from the start. The interrogations yielded damning evidence of Iranian involvement in the plot, but the Clinton administration remained wary of taking action so Freeh decided to wait until a new administration was in the White House to bring the revelations to the Oval Office.

"Mad Dog" Freeh had sunk his teeth into the Khobar Towers case with full force, and he was determined to solve it, using whatever means necessary. Prince Bandar thought Freeh was potentially a loose cannon, ready to act on principle without regard for the political and diplomatic consequences. He rightly sensed that relations between Freeh and the White House had broken down completely, and that Freeh, while a man of integrity, was also very adept at the power game.

"Freeh is a lovely human being," Bandar told *The New Yorker* magazine, "but he is much more sophisticated and deadly than benign."

Freeh was pushing the bounds of the FBI's law enforcement charter into the realm of foreign affairs to resolve the case, letting his moralistic side win out over pragmatism. From a chain-of-command standpoint, Freeh was out of line, but his actions were not unlike that of the young G-man he had been, disgusted with the Washington bureaucracy that threw roadblocks in his way. As FBI director, he had the savvy, determination, and political muscle to get around or bust through them.

At the same time, the war with the White House was taking its toll, and Freeh pondered resigning. He respected authority and knew he was bucking the chief. Sitting back in his desk chair in his seventh-floor corner office in FBI headquarters, Freeh surveyed the portraits of his heroes, among them Teddy Roosevelt, Elie Wiesel, and Giovanni Falcone, the anti-Mafia magistrate memorialized at Quantico in a bust commissioned by the director. Freeh also saw the assorted drawings and paintings by his six boys that covered one of his office walls, and the family pictures on his desk. If he left the Bureau, he could find a lucrative job in the private sector that would ease his personal financial burden and allow him to spend more time with his family. But his deep mistrust of Clinton led him to stay on the job to prevent the president from replacing him with a political hack. He also felt strongly about certain outstanding cases, especially Khobar Towers, which had taken the lives of American soldiers, and he wanted to see them through.

Freeh recalled his first meeting with the president, when Clinton spoke about FBI independence and the importance of family. Had he been snookered, Freeh asked himself, or was Clinton really a well-meaning person who simply let his desires get the better of him? Didn't Clinton's inner conflicts interfere with his ability to work and be a father and husband? Or did he have an uncanny ability to compartmentalize and conceal? Soon enough, Freeh would be asking himself the same questions about Special Agent Robert Hanssen.

18

A LONG AND
LONELY TIME

For eight years, Bob Hanssen kept himself out of the spy game in an effort to protect his security and anonymity. After what at times had seemed like an interminable hiatus, he saw the signs of change in Russia he had been waiting for to resume his activities. With Russian President Boris Yeltsin losing his grip on power in 1999, a former KGB spy, Vladimir Putin, was taking charge. To Hanssen, Putin's arrival on the scene as Yeltsin's successor marked an unmistakable turning point. It also was well timed, since Hanssen, nervously approaching retirement, needed cash to pay various expenses, including renovating his kitchen and putting in new wood floors. Portions of the geopolitical landscape that Hanssen had foretold in his 1991 Active Measures study were becoming increasingly apparent. Many of the authoritarian Russian methods were back, and along with them the old guard that put heavy emphasis on strong, centralized control. Putin and his KGB comrades had grown up in the Soviet culture of deception and duplicity, so well understood by Hanssen and so baffling to many Americans. From Hanssen's perspective, above all else, Putin and his inner circle possessed the temperament and discipline to keep secrets and protect sources.

"Dear friend: welcome!" the Russians wrote to Hanssen, after he reached out to them after the long break. "We express our sincere joy on the occasion of resumption of contact with you."

Most of the remainder of the letter, other than noting that the sum of $800,000 was set aside for him in a Russian bank, dealt with the tradecraft of espionage—a vertical mark of white adhesive tape, six to eight centimeters in length, that Hanssen was to leave on the Foxstone Park signpost nearest Wolftrap Creek as an indication he had loaded the ELLIS dead drop with documents; a horizontal mark of tape to be left by the Russians to indicate they had left $50,000 in return; removal of the tape by Hanssen to show that he had retrieved the cash.

The Russians also suggested, in the event of emergencies, a new set of thumbtack communication procedures in northwest Washington, not far from the Russian embassy. They directed Hanssen to place a white thumbtack sold at a CVS drugstore on an electric utility pole at the southwest corner of Foxhall Road and Whitehaven Parkway to indicate the need for a dead drop at ELLIS on the following Tuesday evening. He was to place a yellow thumbtack in the same spot, about one yard from the ground and visible from a car traveling on Foxhall Road, to indicate a "threatening situation" and the cessation of communication until he replaced the yellow thumbtack with a white one.

"For our part," the Russians wrote, "we are very interested to get from you any information about possible actions which may threaten us."

In a troika of letters he wrote to the Russians in the year 2000, Hanssen, identifying himself as "Ramon Garcia," indicated his desire to spy anew but remained exceedingly concerned about detection. The personal connection and thrill he had felt during his regular, anonymous exchanges with his Russian "friends" years ago had given way, with the passage of time, first to loneliness and then to greater introspection and contemplation of his fate. A letter Hanssen sent to the Russians in March 2000 revealed his increasingly fragile emotional state.

I have come about as close as I ever want to come to
sacrificing myself to help you, and I get silence. I hate silence.

Conclusion: One might propose that I am either insanely brave or quite insane. I'd answer neither. I'd say, insanely loyal. Take your pick. There is insanity in all the answers.

I have, however, come as close to the edge as I can without being truly insane. My security concerns have proven reality-based. I'd say, pin your hopes on 'insanely loyal' and go for it. Only I can lose.

I decided on this course when I was 14 years old. I'd read Philby's book. Now that is insane, eh! My only hesitations were my security concerns under uncertainty. I hate uncertainty. So far I have judged the edge correctly. Give me credit for that.

Set the signal at my site any Tuesday evening. I will read your answer. Please, at least say goodbye. It's been a long time my dear friends, a long and lonely time.

Ramon Garcia

So what does one make of Hanssen's dramatic references to hating silence and insanity? "He's revealing a tremendous amount about himself, about his neediness. He was very needy, he needed the approval, he knew he was at the edge and he talks about it. He can't stand them not giving him positive feedback," suggested psychologist Dr. Mark Siegert. "As you read on, his correspondence becomes flightier," added Dick Alu, one of Hanssen's former FBI colleagues. "It is like he is slowly losing his mind."

Hanssen's reference to Kim Philby appealed to the Russians. A trusted senior British intelligence officer and member of the elite, Philby had spied for the Russians for many years before defecting to Moscow, writing a book about his exploits, and becoming something of an international celebrity for pulling off such daring maneuvers. Former KGB major general Oleg Kalugin, described Hanssen as "bigger than Philby" in terms of the quantity and value of national security and intelligence he gave the Russians. But in Hanssen's mind, Philby was the epitome of "A Citizen Above Suspicion," easily overlooked since he was too senior to be suspected as a spy, and too professional to make stupid mistakes. Some people identify with athletes or musicians as role models or heroes; Hanssen fixated on spies like Philby, appreciating their skill and cunning and the ease with which they beat the system.

"What he said mostly, I recall, was how dumb the counterintelligence services were not to have picked up on it," said a Hanssen confidant. "That seemed to be his main gist; why didn't they figure this guy out? Maybe that is the key here. I don't think he was as impressed with Philby as he was unimpressed with British counterintelligence."

After Hanssen read the Philby book (which actually was published in 1968 around the time Bob turned twenty-four, not fourteen) he talked about it often, "putting it into the 'things are not the way they seem to be' context. That is what fascinated him. I remember him mentioning his fascination and over the years, he would occasionally come back to speculation on the motivations and so on for guys like Philby," a Hanssen associate said.

Several months later, Hanssen wrote the following missive to the Russians:

Dear Friends:

Administrative Issues:

Enclosed, once again, is my rudimentary cipher. Obviously it is weak in the manner I used it last—reusing key on multiple messages, but I wanted to give you a chance if you had lost the algorythm.

Thank you for your note. It brought me great joy to see the signal at last. As you implied and I have said, we do need a better form of secure communication—faster. In this vein, I propose (without being attached to it) the following:

One of the commercial products currently available is the Palm VII organizer. I have a Palm III, which is actually a fairly capable computer. The VII version comes with wireless internet capability built in. It can allow the rapid transmission of encrypted messages, which if used on an infrequent basis, could be quite effective in preventing confusions if the existence of the accounts could be appropriately hidden as well as the existence of the devices themselves. Such a device might even serve for rapid transmittal of substantial material in digital form. Your FAPSI [Russia's espionage communications and technology agency] could review what would be needed, its advisability, etc., obviously— particularly safe rules of use. While FAPSI may move with the rapidity of the Chinese army, they can be quite effective, in juggernaut fashion, that is to say thorough.

New topics:

If you are wise, you will reign in the GRU. They are causing no end of grief. But for the large number of double-agents they run, there would be almost no ability to cite activity warranting current foreign counterintelligence outlays. Of course the Gusev affair didn't help you any. [*Note:* Stanislav Borisovich Gusev was a Russian spy arrested by the FBI while walking back and forth outside the State Department. He was activating a highly advanced remote control bug hidden brilliantly inside a piece of chair molding in a refurbished conference room just down the hall from then Secretary of State Madeleine Albright's office. The tiny bug—difficult

to detect because Gusev turned it off when he was not
nearby—transmitted to a tape recorder in his car. The
folly of the operation was that he parked his car, with
diplomatic plates, at a parking meter, which he regularly
fed quarters while walking around the building. If his
frequent strolls and license plate didn't attract attention,
the parking meter was a surefire sign of something
suspicious, since diplomats in Washington ignore meters
and routinely tear up parking tickets.] If I'd had better
communications I could have prevented that. I was
aware of the fact that microphones had been detected at
the State Department. (Such matters are why I need
rapid communications. It can save you much grief.)
Many such things are closely held, but that closeness
fails when the need for action comes. Then the compart-
ments grow of necessity. I had knowledge weeks before
of the existence of devices, but not the country placing
them . . . I only found out the gruesome details too late to
warn you through available means including the colored
stick-pin call. (Which by the way I doubted would work
because of your ominous silence.) Very frustrating. This
is one reason I say 'you waste me' in the note.

The U.S. can be errantly likened to a powerfully built
but retarded child, potentially dangerous, but young,
immature and easily manipulated. But don't be fooled by
that appearance. It is also one which can turn ingenius
quickly, like an idiot savant, once convinced of a goal.
The [ ] Japanese (to quote General Patten once again)
learned this to their dismay.

I will not be able to clear TOM on the first back-up date
so don't be surprised if we default to that and you find
this then. Just place yours again the following week,
same protocol.

I greatly appreciate your highly professional inclusion of old references to things known to you in messages resulting from the mail interaction to assure me that the channel remains unpirated. This is not lost on me.

On Swiss money laudering, you and I both know it is possible but not simple. And we do both know that money is not really 'put away for you' except in some vague accounting sense. Never patronize at this level. It offends me, but then you are easily forgiven. But perhaps I shouldn't tease you. It just gets me in trouble.

> thank you again,
> Ramon

According to Dr. Siegert, when Hanssen described the United States as a powerfully built but retarded child who was not to be underestimated, he actually was looking in the mirror. "If that is not a self-description, I've never heard one," he said. Hanssen's demeaning reference to the United States also reflected his arrogance and sense of superiority. "Bob is an elitist," said one longtime associate. "In a democratic society, it is the mass that is uncritically thinking and that goes whichever way the wind is blowing today. He was less likely to communicate with somebody who is really in a different social milieu or social world. He is not a guy who would sit there and drink a cup of coffee or have a Coke with the plumber. . . . He does not have a high respect for their ability to judge things and feels they are easily manipulated by shady politicians and the media."

But the KGB's Kalugin said the language Hanssen began using in letters indicated he needed a break from the espionage game, something the Russians failed to encourage. "He was cracking," Kalugin said. "For an intelligence officer, this is a red signal."

To complete the trinity of correspondence in the year 2000, Hanssen transmitted the following letter to the Russians just before Thanksgiving:

Dear Friends:

Bear with me. It was I who sent the message trying to
use TOM to communicate material to you. On reflection, I can understand why you did not respond. I see
that I failed to furnish you sufficient information for you
to recognize that the message you left for me in ELLIS
did not go astray. You do this often (communicate such
assurances through the mention of items like the old
date offset we used), and believe me, it is not lost on me
as a sign of professionalism. I say bear with me on this
because you must realize I do not have a staff with
whom to knock around all the potential difficulties. (For
me breaks in communications are most difficult and
stressful.) Recent changes in U.S. law now attach the
death penalty to my help to you as you know, so I do
take some risk. On the other hand, I know far better than
most what minefields are laid and the risks. Generally
speaking, you overestimate the FBI's capacity to inter-
dict you, but on the other hand, cocksure officers (those
with real guts but not as much knowledge as they think)
can, as we say, step in an occasional cowpie. (Message to
the translator: Got a good word for cowpie in Russian??
Clue, don't blindly walk behind cows.)

I have drawn together material for you now over a
lengthy period. It is somewhat variable in import. Some
were selected as being merely instructive rather than
urgently important. I think such instructive insights
often can be quite as valuable or even more valuable
long-term because they are widely applicable rather
than narrow. Others are of definite value immediately.

My position has been most frustrating. I knew Mr.
Gusev was in eminent danger and had no effective way

of communicating in time. I knew microphones of an unknown origin were detected even earlier and had no regular way of communicating even that. This needs to be rectified if I am to be as effective as I can be.

No one answered my signal at Foxhall. Perhaps you occasionally give up on me. Giving up on me is a mistake. I have proven inveterately loyal and willing to take grave risks which even could cause my death, only remaining quiet in times of extreme uncertainty. So far my ship has successfully navigated the slings and arrows of outrageous fortune.

I ask you to help me survive.

On meeting out of the country, it simply is not practical for me. I must answer too many questions from family, friends and government plus it is a cardinal sign of a spy. You have made it that way because of your policy. Policies are constraints, constraints breed patterns. Patterns are noticed. Meeting in this country is not really that hard to manage, but I am loath to do so not because it is risky but because it involves revealing my identity. That insulation has been my best protection against betrayal by someone like me working from whatever motivation, a Bloch or a Philby.

On funds transfers through Switzerland, I agree that Switzerland itself has no real security, but insulated by laundering on both the in and out sides, mine ultimately through say a corporation I control loaning mortgage money to me for which (re) payments are made. . . . It certainly could be done. Cash is hard to handle here because little business is ever really done in cash and repeated cash transactions into the banking system are more dangerous because of the difficulty in explaining

them. That doesn't mean it isn't welcome enough to let
that problem devolve on me. (We should all have such
problems, eh?) How do you propose I get this money put
away for me when I retire? (Come on; I can joke with
you about it. I know money is not really put into an
account at MOST Bank, and that you are speaking
figuratively of an accounting notation at best to be made
real at some uncertain future. We do the same. Want me
to lecture in your 101 course in my old age? My college
level Russian has sunk low through inattention all these
years; I would be a novelty.)

yours truly,
Ramon

While Hanssen was glib in letters and subdued in manner, the
Russians during 2000 became increasingly businesslike in their communications. Gone was "Dear Friend," and in its place, "Dear Ramon."
Gone were the regards to Hanssen's family, replaced by a "negative attitude" toward his continued use of the U.S. mail to communicate. Gone was the fascination with means and modes of encrypted
communication; instead, the Russians directed Hanssen to give them
specific key numbers and programs so they could crack the code and
read his disks. Gone was the gratitude for whatever Hanssen produced in the way of intelligence; in its place was a numbered wish
list beginning with a request for human, electronic, and technical
penetrations of Russian residences in Washington and elsewhere.
Gone was the sense of a casual comfort with espionage, replaced
by a directive to pass along as much information as possible on a
special FBI-CIA task force actively hunting for a mole inside the
Bureau or the agency.

"We need this information," the Russians wrote, "especially to
take necessary additional steps to ensure your personal security."

19

WATCHING
AND WAITING

FBI Director Louis Freeh purposefully lingered near the end of the line as Attorney General John Ashcroft shook hands with senior Justice Department officials in his private fifth-floor conference room. It was the afternoon of February 2, 2001, Ashcroft's first day on the job under new president George W. Bush, and the former Missouri senator was doing one of the things politicians do best: pressing the flesh. After spending several hours walking the cavernous hallways of the Main Justice building meeting rank-and-file employees, Ashcroft hosted a reception so he personally could greet the heads of all of the major Justice divisions. Though they had spoken by telephone during the attorney general's bruising Senate confirmation process, Freeh and Ashcroft had never met. Freeh had a pressing piece of business he was eager to take up with his new boss as soon as possible. But he also appreciated the value of waiting until the right moment, a trait he had exhibited in the Pizza Connection case and on many other occasions. Preoccupied by thoughts about a classified matter with enormous ramifications for the nation and his FBI, Freeh slowly made his way toward the front of the line and was among the last to extend his hand and congratulate the new attorney general.

"Thanks for your calls, Director Freeh. It is really good to meet you in person," Ashcroft said.

Freeh moved discreetly to the side and waited for the others to shake hands and share a few words with Ashcroft. The reception concluded with punch, cookies, and an impromptu speech by the attorney general. As the crowd departed, the FBI director approached his new boss. "Can I have a minute to talk to you?" Freeh asked. Sensing something big was up, Ashcroft nodded, and the pair walked together into a secure conference room, which was soundproof and routinely swept for listening devices, making it fit for discussion of highly sensitive matters.

Freeh briefed Ashcroft quickly on an unfolding investigation involving the Bureau and the mole. The FBI had received an extraordinary case file from Moscow indicating an enormous breach of security, Freeh said. An FBI agent with expertise in Russian counterintelligence had sold thousands of pages of highly sensitive documents to the Russians since at least 1985. Now, Freeh said, the suspected double agent had been reassigned to a new job within the FBI and was under round-the-clock surveillance. Since it was difficult to prosecute espionage cases without catching someone red-handed—as the Wen Ho Lee case had demonstrated—the FBI was hoping to arrest him in the act. The intelligence breach was severe, though it would take months, or years, to do a full assessment of the damage. In the meantime, if there was a leak in the days ahead, the investigation could fall apart in an instant. Ashcroft agreed confidentiality was of paramount importance, and that no one without an absolute "need to know" would be apprised of the investigation.

Ashcroft walked across Pennsylvania Avenue to FBI headquarters the following week to meet with Freeh and other senior Bureau officials for a more detailed discussion of the case. Ashcroft learned how a joint FBI-CIA task force had continued hunting for a mole since the debriefing of Aldrich Ames six years ago left experts convinced that the Russians had at least one other major source within the intelligence community. Most FBI officials had thought the mole, like Ames, worked for the CIA until evidence from Moscow linking Hanssen to the Russians appeared in the fall.

The Bureau's probe turned upside down the lives of those mistakenly suspected of betraying their country. At least one CIA employee under suspicion for espionage had been suspended since August 1999, part of the human debris created by Hanssen's spying and the FBI's investigation. Ironically, the veteran CIA agent attended the same church as Hanssen, lived on the same street, traveled with him once on a counterintelligence mission, and jogged through Nottoway Park, where the PARK dead drop site was located.

The investigation of the CIA agent recalls stories of FBI intimidation and deception similar to the tactics used against Wen Ho Lee during the same period. The CIA officer passed a polygraph he was given by the Bureau under false pretenses, and the FBI turned down his offer to take a second polygraph in the summer of 1999 to clear his name. Instead, he was escorted out of the building and barred from CIA headquarters. The agent had come under suspicion in part due to his involvement in the investigation of Felix Bloch and because of a suspicious map of Nottoway Park found among his belongings. The FBI tried catching him in a sting by dispatching a Russian to his house who told him the Bureau knew about his spying and then offered an escape plan. But the CIA operative promptly disclosed the Russian's visit to his superiors.

FBI agents had squeezed family members too. Without notice, the CIA officer's daughter, who also worked for the Langley, Virginia–based spy agency, was taken into a small room by FBI agents and told, "We have some bad news for you. Your father is a spy. He's working for the Russians." She cried as they placed their "smoking gun" before her: the marked-up map of Nottoway Park that FBI agents told her designated dead drop sites her father had used. When she denied her father was a spy, one FBI agent shouted, "Come on. We know what he did." An FBI agent also threatened one of the suspected CIA officer's sisters, saying that if she did not cooperate, the Bureau would interrogate their sick eighty-four-year-old mother, who was in a nursing home.

When investigators showed the suspect what they had found in his house, he replied incredulously, "Where did you get my jogging map?" The CIA agent explained that he was a jogger and that the notations of times and routes related to his running through Nottoway Park. The FBI had wiretapped his telephone, secretly searched his home and computers, and pressured him by conducting physical surveillance of his movements. The FBI's heavy-handed tactics took a tremendous emotional toll on the innocent CIA officer and his family.

Eventually, the KGB file and other evidence the FBI received helped clear the innocent CIA agent, who, after passing another polygraph, returned to his job and received a formal apology from the Bureau. But the CIA operative was not the only one unfairly fingered due to Hanssen. A KGB officer mentioned in documents Hanssen turned over to the Russians was arrested and nearly beaten to death after falsely being accused by his superiors of betraying Moscow. He finally convinced them that he had not been a traitor and was released, narrowly averting execution.

Although it was at odds with conventional KGB spycraft, the case file obtained by the Bureau indicated that the Russians never knew the identity of their mole. He used the aliases "Ramon Garcia," "Jim Baker," and "G. Robertson," and was known inside the KGB simply as "B," the signature he used in his initial letter. But one piece of evidence gathered by U.S. intelligence finally pointed the investigation squarely toward a single suspect. The classified documents left at dead drops had been placed in black, plastic garbage bags wrapped with tape, and then placed inside a second garbage bag. An FBI fingerprint examiner ascertained that one of these plastic bags, obtained by the CIA, contained the fingerprints of a trusted Special Agent—Robert Philip Hanssen.

That fall, Freeh made good on a pledge to deliver a speech at The Heights, the all-boys' school where both he and Hanssen had sons enrolled. At the rigorous, tradition-bound Catholic school, where coats and ties were mandatory for high school students, Hanssen introduced his son to Freeh and stayed for the director's speech, which focused on ethics and morality. Hanssen found it amusing that he had been at the school with Freeh at the same time he was spying for the Russians—even the FBI director couldn't keep up with him, he thought. Freeh later told senior Bureau officials that it had been awkward and surreal to deliver a speech about character in front of a double agent who had abused his relationships with family and country, and whose investigation Freeh was personally overseeing.

The CIA had recovered thousands of pages of original classified documents from the KGB file, which was filled with intelligence and defense matters involving the FBI, the CIA, the National Security Agency, and the Pentagon, and a tape recording of a telephone call between a known KGB agent and the mole. A number of FBI agents listened closely to the secretly taped telephone conversation between the spy and the KGB agent Fefelov in August 1986. A pair of FBI officials who worked closely with Hanssen concluded that both the two-minute tape and an FBI-enhanced version of the recording that blocked out background noise contained Hanssen's voice. The longevity and breadth of Hanssen's successful espionage ultimately proved a liability, making his case file a valuable bargaining chip for a Russian mole doing business with the CIA. "He forgot that the better he was, the more at risk he was," said David Major, founder of the Centre for Counterintelligence and Security Studies and one of Hanssen's few friends at the Bureau.

The FBI obtained permission from the Foreign Intelligence Surveillance Act court to bug Hanssen's office, home, and car, and to conduct covert searches. The FBI secretly purchased a house on Talisman Drive across from the Hanssen residence, and equipped it with tools for eavesdropping and visual surveillance to monitor Hanssen and other family members closely. Hanssen, who had been working as the FBI liaison to the State Department, ferrying classified documents from one building to the other, had been given a new job and office inside the FBI where his every move was recorded and transmitted live to an office on another floor inside the Bureau's National Infrastructure Protection Center. At the same time, FBI computer mavens unearthed a curious pattern. Hanssen had been furiously checking the FBI's online investigation tracking system, known as the Electronic Case File, to detect whether any of his espionage activities were under investigation. From June 1997 until January 22, 2001, Hanssen had searched the system using keywords like "Robert Hanssen," "Dead Drop," and "Talisman Drive" nearly eighty times. But the FBI had entered into the system nothing about its massive probe of Hanssen in order to prevent him from detecting that he was under investigation.

Only days before Freeh first alerted the attorney general to the investigation, the FBI had searched Hanssen's Ford Taurus and photographed a roll of white Johnson & Johnson medical adhesive tape and a box of Crayola colored chalk. In the trunk, FBI agents discovered seven classified documents printed from the Bureau's online case-tracking system, several of which related to active foreign counterintelligence probes; a roll of Superior Performance Scotch clear masking tape; and dark-colored Hefty bags. To avoid tipping Hanssen, none of the materials were removed from his car. A second search of the vehicle nearly two weeks later revealed that the glove compartment contained a small plastic box of colored thumbtacks.

Between December 12, 2000, and February 5, 2001, FBI agents secretly watched Hanssen drive past or stop at the Foxstone Park sign near his home—the signal site connected to the ELLIS dead drop site—fourteen times. This followed a letter from the Russians in mid-2000 saying that a dead drop and exchange of cash would take place in that park on "12 August." Under the formula that Hanssen and the Russians were still using to avoid detection in the event of intercepted communications, the actual date of the dead drop would be February 18, 2001.

Freeh emphasized repeatedly to everyone involved at the FBI how critical it was to avoid any leak. Ashcroft, though troubled by the long-running espionage, was pleased that the potential existed for the FBI to nab Hanssen within a matter of weeks in Foxstone Park. But in a town where the passing of secrets is the coin of the realm, both Freeh and Ashcroft worried about the potential for some type of embarrassing foul-up in a counterintelligence operation where the FBI was being forced to hunt down one of its own.

There was other evidence, much of it circumstantial, linking Hanssen to espionage in the dossier received by the FBI. There was the proximity of two of the most popular dead drop sites to the two houses where Hanssen had lived in Vienna. The FBI learned that his first letter to the KGB, postmarked in Prince George's County, occurred while he was in Washington on administrative business in October 1985 after he had been reassigned to work in New York. Several FBI employees recalled Hanssen quoting General Patton and one remembered him saying something like, "Let's get this over with so we can go kick the shit out of the damn Japanese," the same language he had used in a letter to the Russians. There were numerous correlations between Hanssen's assignment to specific jobs that would have given him access to intelligence information passed to the Russians, including the debriefing of KGB defector Victor Sheymov. And the FBI ascertained that Hanssen's Palm III contained a reference to the ELLIS dead drop site and the date February 18.

Hanssen told several people at the FBI, and some family members, that he was considering accepting a lucrative $200,000-a-year job with Sheymov upon his retirement from the FBI in April 2001. Still, Hanssen wore a look of resignation, reflecting a weariness that some friends and family members surmised was due to his more than two decades at the Bureau. "He looked tired," said Paul Moore. "He was heavier than when I saw him last. . . . He looked like someone who was at the end of his career and was ground down by the system."

Hanssen had become fixated on a new approach to Internet security developed by Sheymov's northern Virginia firm, Invicta Networks Inc. The company's software possessed a secret offensive capability to strike back at hackers with a virus, as well as a novel way to ward off cyber-attacks. Hanssen had arranged for FBI officials to meet with Invicta executives to review the software. But while he showed audacity as a double agent, the potential move into the private sector seemed daunting to Hanssen after decades as a federal employee.

On the morning of Friday, February 16, 2001, after dropping off Jack Hoschouer at the Vienna metro stop, Hanssen drove out to Herndon, Virginia, near Dulles International Airport, to meet with his old friend Sheymov and other executives at Invicta. Sheymov was unaware that the agent who had helped him settle in Virginia years earlier, serving as his FBI handler and pretending to be a loyal friend since the late 1980s, had secretly informed the KGB about his whereabouts and plans, as well as his debriefing by U.S. intelligence. Still, by his very nature, Sheymov was suspicious of Hanssen as he pressed hard for a job at the firm. Sheymov was worried, among other things, about the appearance of impropriety—if he hired Hanssen and the FBI decided to use his technology, some might say he had engaged in an unethical quid pro quo as a government contractor.

After the meeting, Hanssen headed to his office downtown at the FBI. Shortly thereafter, Hoschouer, who had been at a business meeting, drove to Bureau headquarters and picked up Hanssen, who was waiting for him out front on Tenth Street. The pair headed to the D.C. waterfront for a casual lunch. After eating, Hoschouer dropped Hanssen off at the FBI and spent the remainder of the afternoon working on potential sales for his employer. But the duo managed to find time later to go to the National Rifle Association's firing range in northern Virginia and shoot some of the guns stored at Hanssen's home, most of which belonged to Hoschouer. Hanssen fired his FBI service pistol, as well as one of Hoschouer's guns. Hanssen attended gun shows from time to time, and felt so passionately about the constitutional right to bear arms that after an area store stopped selling ammunition he refused to shop there for anything else.

On Saturday evening, February 17, Hoschouer joined Hanssen for dinner along with some other friends at an Italian restaurant near Hanssen's home. Bonnie Hanssen stayed home, as she often did when Jack was around, saying there were children to feed and chores to do. Bob was quieter than normal at dinner, seemingly preoccupied in thought. This would be his last meal with Hoschouer, the final time they would decide freely where and when to eat.

There is an old Russian saying that every great intelligence success eventually ends in failure. Robert Philip Hanssen was about to learn, firsthand, just exactly what that meant.

20

WHAT TOOK
YOU SO LONG?

Bob Hanssen listened closely as Father Franklyn McAfee posed provocative questions about God. Sitting with Bonnie and the kids in their traditional pew on a chilly February morning, Bob tried to brush aside his sense of foreboding by tuning into the challenging homily. His mind was racing. Could it be that Father McAfee was speaking directly to him, or did it just seem that way? Was that FBI Director Louis Freeh sitting across the way, flanked by a statue of Jesus and the Vatican flag, or were his eyes playing tricks on him?

"If I were to ask you this morning, 'Does God love you?' what would be your answer?" the priest asked those assembled for Sunday Mass. "I say what would be *your* answer, rather than what would be *the* answer, because I know the answer, although I may not know your own. Regardless of your answer, the answer is 'yes.' Your own answer may be different, but I am here in this pulpit this morning to tell you infallibly that you are absolutely wrong. God loves you.

"But I am an alcoholic? God loves you.

"But I am an adulterer? God loves you.

"But I am a hate-monger? God loves you.

"But I am an atheist? God loves you."

He had sinned, Hanssen thought, but so had the guy sitting in the row behind him and the guy in the next row too. What married man hadn't lusted after a sensual woman? And what was the difference between lusting and committing adultery? Evil is evil, but God saves the righteous. He was a good father to his six children, a devout Catholic, a husband who was home on time for dinner, a grateful spouse who praised Bonnie's cooking and helped do the dishes. He was also a strict devotee of Opus Dei. Of course God loved him.

Louis Freeh also felt the presence of the Divine in the sunlit nave of St. Catherine of Siena Church. He had a much closer relationship with Father McAfee than the one Hanssen enjoyed, and demonstrated a sense of humility in this house of God that impressed the pastor. Among McAfee's other congregants were a Supreme Court justice, various members of Congress, a coterie of FBI officials, and wealthy real estate magnates, none of whom surpassed Freeh's extraordinary commitment to family and faith. "Louis Freeh is very devout," McAfee said. "When he receives communion, Louis genuflects. Most people stand. He goes down to the floor."

As far as McAfee and others could tell, however, Bob Hanssen was a man unbowed.

"Seasons come and go, friendships wax and wane, yet one fact remains that changes not: God loves you," McAfee continued from the pulpit that Sunday. "His love is unconditional—not that his tremendous love makes no demands nor carries with it expectations because it does. But it is unconditional insofar as we cannot lose it nor earn it. The Bible often describes the love of God in terms of a mother's love. You may earn or lose your mother's trust, you can earn also your mother's respect, but you cannot earn a mother's love nor can you lose it. A mother's love is unconditional, even if the child betrays."

The words resounded in the church and rung in Hanssen's ears. In his clandestine world, Hanssen had betrayed no one; he had only made new friends. Everyone knew betrayal was some kind of public or familial act. And Bob was a good son, visiting his mother in Florida at least once a year and regularly checking up on her since she moved there from Chicago in the 1970s. Things had been rough when his father was alive, but decades had passed since Howard Hanssen's death. Just before he died, the two men had been alone in a Florida hospital room when Howard told Bob that he loved him—words that Bob had longed to hear since he was a child. At least that was the way he remembered it. As Bob ambled out of the room, his father shouted after him that he wanted a copy of the daily racing form. Then, he died. Just like that.

"Some people wounded by sin and chained by guilt mistakenly believe that they have lost God's love," Father McAfee intoned. "As the father in the parable of the prodigal son was always waiting, always looking out the window and down the long dusty road for the son who had broken his heart and run away, so God waits for us to repent and He loves us as He waits. And that constant passionate love prompts us, enables us to change, to come to Him, to go to confession and place our weaknesses before Him."

Hanssen knew there were hundreds of others present in church, but he believed McAfee to be talking to him. He had confessed and confessed, so much so that he felt no guilt, no remorse, no self-pity—only anxiety, animus, and arrogance. And he felt them with good reason. In his fantasy world, Hanssen had lived life just the way he wanted, unlike the rest of those loathsome bureaucrats and political animals like Louis Freeh whose definition of success in life began and ended with their own career advancement. He knew there would be a reckoning, and that day was coming. For an instant, he might feel a sense of relief; no longer would he have to juggle the obligations of his multiple lives. But the comfort would prove fleeting. After living in the shadows for so many years, the reality thrust upon him would be too much for him to bear.

"When you were a child, what did you do when you hurt yourself?" McAfee asked. "Did you go to your friends? Did you run to your room and stay there alone and bleed, or did you not run to your mother and want her to bandage your wounds and to kiss your hurt away?"

Hanssen thought back to the times he had hid from his father in his bedroom, afraid to venture out. He had such painful memories, knowing that neither his mother, nor anyone else, could protect him.

Hanssen listened but didn't hear the rest of what Father McAfee had to say. He wouldn't hear it next Sunday either. After returning home to Vienna from the church in Great Falls, he made some final preparations, including making sure that a stack of classified FBI documents and a computer diskette were secured in a plastic garbage bag. The encrypted diskette contained the final letter he had written and concealed.

Dear Friends:

I thank you for your assistance these many years. It seems, however, that my greatest utility to you has come to an end, and it is time to seclude myself from active service.

Since communicating last, and one wonders if because of it, I have been promoted to a higher do-nothing Senior Executive job outside of regular access to information within the counterintelligence program. It is as if I am being isolated. Furthermore, I believe I have detected repeated bursting radio signal emanations from my vehicle. I have not found their source, but as you wisely do, I will leave this alone, for knowledge of their existence is sufficient. Amusing the games children play. In this, however, I strongly suspect you should have concerns for the integrity of your compartment concerning knowledge of my efforts on your behalf. Something has aroused the sleeping tiger. Perhaps you know better than I.

Life is full of its ups and downs.

My hope is that, if you respond to this constant-conditions-of-connection message, you will have provided some sufficient means of re-contact besides it. If not, I

will be in contact next year, same time same place.
Perhaps the correlation of forces and circumstances then
will have improved.

your friend,
Ramon Garcia

Outside the house playing Frisbee with the Hanssens' dog, Sun-dae, Jack Hoschouer sensed that something was wrong with his pal Bob Hanssen. It was more than the usual preoccupation or fixation on his latest idea; he appeared melancholy. Bob went inside to an-swer a phone call about Invicta, Victor Sheymov's firm, but he cut the conversation short, saying he needed to take Jack to Dulles Air-port and would resume the discussion that evening. Meanwhile, dur-ing a conversation with Jack about ethics, Hanssen abruptly left the room and returned with a prized possession, his worn copy of *The Man Who Was Thursday*. He gave the book to Jack, along with a final piece of wisdom: "Things are not always the way they seem."

Before they departed for the airport in Hanssen's light-gray Ford Taurus, Jack pulled Bonnie aside.

"Something is wrong with Bob," Jack whispered to Bonnie. "He is not happy."

When he took Jack to the airport, Bob would usually park the car and go inside so they could chat. He would have a Coke, and Jack would drink a beer. But not this time. They said their good-byes at the curb, Jack headed to the gate to catch his westward flight, and Bob drove directly to Foxstone Park, where he placed a piece of white adhesive tape on a pole to signal the Russians that he had loaded the ELLIS dead drop. Then, carrying the documents he had prepared for his Russian friends, he walked through the cold, breezy park to the footbridge and placed the package wrapped in plastic in the usual safe, concealed spot.

Hanssen headed back to his car, but before he could open the door FBI agents descended on him with their weapons drawn.

"Freeze!" the agents shouted, ready and eager to fire if Hanssen went for his gun. They slapped a pair of handcuffs on him, locking his wrists together behind his back. Neither impressed nor shocked, Robert Philip Hanssen taunted his FBI colleagues with a question destined to haunt Freeh and the Bureau for years to come:

"What took you so long?"

21

FREEH FALL

With each passing hour that her husband didn't return from Dulles Airport, Bonnie Hanssen grew increasingly anxious. Bob was always on time. She wondered if he had been in a car accident, whether the arrhythmia he had developed had led to a heart attack, if he had been hospitalized or, worse, was slumped over the wheel of the car in one of those giant parking lots at the airport. She called Bob's cell phone. It was dead. Bonnie prayed that her husband was not. With Sunday supper ready at 5:00 P.M. and no sign of Bob, Bonnie nervously served her hungry family one of her specialties, Moroccan beef over rice. Bob's chair at the head of the table in the dining room, where the family always ate on Sundays, remained empty.

After dinner, accompanied by her best friend and fellow Opus Dei member Donna Serby, Bonnie headed toward Dulles to see if she could find Bob. On the car radio, the news was dominated by the stunning death of stock car racing legend Dale Earnhardt in a crash at the Daytona 500, which Bob had planned to watch that afternoon on TV. On the way, Bonnie scoured passing cars in hopes of finding her husband. Instead, after arriving at Dulles, she was approached by FBI agents who told her that Bob had been arrested on espionage charges.

"He did it, didn't he?" Bonnie blurted.

The FBI escorted her home to gather some belongings, even as agents were cordoning off and canvassing the Hanssen residence for clues. The agents seized computer monitors, hard drives, printers, diskettes, CDs, cameras, film, and a video surveillance catalog. They also removed Bob's photo of Gen. George Patton's gravesite. They took a dozen guns from the house, including the matching Walther PPKs purchased by Hanssen and his friend Jack Hoschouer (the same type of semiautomatic weapon James Bond used), two Colt pistols that had belonged to Bob's father, Hanssen's FBI-issued gun, his 9mm Beretta, and magazines of ammunition.

The FBI found that Hanssen had not amassed any wealth from his espionage. The family's $290,000 house was heavily mortgaged and, though Bob had opened a Swiss bank account, there was very little money in it. He supposedly had accrued $800,000 in the account the KGB had established for him at the Moscow-based Vneshtorg Bank. But he would never see a penny of it.

The Bureau seized Hanssen's Swiss bank account records; his last will and testament; his Republican National Committee card; his passport; his Rolodex; his FBI-issued Palm Pilot; a newer Palm IIIx given to Hanssen by his children for Christmas; and a DVD of the movie *The Mask of Zorro*, starring Catherine Zeta-Jones, an actress Bob had become so obsessed with that he kept photographs of her in his car. The Bureau took Hanssen's personal copy of his manifesto, "Soviet Active Measures in the Post Cold War Era"; an unsigned letter he wrote to a publication called the *Proletarian Revolution*; photocopies of articles about Communism, the KGB, and espionage; and the pin presented to Hanssen by the FBI for twenty-five years of loyal service.

During the search, Bonnie, reeling from the devastating news about her husband, picked up a phone and called her oldest daughter Jane's house on a line that the FBI had tapped.

"Bob has been arrested," Bonnie whispered in the way she did whenever anything really bad happened. "He's been arrested for spying for the Russians."

"There must be some mistake. Do they know he's an FBI agent?"

"No, no," Bonnie replied. "He did it. He did it. I know he did it."

The FBI agents drove Bonnie and two of her children, Lisa and Greg, to a nearby Marriott hotel where they had reserved a suite for questioning. Shivering and wrapped in a comforter, Bonnie answered questions for hours and hours from a pair of FBI agents who won her trust. They seemed more like a friendly married couple who empathized with her plight than shrewd adversarial inquisitors. Until she collapsed from fatigue around 4:00 A.M., Bonnie told them everything she knew, including the time she had caught Bob apparently committing espionage for the Soviets more than twenty years earlier.

Over the following months, Opus Dei members, families with students at The Heights and Oakcrest, and fellow parishioners all prayed for Bonnie, Bob, and their children. Even as the schools raised money to assist them, friends and family offered shelter and comfort. The Missionaries of Charity, the nuns who carried on the work of Mother Teresa, also prayed for Bonnie; they sent pictures of Mother Teresa encased in plastic, each containing a lock of her hair. Bonnie and the children found solace in the outpouring of support and affection, and were comforted and excited that they had received a relic from the modern-day saint.

But their anguish over Bob's actions would be reawakened. On September 11, 2001, more than 4,500 men, women, and children were killed when terrorists linked to Osama bin Laden hijacked several airplanes and crashed them into the Pentagon and the World Trade Center. It was the worst terrorist attack in American history. On the day the planes hit their targets, Bonnie and other family members watched the news in horror, terrified that Bob would be blamed for the carnage. A published report several months earlier had claimed that sophisticated software Hanssen passed to the Russians had been sold to bin Laden for $2 million, permitting the FBI's Most Wanted Fugitive to monitor U.S. efforts to locate him. The Russian government has denied selling the software to bin Laden, who spearheaded a bloody campaign to drive the Soviets out of Afghanistan and who is regarded in Moscow as an enemy. Any such sale, if it took place at all, might have been carried out by individual Russians eager to profit from their access to information compromised by Hanssen. Shortly after the terrorist attack, one of the FBI agents who had interrogated Bonnie on the night of Bob's arrest called to tell her that the attacks were not her husband's fault.

For the FBI, the CIA, and other agencies, however, the terrorist strike was a total intelligence failure, prompting calls on Capitol Hill for an independent probe for what went wrong. Specifically, the Bureau's round-the-clock "bin Laden watch" begun under Freeh failed to provide any advance warning of the terrorist strike. Despite shifting considerable resources into fighting terrorism, Freeh's top strategic goal—preventing terrorist acts against Americans— had gone unfulfilled.

For Freeh, Hanssen's arrest marked the beginning of the final phase of his tenure atop the Bureau. Though the two men had taken radically different paths over the past quarter century, their destinies were inextricably intertwined in the Bureau that one loved and the other loathed. It was no longer just the deep interest they shared in clandestine FBI operations, their respective families of six children, their membership in the same church, and their decision to send children to the same school that bound one to the other. Now, they would share something else—a bond forged by their exits from the Bureau. If Freeh's FBI had seemed charmed before Hanssen's downfall, the following months seemed cursed.

Initially, Freeh still had some of his old magic. Before a closed-door hearing of the Senate Intelligence Committee, he made the case for greater counterintelligence funding in response to the devastating Hanssen case. He also pledged to increase the use of polygraphs within the FBI, which he had long resisted, and tighten document control. But as revelations poured forth about the scope of Hanssen's espionage and its massive damage to national security, the once untouchable Bureau became vulnerable. The case set off an international incident, as the United States and Russia expelled legions of suspected spies and traded harsh words. Freeh's attempt at damage control by naming former FBI director William Webster to chair a blue-ribbon commission on the Hanssen case proved ineffective. Confidence in the FBI, and in its ability to police itself, dissipated. Attorney General Ashcroft directed the Justice Department's Inspector General to launch an aggressive review of the FBI that could lead to sanctions as a result of the most damaging intelligence breach ever of America's national security. Congress was not far behind, with bipartisan commissions established and legislation passed to beef up oversight.

On May 1, with slightly more than two years left in his ten-year term, Louis Freeh announced his resignation as FBI director. In addition to troubles wrought by the aftershocks of the Hanssen case and other matters, Freeh faced immense financial pressure from hundreds of thousands of dollars of home loans, looming college tuition, and twenty-seven years in public service that had left him with little savings.

In a written statement, Freeh cited accomplishments on his watch that were a testament to his enormous influence on the FBI, including increasing the Bureau's budget by 58 percent to $3.4 billion; pushing legislation to bolster the FBI's ability to fight crime by monitoring e-mails, cell phones, and other communications; and more than doubling the Bureau's overseas presence—with agents now based permanently in forty-four countries to fight terrorism, cyber-hacking, and other international crimes.

Rather than departing immediately, Freeh had one last matter he wanted to see through: the indictment of suspects in the 1996 bombing of Khobar Towers in Saudi Arabia. Though it would require him to stay on until sometime in June, Freeh wanted to announce criminal charges in the case before he left office. That delay would prove to be a colossal error in timing on Freeh's part, as one incendiary issue after another ignited in the final days and weeks of his tenure and immediately following his exit, raising questions about the basic competency of the FBI and his stewardship. Privately, Freeh told associates that the Bureau had a "hollow middle" between its new agents and senior officials that left it susceptible to error and shoddy work. In his final months, that gap was on display for all the world to see.

Of all the new issues that arose, none was more embarrassing than the discovery that the FBI had failed to turn over thousands of pages of documents to lawyers for convicted Oklahoma City bomber Timothy McVeigh. As McVeigh prepared to become the first federal inmate to be put to death in nearly forty years, families of victims gathered to watch the execution via closed-circuit television. The FBI's admission that forty-five of its fifty-six field offices failed to provide documents repeatedly requested by Freeh was devastating, forcing Attorney General Ashcroft to delay the execution and causing further pain to the families of victims. In the aftermath of the Hanssen spy case, the McVeigh debacle prompted a wave of negative publicity about the FBI and its outgoing director. With the nation watching every move in the McVeigh case, public confidence in the FBI plummeted.

For Freeh, who had called the FBI "the greatest organization for law enforcement ever created by democratic society," things could not have been worse. Before he could leave office, millions of Americans were asking what was wrong with the FBI. Under the bright lights, Freeh's FBI became the butt of jokes from late-night talk show hosts who said its initials stood for "Fumbling Bunch of Idiots." Public officials and newspaper editorials called for a new kind of leader who had strong management skills and the will to change the FBI's culture. Once again, Attorney General Ashcroft ordered the Justice Department's Inspector General to dig into the FBI, this time undertaking a "comprehensive review" of the entire Bureau. On Capitol Hill, congressional panels launched fresh inquiries of their own.

After a multiweek delay and skirmishes in court, McVeigh was executed on June 11. But the damage to the Bureau was so severe that Freeh uncharacteristically refused to appear after being invited to be a witness at a Senate Judiciary Committee hearing on "Restoring Confidence in the FBI." The director said he had other obligations, avoiding an expected tongue-lashing that would have further sullied his image. While the congressional hearing was taking place, Freeh stood in the blazing sun of the FBI headquarters courtyard, giving a pep talk to employees bombarded by unyielding criticism of the Bureau. Freeh likened the FBI's predicament to the situation at Reagan National Airport, where attention typically focused on those planes that had trouble rather than on the vast majority that took off and landed without incident. "Please," Freeh implored them, "don't for a moment think that we are an institution in trouble or crisis. We are not."

Even so, the problems were daily mounting for Freeh and the FBI, and he was no longer able to talk his way out of a jam. That same week in June, prosecutors disclosed that an FBI official in Las Vegas had been charged with stealing classified information and selling it to the Mafia and defense lawyers. The Justice Department issued a scathing report on the FBI's handling of the Wen Ho Lee case. The report cited a pattern of gross negligence, though it absolved the FBI of charges of discrimination. "This investigation was a paradigm of how not to manage and work an important counterintelligence case," the study said. Democratic and Republican senators alike concluded that the Bureau's problems were so widespread that the Justice Department needed an independent Inspector General whose sole responsibility would be to probe FBI misconduct.

"The FBI has long been considered the crown jewel of law enforcement agencies," said Senate Judiciary Committee Chairman Patrick Leahy of Vermont. "Unfortunately, the image of the FBI in the minds of too many Americans is that this agency has become unmanageable, unaccountable, and unreliable. Its much vaunted independence has transformed, for some, into an image of insular arrogance."

It was the same critique of the FBI that Bob Hanssen, who knew something about insularity and arrogance himself, had voiced many years ago. And ultimately, his comeuppance was theirs.

EPILOGUE

*All men long to confess their crimes more than a thirsty beast longs for
a drink of water.*

—G. K. Chesterton

On the morning of July 6, 2001, Robert Philip Hanssen pleaded
guilty to thirteen counts of espionage. As part of his plea
bargain, the gaunt-looking double agent, wearing green cov-
eralls with prisoner emblazoned across his back, agreed to spend the
rest of his life in jail. Prosecutors, in return, promised not to seek the
death penalty. Hanssen, blinking frequently and fidgeting with his hands
behind his back, responded tersely to queries about his plea from U.S.
District Court judge Claude Hilton. The fifty-seven-year-old spy, who
had lost about twenty pounds since his arrest, promised to respond
truthfully to questions from the FBI and CIA about the billions of dollars of secrets he had sold to the Russians, enabling U.S. officials to assess
the damage to national security. The spy whose children's favorite
storybook was *Pinocchio* also agreed to take lie detector tests during his
debriefing, something the Bureau had failed to give him even once
during his twenty-five-year career. In addition, the computer whiz
agreed to have his access to computers restricted forever. The Justice
Department, after concluding Bonnie Hanssen played no role in her
husband's espionage, allowed her to keep their home, three cars,
and the annual $40,000 survivor's portion of Bob's pension—the
same amount she would have received if he had died.

Hanssen's secret life as a spy left his wife and children, who range in age from fifteen to twenty-nine, and their friends struggling to understand his motivation. But before they could ask him about it, Hanssen needed to finalize his deal with prosecutors. That deal nearly fell apart when Hanssen, who had been so proud of his espionage, could not bring himself to answer questions from his fellow FBI agents. After a talk with his attorney, Plato Cacheris, Hanssen's responsiveness improved markedly. During jailhouse visits, Bonnie and other family members—separated from Hanssen by thick glass and aware that every word spoken on prison phones was reviewed by the FBI—avoided asking certain questions. But with debriefings proceeding apace a few weeks after Hanssen's guilty plea, the time had arrived for Hanssen to explain his deception.

"Why did you do it? Why did you spy?" Hanssen was asked.

"Fear and rage," he replied.

"Fear of what?"

"Fear of being a failure and fear of not being able to provide for my family," Hanssen said.

As a double agent, he had been the best, excelling at espionage, feeling important, and easing financial pressures too. He had been bored most days at work. In contrast, he found the spy game exhilarating. "I'm like Dr. Jekyll and Mr. Hyde," he said, "and sometimes Mr. Hyde takes over."

Hanssen's "rage" at the FBI erupted each time he was passed over for a promotion. He fought back by attempting grand, daring feats of espionage. He failed to recognize that his progress at the FBI was inhibited by his personality. In Bob Hanssen's world, the problem revolved around other FBI agents, who lacked his commitment, and with the FBI itself, which was not fighting the war against the Russians the right way.

Hanssen viewed the FBI as a corrupt father figure. As he had in his youth, Hanssen largely remained silent, lacking the self-confidence and skills to try to change things. He detested the FBI hierarchy, and his job became something he tolerated only for the opportunity to live

226 David A. Vise

out his fantasies. Filled with unrealized ambition, he looked to the KGB to validate his intelligence and importance, in much the same way he turned to Jack Hoschouer to confirm his masculinity and sexual prowess.

In explaining his spying, Hanssen avoided discussion of how he compartmentalized his fiendish deeds from the morality play he lived through family and church. Finances played a role, but Hanssen's fantasies were largely the product of a fractured ego seeking recognition.

"How do you develop a dynamic and say, 'I am better and smarter than all of you authority figures? I can give the Russians information but they don't know who I am.' That is power," said Dr. Stephen Hersh. "What better way to show his vengeance and his power than to sell secrets to the Communists?" Added Dr. Mark Siegert, a psychologist at Columbia Teacher's College in New York. "I really see him as a very frustrated, very childlike man who had a tremendous need to prove something, and what he needed to prove was that he wasn't a sucker."

Dr. Alen Salerian, a psychiatrist who spent thirty hours talking with Hanssen after his arrest, said he suffered from a "very severe," multi-faceted mental illness that was biological in origin and triggered by a stormy childhood, and which factored in his spying. The doctor said the Bureau trusted Hanssen with secrets for decades while he had a "serious psychiatric illness," and desperately needs to implement an ongoing psychological-testing program for agents. According to Salerian, Hanssen also was plagued by migraine headaches and tormented by guilt—not from spying, which he rationalized by saying that the Soviets were too weak to be a threat, but from deceiving Bonnie. After Salerian pushed him to inform his wife about his obsession with pornography and other indiscretions, the psychiatrist served as an emissary, conveying the sordid details. "She is very trusting," he said.

Though disgraced in the United States, Hanssen will be celebrated in Russia, where his passing of vital U.S. intelligence and national security secrets reaffirmed the prestige and strength of the nation to overcome setbacks. "He was a great spy," said Oleg Kalugin. "That's the way he'll be described in Russian textbooks and the media. This was one of the greatest feats of Russian intelligence."

Louis Freeh, who had gone to work as an FBI agent within months of Hanssen's joining the Bureau a quarter century earlier, stepped down as director at almost the same time as Hanssen cut his plea bargain. Freeh had presided over a highly successful counterintelligence operation in arresting Hanssen. But the spying had gone on too long and cost too much. Under the circumstances, there would be no grand send-off for Freeh, no series of standing ovations, public accolades, or formal ceremonies. Instead, the most influential FBI director since J. Edgar Hoover engineered his own farewell, calling a press conference on his last day to announce indictments in the 1996 Khobar Towers bombing case. The "presidentially appointed case agent" went out declaring the FBI as the victor in a matter he had doggedly pursued, generating front-page headlines and praise from the attorney general. But privately, Freeh acknowledged that the indictments merely marked the next preliminary step in an ongoing probe with an uncertain future. Nearly all of the fourteen alleged terrorists who were charged remained at large in Saudi Arabia or elsewhere, and the Saudis refused to extradite anyone to the United States. Freeh, convinced Iran had played a major role, had hoped the Iranian government would be charged, but the court papers stopped short of that.

A few weeks after he left the Bureau, a credit card company that already employed a coterie of Freeh's FBI cronies announced it would hire him. "Former FBI director Louis Freeh, who managed agents accused of spying and withholding documents in the Timothy McVeigh case, has been hired by credit card giant MBNA to oversee personnel functions and legal affairs," the Associated Press reported. MBNA spokesman David Spartin called Freeh a "proven leader," adding that the negative publicity that marred his exit from the FBI did not give the company pause in hiring him. The overseas connections Freeh had developed at the Bureau undoubtedly would help the company grow abroad. After twenty-seven years in public service, Freeh was ready to cash in.

The FBI he left behind was reeling and vulnerable amid disclosure of a litany of embarrassing new problems. Soon after his departure, the FBI admitted that 449 of its guns were stolen or missing and that one of them had been used in a homicide. The Bureau also disclosed that it had lost 184 laptops, at least one of which contained classified information. Senior FBI officials acknowledged that the Bureau's computer and record-keeping systems were antiquated and vulnerable. After probing the FBI, former senator John Danforth said honest people were stuck in a culture that did not allow for mistakes and punished those who admitted them. FBI agents and others publicly said the Bureau had made scapegoats out of those in the ranks while glossing over serious mistakes by senior officials, including Freeh.

Attorney General John Ashcroft stripped the FBI of its protective shield—which Freeh had fought to maintain—by declaring that it would no longer enjoy special immunity from full-fledged, independent investigations of mismanagement and malfeasance. Soon, seven major investigations of the FBI were under way amid sinking morale. "It's hard to believe the situation has deteriorated and disintegrated the way it has," said Senator Richard Durbin of Illinois. "How did this great agency fall so far so fast?"

With the Bureau imploding, the Republican attorney general launched new probes, hired a management consulting firm to propose changes, and marched across Pennsylvania Avenue to FBI headquarters to deliver a sober message. "Each of us has the responsibility to protect the public trust," Ashcroft said. "We have the responsibility as well to recognize when that trust has been shaken."

Within Hanssen's family, meanwhile, bonds of trust were shattered by the disclosure of his spying and sexual escapades. Contemplating his fate, Hanssen told a friend he understood how penitentiaries got their name. They were houses of penitence and that was where he belonged. Yet he didn't seem overwhelmed by contrition. On the day before he pleaded guilty, Hanssen wasn't focused on the fate that awaited him or on the pain he had inflicted. Instead, he held forth with family on why one of Albert Einstein's theories was flawed. Following his guilty plea, Bob repeatedly expressed his love for Bonnie, promising that he never considered leaving her to flee the country and telling her that she was the best person in the world and the source of all happiness. Meanwhile family members expressed frustration at Bonnie's determination to rationalize her husband's behavior, both in his job and in their marriage. Bonnie, her faith in God unshaken, continued to visit Bob weekly at the jailhouse, prayed daily for his soul, refused to believe he had wronged her, and once again forgave him.

The FBI, however, would not forgive Hanssen for what he had done. Due to careful crafting of an infallible image, the FBI, a fraternity built on "Fidelity, Bravery and Integrity," held a special place in the American psyche. With its reputation as the world's premier law enforcement agency, the Bureau was accustomed to being held to a higher standard. But with the damning revelations about Robert Philip Hanssen, the FBI was knocked from its lofty pedestal. Said Attorney General Ashcroft: "No American has escaped injury from the espionage to which Robert Hanssen pled guilty. But for the men and women of the FBI, the wound is deeper. Together, Americans have felt the shame caused by the treachery of a countryman; the FBI has felt the pain inflicted by the betrayal of a brother."

Howard Hanssen enjoyed fishing with his son Bob, but their relationship was often turbulent.

Below: Bob Hanssen met his best friend, Jack Hoschouer (right), at Chicago's Taft High School. They graduated in 1962.

Bob Hanssen (second from right) and dental school classmates enjoy the snow along Lakeshore Drive in Chicago.

In 1968, Hanssen married Bonnie Wauck. A schoolteacher and mother of six, she remains devoted to her husband.

On a weekend trip to Washington, D.C., Hanssen took fellow FBI recruits to see the Soviet embassy.

Robert Hanssen showered stripper Priscilla Galey with gifts and attention as he tried to save her from a troubled life.

Below: While President Bill Clinton congratulated Louis Freeh (pictured with one of his sons) when he took the helm as FBI Director in 1993, the two came to mistrust each other.

CIA Agent Aldrich Ames, who spied for the Russians in the late 1980s at the same time as Robert Hanssen, is serving a life sentence for espionage.

Viktor Cherkashin (left), the KGB's number two man in Washington, handled double agents Hanssen and Ames while Vladimir Kryuchkov supervised from Moscow.

Dmitri Polyakov, Valery Martynov, and Sergei Motorin were executed by the KGB after Hanssen and Ames identified them as U.S. spies.

Dressed in his trademark dark suit, FBI agent Robert Hanssen earned the nickname "The Mortician."

Louis Freeh (pictured with Attorney General Janet Reno) was a favorite on Capitol Hill, even as scandals tarnished the Bureau's image.

The FBI monitored Hanssen from the house it bought on his block in Vienna, Virginia. Freeh oversaw Hanssen's arrest from inside the Bureau's Strategic Information Operations Center.

DEAD DROP
"ELLIS"—On February
18, 2001, Hanssen was
arrested after leaving
a package of classified
documents under this footbridge in Foxstone Park.
Hanssen placed white
tape on a sign (left) to
signal the Russians that
the site was loaded.

Nearby, the FBI found a black garbage bag filled with $50,000 and a note from Hanssen's Russian handlers.

Robert Philip Hanssen, with defense attorney Plato Cacheris (left), pleads guilty to espionage charges before Judge Claude Hilton in federal court in Alexandria, Virginia, and agrees to a sentence of life in prison.

After disclosing Hanssen's betrayals, the virtually untouchable Louis Freeh suddenly found his steward-ship questioned, and the fallout ulti-mately spoiled his exit from the FBI. Attorney General John Ashcroft (background left) and CIA Director George Tenet look on.

APPENDIX I

THE BETRAYALS
OF A SPY

R obert Philip Hanssen was a traitor of unparalleled dimension. His access to national security and intelligence secrets was broad and deep, and his betrayal of those secrets was far-reaching, given his computer expertise and access to secret FBI, CIA, National Security Agency, National Security Council, and Pentagon documents. Aided by the efforts of federal agencies to share more information with one another, Hanssen obtained an extraordinary array of classified materials. Several counterintelligence experts, including former FBI and CIA director William Webster, have equated Hanssen's treachery with a "five-hundred-year flood." He compromised thousands of pages of intelligence sources and methods; cryptology; communications and technical surveillance programs; counterintelligence operations; and military, logistical, and political strategy for surviving a nuclear attack.

In the world of espionage, there is an acronym—MICE—that helps to explain why Hanssen and others spy. MICE stands for Money, Ideology, Compromise, Ego. In Hanssen's case, ego was considered the most important factor, though money also played a contributing role.

Nearly everything that Hanssen passed along to the Soviets and Russians during his espionage career was "classified." The classification system used by the U.S. intelligence community is based on the damage that would ensue if information were compromised. Data that would cause "serious" damage is classified SECRET, and information that would cause "exceptionally grave" damage is TOP SECRET. Highly sensitive information at any level may be further restricted as SENSITIVE COMPARTMENTED INFORMATION, or SCI. Access to material bearing an SCI designation requires specific additional security clearances. Hanssen held TOP SECRET clearance from his first day at the FBI in 1976. He received his initial SCI clearance in June 1980, roughly one year after his first counterintelligence assignment, and would be cleared for at least five more SCI programs over the course of his FBI employment.

According to court documents and interviews, while working as a double agent for the GRU, the KGB, and its successor intelligence services in Russia, Robert Philip Hanssen:

> —increased the prospect of nuclear war by compromising the Continuity of Government Plan, the supersecret program to ensure the survival of the president and U.S. government operations in the event of a nuclear attack. This crown jewel of U.S. national security was an important element of the "mutually assured destruction" (MAD) theory, in which both the United States and the Soviet Union refrain from using nuclear weapons because a retaliatory strike would prove as deadly as a first strike. However, with knowledge of the U.S. continuity program, the Soviets believed they could win a nuclear war and began to devise an offensive nuclear strategy.

> —divulged the identities of at least nine Soviet officials recruited to spy for the United States. In the 1979–80 period, Hanssen revealed the identity of Dmitri Polyakov, a Soviet general code-named TOPHAT who was executed by the U.S.S.R. in 1988 for espionage. In his initial letter to the KGB in 1985, Hanssen also exposed the identities of three KGB officers serving as double agents for the FBI. Two of them, Valery Martynov and Sergei Motorin, were ordered to return to Moscow and were put to death.

—revealed the existence of the "spy tunnel" constructed beneath the Soviet embassy in Washington, D.C., to eavesdrop on conversations and communications. The tunnel, orchestrated by the FBI and the NSA, was installed in the 1980s as the Soviets were completing an expansive new diplomatic compound on a hilltop just north of Georgetown. Hanssen's tip rendered the several-hundred-million-dollar tunnel a completely worthless intelligence tool that the Russians in turn manipulated to feed disinformation to the FBI.

—disclosed the National Intelligence Program, which detailed everything that the U.S. intelligence community planned to do for a given year, and how money would be spent. Hanssen compromised this "Holy of Holies" of the U.S. intelligence community in September 1987, covering that year in progress, and again in May 1989, for the upcoming 1990–91 period.

—severely hampered the U.S. intelligence community's ability to recruit foreign double agents, by revealing both overall strategies and key operational details, such as the identities of potential targets. Hanssen divulged a document entitled "The FBI's Double Agent Program," which included an internal evaluation of double agent operations worldwide, including joint operations with other U.S. intelligence agencies, and he later handed over another management review of U.S. double agent recruitment efforts.

—divulged information about at least five Soviet defectors, including high-ranking KGB officers Victor Sheymov and Vitaliy Yurchenko. Hanssen passed along debriefing reports on Sheymov and disclosed the defector's whereabouts in the United States, making him susceptible to reprisal from the KGB.

—revealed the ongoing FBI espionage investigation of Felix Bloch, a State Department officer who was believed to be spying for the Soviet Union. Hanssen's revelation allowed the KGB to alert Bloch to the investigation, foiling the Bureau's attempts to arrest him.

Between 1985 and 2001, Robert Hanssen also:

—described the location, methods, and technology involved in FBI eavesdropping and surveillance of a particular Soviet spy station

—warned the KGB of a successful new intelligence operation by the NSA against a Soviet target

—disclosed that the United States was listening in on Soviet satellite transmissions by exploiting a technical vulnerability in the Soviets' communications systems

—shared TOP SECRET documents from the National Security Council, which advises the president on intelligence and national security matters

—handed over details about a meeting between the United States and "M," a potential Soviet double agent; the accused agent, Gennadiy Vasilenko, was nearly beaten to death by the KGB after Hanssen's betrayal but was ultimately released after convincing his captors that he wasn't a turncoat

—provided a technical document describing the U.S. intelligence community's classified intranet system, called COINS-II (Community Online Intelligence System)

—disclosed specific NSA limitations in reading certain Soviet communications, giving the Russians secure channels through which to pass information

—divulged a document from the director of Central Intelligence entitled, "Stealth Orientation"

—disclosed intelligence relating directly to the United States' preparations and means of defense and retaliation against a large-scale conventional or nuclear attack

—released a document prepared for the director of Central Intelligence entitled "Compendium of Future Intelligence Requirements: Volume II," which contained a comprehensive listing of data sought by the United States, including information about the military capabilities and preparedness of Russia and other nations

—divulged information that Soviet spies and defectors had provided to the United States about Soviet intelligence successes against the United States.

—disclosed what the United States knew about KGB double agent recruitment operations targeting the CIA

—revealed details of a U.S. technical program to penetrate Soviet communications intelligence

—handed over an FBI memo about a suspected KGB counterintelligence officer stationed in New York City

—handed over the transcript of a meeting of the CI Group, an association of senior counterintelligence officials from all U.S. intelligence agencies that sets national priorities

—released documents regarding the National HUMINT (human intelligence) Collection Plan

—divulged, on at least two occasions, intelligence reviews of the Russian armed forces and their capabilities for conducting strategic nuclear war during the 1990s

—revealed, on at least two occasions, that the United States was targeting a particular category of Soviet communications in an operation related to American national defense

—provided the Soviets with a highly specific and technical document regarding the MASINT (measurement and signature intelligence) program, which monitored keystrokes and other elements of communications in a clandestine fashion

—revealed that the United States had the capability to read certain Soviet communications

—handed over a report for the director of Central Intelligence entitled, "The Soviet System in Crisis: Prospects for the Next Two Years"

—divulged the identity of a particular NSA employee and the sensitive office where the person worked

—passed along documents about nuclear and missile weapons proliferation

—divulged how the United States planned to conduct surveillance of a Soviet intelligence officer

—disclosed the specific methods the NSA employed to read communications of foreign countries

—alerted the Soviets to an FBI "dangle" operation initiated at a U.S. military facility that aimed to entice the KGB into recruiting an apparent FBI informant who actually would supply disinformation

—suggested that the KGB recruit his best friend, Jack Hoschouer, who was serving in the U.S. Army in Germany (They didn't)

—divulged to the Soviets what the United States knew about the KGB's foreign intelligence and counterintelligence operations by providing a CIA report entitled, "The KGB's First Chief Directorate: Structure, Functions, and Methods"

—disclosed budget planning of the FBI's foreign counterintelligence program for 1992, giving the Russians detailed information about counterintelligence programs and resources

—revealed that the United States was successfully intercepting the communications of a specific foreign country

—disclosed how FBI counterintelligence probed a suspected Soviet penetration of U.S. intelligence

APPENDIX II

THE E-MAILS
OF A SPY

In addition to his extensive correspondence with the Soviets, Bob Hanssen was a voracious e-mailer, sending his lifelong friend Jack Hoschouer in Germany, family members, and others dozens of e-mails daily expounding on his worldview. What follows are excerpts from some of the e-mails Hanssen sent in 1999 and 2000 on topics ranging from his contempt for President Clinton, a sentiment he shared with FBI Director Louis Freeh, to his lack of respect for members of Congress, to his views on Cuba, Israel's Mossad intelligence service, and other matters. The brackets [ ] in these e-mails, first published by *Insight* magazine and independently verified for authenticity, denote names that have been left out for security purposes; the blanks indicate names omitted to preserve privacy.

Subject: Clinton
Date: Thu, 25 Feb 1999 09:1505 -0500 (EST)
From: root <root@orion.clark.net>
To:

The NSA representative told me two things yesterday I found interesting.

1. When Clinton first came to office NSA prepared an intelligence report from an intercepted conversation between two world leaders discussing how incompetent Clinton was. They

published it and were reprimanded and told never again to publish negative comments intercepted about the administration or the president. Previously such things were routinely published to give analysts insight into the thinking of foreign leaders.

2. Prior to Clinton's presidency, for all prior presidents back to Truman, NSA published a daily classified schedule of the president's detailed where-abouts and who was accompanying him as security updates. They were told to stop including the detail of who accomanied the president because it was showing which female staff he taking to the hotels at night for sex.

This was told me by the thoroughly disgusted NSA representative, [ ] now assigned here. [ ] worked in the policy shop and has been abroad often in support of presidential travels and conferences. [ ] never saw anything close to the outrageous behavior shown by Clinton and his staff during the Bush administration. Bush was a man of real character, the Clintons pure slease in her assessment.

Subject: M
Date: Fri, 5 Mar 1999 11:06:09 -0500 (EST)
From: root <root@orion.clark.net>
To:

Our agents investigating the M case don't believe M is the code name of the technical operation. They are still working full speed to identify M as a human source. Their belief is based on a careful analysis of the original Hebrew intercept between the Ambassador and the MOSSAD Chief of Station. I talked to the case agent yesterday. Of course, they have a vested interest in that they've always wanted an excuse to tear into the Israeli network, and now they've gotten it and are hell bent on identifying every agent in the Israelis network while they have the excuse.

Check in when you come to town. Life is full of rich and terrifying insights. I always wondered, when I was young, why FBI agents so often retired to cabins in the woods. Now I know.

Subject: Re: Questions!
Date: Tue, 09 Mar 1999 21:39:17 -0500
From: "Robert P. Hanssen" <hanssen@orion.clark.net>
To:

The problems with genius is that it often borders insanity. The problem with truth is that it sometimes seems utterly fantastic. I don't see how the Israelis could have altered our desire to look into the [TWA Flight] 800 crash up or down. They didn't know it wasn't terrorist-related. Nobody did. The flight which left just before it, (which was delayed) was an El-Al flight to Israel. Further, the Israelis have no desire to tie up our counter-terrorist resources. Their interest is in having the FBI dedicate 100% of our counter-terror resources to the protection of Israel. They wanted to know if it was a terrorist action and if so did it hit the wrong plane and if so who launched it so they could kill them as quickly and publicly as possible.

Did you know that we grabbed some Israeli students in Newark with walkie talkies hanging around the inbound flight path of the El Al flight? They said they were hired by the Israeli Consulate in NY to look for anything suspicious like someone getting to shoot at the plane. If they saw anything suspicious, they were to use the radios. The radios were on a secret security channel directly to the El Al flight to wave it off. This is not stupid. This is careful. Israel, as a nation, hasn't stayed alive by dumb luck. Israel is thorough. You don't want to underestimate them. Whenever we do, we get burned. They have a lot of smart people. It isn't for nothing that God chose them to carry the message. Remember, God is Jewish. He was born of the House of David. He had His choice.

Subject: Weapons/DOE [Department of Energy]
Date: Tue, 25 May 1999 18:13:20 -0400
From: "Robert P. Hanssen" <hanssen@orion.clark.net>
To:

You know, I listen to these congressmen talk and I shake my head. They just don't get it. I listen to them saying this is a counterintelligence failure on national TV, and I say they just don't get it. This is a SECURITY FAILURE and a tremendous COUNTERINTELLIGENCE SUCCESS. Counterintelligence [CI] investigates the enemy, or if you will in the modern world, the opposition, to learn their capabilities, intentions, methods, and focus. It is not security work. Security protects. It does not attack. CI attacks the actor. It attacks opposition intelligence structures. CI studies that actor. CI learns what he is, in fact, doing. It is not speculative. CI feeds security because it helps them focus on meaningful measures and safeguards. But CI is not security. It is not part of the security apparatus. Using CI to help security is just smart security. Now in this case, CI learned what the Chinese were doing early on. It tried repeatedly to convey the importance of that to DOE. No one listened. Whose fault is that? DOE had different agendas—social agendas, economic agendas. They didn't want to hear. They refused to secure the labs.

Subject: And Another Thing
Date: Tue, 25 May 1999 19:57:35 -0400
From: "Robert P. Hanssen" <hanssen@orion.clark.net>
To:

The Clinton administration's problem is that while other administrations didn't move DOE in the right direction (toward good security), the Clinton administration ran headlong in the opposite direction. It then got scared, turned 180 degrees, and started running hard back. Now it wants a pat on the back because it is the first administration in history that is running headlong in the right direction. Commendable? Well you've got to turn some bleak historical pages pretty rapidly to call it that. But they're not running out of being so smart, they are running from being totally stupid, and they only changed direction because they got terrified at the potential public repercussions they started to envsion at the ballet box.

Richardson deserves some credit in this reversal, for he is the first DOE-Secretary to realize that he needs both a CI chief and a Security Chief reporting directly to him. Security, he sees, is one of his primary responsibilities. (They're nuclear weapons for God's sake.) And he also seems to know that CI needs independance from security to an effective critic (and not to get swamped bugetarily). Others thought security was a sideshow.

Clinton deserves no credit, for he is the one who picked the people who wanted to run the wrong way in the first place, and then he allowed them to do so. If it hadn't been a mess in the first place he certainly would have made it one, for he disassembled even what limited security they had, or tried to.

Now the Clinton administration has turned DOE around. Well just wait until no one is looking again. I wonder whey they only implemented 85% of the recommendations. What is it about the others they don't like? Does anyone want to ask that? Could it be that they conflict with basic errors strongly held by the administration. Who knows? It is a good question. In the history of this country, no one has held more basic errors about the world than this administration.

That's my take.

Subject: Depressing Things . . .
Date: Mon, 1 May 2000 09:14:03 -0400 (EDT)
From: "Robert P. Hanssen" <hanssen@orion.clark.net>
To:

. . . which have depressed me recently.

Coming down to pick up [ ] from the train last night I ran into
the gay and lesbian rally. Most of it was over and being taken
down. Two of the dikes are pushing hand trucks with boxes
from their booth down Constitution Avenue. I recognized the
first. It was Deputy Assistant Director [ ] of the National Security Division of the Federal Bureau of Investigation.

In a meeting (video conference with White House, Justice,
State, Coast Guard, Marshall's Service, FAA [Federal Aviation
Administration], JCS [Joint Chiefs of Staff]) State agreed to
place travel controls on Cubans visiting Wye [a Maryland estate where Elian Gonzalez was temporarily housed]. They were
to call them in at 3pm and tell them. State called them in but
unilaterally decided not to place the controls on them. (They
said they were afraid they might retaliate against us somehow
in Cuba. They had presented that argument at the meeting but
had gotten slapped down.) This week the Director of OFM
[Office of Foreign Missions] is out of the country. There is no
one to fight the fait accompli.

Subject: Re: Where'd You Disappear to?
Date: Wed, 3 May 2000 16:21:32 -0400 (EDT)
From: "Robert P. Hanssen" <hanssen@orion.clark.net>
To:

Why Castro is so insistant that the Interest Section keep this
story (Elian) on the front page?

Answer:

If Cuba is on the front page everyday, Cuba must be important. People have forgotten about Cuba. The American people's and the world's frame of reference needed to be distorted so they think Cuba is important. The more you write about Cuba, the more important it is to the public and the more likely that the public will support normalizing relations. Interestingly, it makes no difference what is written, positive or negative. It is the amount of time spent discussing Cuba that counts for Castro. Elian means nothing to Castro. He is a convenience. Justice, by moving Elian out of the Florida court system on custody, played into this because they are:

Multiple Choice:

1. Stupid

2. Complicit

3. All of the Above

Individuals fall into either 1, or 2, above and are all that was needed.

While "You can fool some of the people some of the time and some of the people all of the time, ... you can't fool all the people all the time," unfortunately you don't have to do the latter, the former is usually sufficient.

Subject: Re: Where'd You Disappear to?
Date: Wed, 3 May 2000 20:42:15 -0400 (EDT)
From: "Robert P. Hanssen" <hanssen@orion.clark.net>
To:

National Security is not the Clinton administrations long suit. You might think that security concerns regarding intelligence methods don't even get to the table. But it is far worse than that. Here's some examples.

NSA was instructed not to report derogatory comments about the President by other world leaders because the administration thought they might leak. Furthermore, this administration selectively and actively tries to blind national collection means which have proved embarrassing.

The NSA representative to OFM said [ ] personally saw reports that were highly relevant to ongoing negotiations, e.g., that the opposite side had no intention of carrying out promises they made because they didn't trust Clinton to keep his word, because the White House had instructed that no reports of comments by foreign leaders derogatory to Clinton could be issued. [ ] also complained that currently the Justice Department is returning FISA [Federal Intelligence Surveillance Act] court applications groundlessly—wrong type face, (the same one NSA's always used) etc. It has gotten to the point that the FISA court judges are considering instructing NSA to go around Justice and make their applications direct without justice review because the administration is obstructing collection on places such as China where the take could embarrass the president. Such collection initially tipped the intelligence community to Clinton's illegal fund raising. I believe they don't want this to happen again. I hypothesize that the Clintons came in doing business in their usual extortionate Arkansas way and were truly shocked when they learned that their practices were so open to view when tried on a nation-to-nation level. They really thought you could deal with the Chinese the way you could deal with an Arkansas savings and loan and no one would be the wiser.

I guess from this you can determine that I am not a big fan of Clinton. But then, you suspected that.

Subject: Flash: NSA Loses Battle to Virus
Date: Thu, 4 May 2000 15:59:54 -0400 (EDT)
From: "Robert P. Hanssen" <root@orion.clark.net>
To:

NSA's secure e-mail system because infected with the ILOVEYOU virus today. Now everyone is asking how did it get into a system which supposedly is secure.

APPENDIX III

THE SEXUAL
FANTASIES OF
A SPY

Bob Hanssen posted the following tales of sexual fantasy about his wife, Bonnie, on adult Internet sites in the late 1990s. The events covered their early years of marriage when they lived in Chicago. Neither the titles nor the stories below, which contain sexually graphic descriptions, have been edited or altered in any way. While there are elements of truth in the two stories about that period in their lives—Bob was a dental school student, for example—the descriptions of sexual feelings, emotions, and actions attributed to Bonnie are based solely on Bob's fantasies. Bonnie Hanssen declined comment on the stories.

THE "UNEXPLICATABLE" GAME

Beach time with Bonnie, in our early years of marriage, was wonderful. We lived in a little apartment on Chicago's north side only a couple of blocks from Lake Michigan. Now Lake Michigan isn't much for swimming unless you like it cold. The lake freezes out hundreds of yards in the winter and in the warmest August might make it up to 60 degrees once the ice melts. Usually it would turn you blue in short order, and Bonnie never liked turning blue. She was more one to enjoy shades of suntan and would bask in the sun to achieve the right color. She dragged me to the beach often each Summer, not that I objected. I'd find little entertainments there like seeing how small I could roll her bikini before she'd object. I just loved showing her off.

Bonnie was 5'4", around 120 lbs. of 34–23–36 scrumptious legginess that would often gain gawks from men and honks from the more lecherous truck drivers. Letting her walk to the beach in her beach coverup was positively dangerous to traffic. Sometimes I thought I should charge a fee to auto body shops to let her walk around. It would build their business. Bonnie was a doll. When she'd strip off her coverup at the beach men would take note. Women dragging husbands would decide to leave. It was always a laugh. Other women didn't like to stick around in potential comparison to Bonnie in a bikini.

Now, as gorgeous as Bonnie was, she was a bit naive and also strangely unconvinced about her looks. At least she always seemed truly surprised when men found her pretty. She didn't have a lot of confidence. Perhaps this was because she'd bloomed late after suffering ovarian problems as a teen which had delayed the onset of maturation. That was about the time when she was comparing herself to other girls and forming her self-image. Well, nature made up in elegance what it shorted her in promptness, but unfortunately (for her) not before she'd become insecure about her looks and had developed a need for the constant reinforcement that seemed to come only from attracting the eyes of men. Bonnie liked to be looked at.

Well, as I said, sunning in Summer was Bonnie's avocation. The water held no interest for her. We'd pick a nice spot on the grass near the edge of the bluff that overlooked the sand at Hollywood Beach just north of Foster Avenue, the beach where Hollywood Blvd., with its funny rush-hour reversing signs, intersects with Sheridan Road near the lake. Hollywood Beach was a great place to sun. That bluff area was sparsely populated with the serious sun people, and the bluff made it about eight feet higher than the level of the sand where the seriously ac-

tive deployed to periodically dunk their bodies in the ice water. Bonnie would bring a book and a big beach bag hat and lie
on her blanket on her stomach reading with her bikini top un-
tied. (She hated bathing suit lines on her back.) For my part, as
I said, I would entertain myself by rolling Bonnie's bikini bottom into progressively smaller triangles of coverage. It was thin
enough that I eventually could get it down to just a virtual two
inch triangle rolled down low across the middle of her gorgeous
buns and in from the sides into the crack of her ass, that is, when
she'd let me. She'd look at me askance at first, but the more I
did it, the more sexually aroused she'd get. It was great fun.

Now we would generally be fairly alone up there, above the
main fray of revelers. It was always a bit of a race to see if I could
get Bonnie aroused enough that she would ignore the increasing volume of male strollers who chose, for some perhaps not
so obscure reason, to walk along the cliff edge past our blanket
when her suit was rolled nice and tight. Bonnie looked stunning. I was always interested also to see how low I could actually pull down her suit, as opposed to just rolling it, and that
would vary. It would vary with how hot she got, and I don't
mean from the sun. Several times I managed to get it and keep
it for long periods down around her mid thighs, completely
exposing her little tight bare ass. Now that was quite a sight
indeed. As I said, I did like showing her off. At those times,
Bonnie had to make quite an effort to avoid noting the traffic
going by, but she'd manage. She'd feign sleep.

Of course Bonnie didn't always lie face down. How could she.
She needed a good tan on both sides. When she was on her
back it was always more difficult for her to ignore the passing
guys who'd pause and look at her as best they could, never
enough to get her nervous and spoil her little show of course.
They were smarter than that. On her back, she'd use the hat
effectively to cover her eyes. That was she could avoid noticing that her bikini was pull down sometimes completely
exposing her pubic hair. Ah, those were wonderful moments
in the annals of exhibitionism. Bonnie had a knack for it. We
were a great match.

Both of us knew it was a game. The cardinal unspoken rule that we could never discuss playing it or even acknowledge that she had in any way been seen injudiciously exposed where anyone could "really" see her. Yes, the game had rules. It had to be done covertly. Bonnie had to preserve a decorous deniability about it. If I played by the rules, she'd play with all her heart. The rules made that possible. Rules, you will find, are enablers. They are not restrictions except when seen by the unwise.

After such sessions at the beach, we'd go back to our apartment and Bonnie would fuck like a bunny. Bonnie was a lot of fun.

SHE LAID THERE NAKED AND "UNKNOWINGLY" LET THEM ALL LOOK

When I was in dental school and we were newlyweds, my wife Bonnie and I lived in an inexpensive apartment on Winthrop Avenue on Chicago's north side. The primary reason it was inexpensive was that the elevated tracks ran right behind it. The trains made an ungodly noise especially during the rush-hours. They ran on a concrete-sided, raised roadbed level with the windows of our second-floor apartment and just across an alleyway. Our bedroom window, in fact all our windows, looked directly on them. Our bed was pushed up against the windowed wall and stood about six inches beneath the level of the sill of the bedroom's large two-paneled, horizontally-sliding picture window. In the morning you could see the faces of hundreds of people whizzing past perhaps 100 feet away. Such is life; we got used to the noise.

Now Bonnie was and remains a pretty straight arrow, but I learned early-on that when she was sexually aroused she was stimulated enormously by situations where she might be seen naked by other men or be seen in sexual activity. Why this was true, I wouldn't hazard a guess. It was just a conclusion I finally drew from incidents. She would never admit it or even think to address it openly. For example, I found she enjoyed having sex most when she was top-less in my Volkswagen facing me on my lap with her tits bouncing wildly in the passenger side window. We'd often do this while parked right on suburban side streets, albeit at night, and even in lover's lanes along with other couples. (Yes, alas, we were only engaged at the time and had no better place.) She would be discrete until she got really around and then it was show-time! She didn't seem to want to get caught, but it seemed to be that the risk of being seen aroused her. I gradually saw that such risks were more than a passing fancy for her. They drove her wild. Underneath I had to assume that she did have fantasies of putting on a show which stimulated her. Who knows. We never discussed it. I'm sure she'd never admit to it, but it was there as sure as I know anything.

Well we were a perfect match in this regard because what turned me on most was the thought of other men seeing her, wanting her, being aroused by her. We were well matched.

I must say, having the bed next to the window like that led to plenty of fun. There were times when she would ride me in the mornings naked right in the window. The passage of a train would throw her into instant orgasm. Even with the shade down in the evenings leaving the bright dresser light on cast a magnificent shadow of her naked silhouette on the shade with her tits bouncing. It was great.

This window situation did lead to one debacle for her though which she later described to me in detail and which I can only now relate as she told it. I wasn't there.

Bonnie would shower in the mornings and sit perched on a high stool in front of her dresser mirror in that bedroom to do her hair while still naked. She'd never draw the shade despite the elevated trains breezing past. She said she liked the light, couldn't stand being boxed into a shaded dark room, and anyway the trains went so fast no one could 'really' see her. It was three explanations where one would do. The last, was a plausible theory. Of course when I looked out the window from the train in the mornings on leaving for school I could see her, but why object. She was enjoying herself. She was only 21 then.

Bonnie had long brown hair in those days past her shoulders and often wore it up which means she'd sit there and fuss with it until it satisfied her. Then she'd go off to teach second grade. She'd do the same on evenings when we were going out—putting her makeup on there too, with the lights on, always naked with the shade undrawn. One can only guess why, but I know it did arouse her. After doing it she'd be all cuddly. Partly perhaps, she probably did it because she sensed it pleased me, and it aroused me when she did. I don't know. Women are hard to figure.

One afternoon Bonnie was fixing her hair as usual completely nude. She'd been putting it up in different styles to see how to wear it that evening. After quite a while, she noticed some movement out the window. She looked and saw five track workers standing on the roadbed leaning on their shovels looking at her. She was horrified. Her only thought was to get that shade down and get it down quickly. To that end, she jumped up and clambered across the bed, using it to stand on to reach the shade pull. Now Bonnie is only 5'4" and has a knock out figure. Her legs were once voted best on campus by the fraternity poll, so I can imagine it must have been a gorgeous sight for the workers to see her standing on the bed full frontally naked in the window trying to capture the drawstring. In her rush, she yanked it down hard and let go only to have it pop up again. She became flustered. She pulled it down a second time, this time even more vigorously with the same result. Worse and to her horror, this time the string wrapped itself around the roller. Her hands were shaking. She then "had to" stand there on the bed right in the window untangling it for what she described as "forever" before she got it loose and finally locked down. I asked her why she didn't just duck down below the bed and she said, "I guess it never occurred to me; all I could think of was getting the shade down." Well that was Bonnie. We had great sex that night after she told me. Such things make life interesting. She could see it aroused me.

Bonnie could always justify such incidents as accidents. But there was one occasion where Bonnie really lost it and ended up purposely exposing herself to other men with my covert encouragement. She wouldn't have done it if she hadn't been intoxicated. It occurred when we had a party at our apartment for some of my classmates. All were single except one who brought his wife, and they left early. Liquor flowed and Bonnie had consumed a few mixed drinks. Now Bonnie isn't used to drinking at all plus she is small, so alcohol affects her dramatically. Well it turned out that one of the guys at the party had a couple of marijuana cigarettes, and they began to smoke them. Before I could stop her and get them to knock it off, they had gotten her to take a few puffs of one, under the guise of showing her how. She finally managed a deep puff, and held it, as they insisted. She seemed fine for a second. Then, she stood up and took about five steps before the swirl of the room got to her and she slumped down grasping the floor to steady herself on it. By the time I got there, she was lying head on her folded arm in the middle of our living-room floor.

I must say though that she looked great. She was wearing a beautiful, short dark-brown velvet dress that buttoned down the front and heels. One knee was pulled up, and the dress was pulled up high enough to expose the lower half of her pantyhose covered bum. She really looked gorgeous. I was down at her side in an instant receiving her complaints about the room spinning. I wasn't into marijuana. During her ramblings, she said, "Check my dress and make sure I look decent." I looked at it and it looked OK to me. I'd had a couple of drinks too but I was not plowed. I took the hem of her dress and lifted it all the way to her waist, leaving it up and said, "There, now you look fine." She thanked me. Then she said, "Oooww," and hugged the floor some more. She said she just wanted to lie there for a while, so I stayed with her.

The guys were mostly congregated in the kitchen area eating finger food which Bonnie had made, but they'd occasionally walk around wandering by to look down approvingly at Bonnie's tight little ass. Everyone seemed to be enjoying themselves. Then Bonnie told me she was going to get sick.

What she was, was a strange combination of sick, cuddly and turned on. I managed to get her curled on the floor of the bathroom where she threw up in the toilet.

Sick as she was, she still wanted me to stroke her and take her pantyhose off to rub her pussy. She was mightily turned on, for someone sick. All her inhibitions had apparently evaporated. She tried to help me get her out of her pantyhose, dress, and bra as fast as she to go play on the bed but she was pretty useless. Still I managed the task.

Now, we had only a three-room apartment not counting the bathroom which was sectioned from the bedroom. The kitchen eating area was not really separated from the living room. The four guys remaining still roamed free exploring occasionally but centered their forages on the food and liquor in the kitchen. None of that phased Bonnie in the least. She wanted me to play with her on the bed and I was more than glad to comply. She dilated rapidly and was kissy and cuddly as can be as I moved from one to two, then three, to four fingers pumping her. She was as hot as a rocket, but strangely, still the hostess somehow. She stopped me and wanted me to leave her for a while and go out to check on our guests. I did.

They were wandering aimlessly and all in good spirits, prowling for more liquor, which I gave them, after I'd made them get rid of the marijuana When I went back to Bonnie, she had pulled the bedspread which hung below her over her a bit to cover herself but it hadn't worked. I told her she shouldn't do that, that I wanted to see her naked when I came back. She acknowledged that she liked me. I told her, "No more silly covering yourself now," and she said, "OK." She began holding her pussy open for me to show me how aroused she was. After stoking and fingering her some more, I tucked the spread back down hard and said that I was going to check the guests again and that this time when I came back I wanted "to see you holding yourself for me just like you are now." She promised she would stay like that. She was almost gyrating with excitement, drippingly luscious, totally naked.

At this point, I went out of the bedroom back to the living-room to see if anyone might wander in and see Bonnie. I maneuvered one of my friends, "Jay" Sullivan, that way and he did wander into the bedroom. Now Sullivan was a wacko of the first water. He was so handsome girls would actually accost him on the street for concocted reasons trying to talk to him. He always thought somehow they were making fun of him. He was totally out of it on a good day.

I watched him go in through the short closet-depth hall to the bedroom and turn the corner toward Bonnie on the bed. He disappeared from view for awhile, apparently had a nice wander have and came back out about 10 seconds still in a complete fog. I think that in his state if he'd seen an elephant in that room, he wouldn't have thought it unusual. Jay was wasted. Then Marty wandered up. Now Marty was stable, not a pot-smoking goof like Jay. He saw Jay coming out so he wandered in. I could see that he too left the door area and went over toward the bed where Bonnie lay maybe 10 foot from the entry-way. He was in there longer. He at least wandered back out looking satisfyingly impressed.

Now I had to see what they saw, so I walked in myself. Bonnie was there lying completely nude on her bed with her pussy held open, her legs splayed wide, just as I had told her. She was a good obedient wife. She saw me through her mock closed lids and smiled at my hungrily. Now she was hotter than ever. She said, "I think somebody may have come in and seen me while you were gone." I thought to myself, "Now that was a masterful understatement," but I told her not to worry about it, that it was OK. That seemed to make her extremely happy, and she began begging for sex. She knew she had done what I wanted. This was good.

I told her that we had to get the guests out first though, and she agreed. She seemed likely to agree with anything at this point. Bonnie, it turned out, had been lying with her legs across everybody's coats, not a place where one might think to stay hidden from departing guests. It was winter. She foggedly wanted to get her dress back on so she could go to the door to say goodbye. She insisted on it. She slipped it on but couldn't button it and settled instead for just holding it closed. The dress hem was only at her mid-to-upper thigh—about the length of most leggy Star-Trek women, a nice length for a girl with good legs. The buttons went down to well below the waist but not completely to the hem and it flowed down from the shoulders, sculpted, but with no a formal division or waist-band, so holding it closed shortened it further. She looked great. Somehow I got her to the door. It was a little hard for her to walk in the spinning room.

I managed for people to get their coats, etc. It all worked out. I stood almost in the doorway with my hands supporting Bonnie around the waist. Bonnie, doing her part still as hostess, felt she had to kiss everyone goodbye, which she did, looking damn sexy as she'd lean forward from her waist and lifted onto her toes while pressed against me. I'd never seen her so horny. She was playing games with her ass rubbing my crotch. We stood briefly in the hall outside the apartment and waved goodbye to the last departing three. By then she seemed to have forgotten about holding the dress completely. She looked great. The instant they rounded the hall corner, she slid her dress off right there in the outside hall and turned to me wanting sex. I somehow got her back to the bed, and we both just had a wonderful time.

Bonnie has never mentioned the evening since except to fuss the next day over whether I thought that everyone had a good time. She was concerned that she hadn't been a good enough hostess. I assured her that she had done just fine and had entertained everyone greatly!

SOURCES

T his book is based on interviews with more than one hundred people, as well as a review of thousands of pages of
public documents, internal memos, Internet postings, and e-
mails. Many of the interviews were conducted "on the record," and
those individuals are cited by name wherever possible. Numerous other
interviews were conducted on "background"—those people talked with
me only with the assurance that I would not identify them as a source.
The desire of current and retired FBI agents for anonymity grows out
of loyalty to the Bureau's long-standing tradition of secrecy. In some
instances, sources cited the need to remain anonymous so they could
protect ongoing law enforcement and national security matters.

I want to thank everyone who spoke with me and so generously
took the time to assist in my efforts to write a fair, accurate, and compelling account of double agent Robert Hanssen and FBI Director
Louis Freeh. Without your help, and you know who you are, the
inside story of *The Bureau and the Mole* would have remained a secret.

In addition to present and former FBI agents, I interviewed
people who served in the White House, Congress, the Justice Department, the CIA, the National Security Council, the Pentagon, the
State Department, the National Security Agency, and other branches
of federal, state, and local government. I also talked to Russian intelligence officials. I interviewed representatives of the Catholic Church
and Opus Dei, as well as religious scholars. I interviewed psychia-

trists and psychologists in an effort to understand Hanssen, and spoke with his relatives, classmates, childhood and adult friends, legal counsel, and professional colleagues. I talked to experts on espionage, counterintelligence, foreign affairs, the Soviet Union and Russia, and the KGB and its successor, the SVR. I did much of the reporting in Washington, D.C., and northern Virginia, but the work also took me to other locales, including New York and Hanssen's birthplace in Chicago. I also communicated by telephone and e-mail with people throughout the United States, the Middle East, South America, Russia, and elsewhere in Europe.

I am aware of the difficulties presented by any attempt to reconstruct events after the fact. Wherever possible, I relied on transcripts, contemporaneous notes, court papers, congressional records, speeches, studies, and other documents that, unlike memories, do not change over time. I relied on confidential FBI memos and letters in some instances. In other cases, I gained access to FBI and Justice Department documents by making formal and informal requests. I also reviewed the Justice Department's lengthy affidavit in support of Hanssen's arrest, the criminal complaint and indictment in the case, the arrest warrant, the search warrants, the list of items seized, the statement of facts in support of Hanssen's plea agreement, and the plea agreement itself.

The exchange of correspondence between Hanssen and his Soviet and Russian contacts was not corrected for grammar or spelling. The same is true of e-mails and Internet postings written by Hanssen.

I was assisted enormously in my research by the high-caliber work of other journalists and authors. In relating the story of Louis Freeh, his early years and his actions as FBI director, I drew heavily from several outstanding articles that Bureau officials confirmed were accurate: "The View From the Bench," by Ralph Blumenthal (*New York Times*, March 11, 1992); "The American Connection," by Steve Coll (*Washington Post Sunday Magazine*, October 31, 1993); "The FBI's Freeh Agent," by Lloyd Grove (*Vanity Fair*, December 1993); "Running the FBI," by Bruce Porter (*New York Times Sunday Magazine*,

November 2, 1997); and "Louis Freeh's Last Case," by Elsa Walsh (*The New Yorker*, May 14, 2001).

In learning about Freeh and Hanssen, I relied on outstanding reporting in the *Washington Post*, as well as on a vast array of well-researched and carefully crafted articles in the *New York Times*, the *Los Angeles Times*, the *Chicago Tribune*, the *Wall Street Journal*, *USA Today*, *Legal Times*, *Newsweek*, *Time*, *U.S. News & World Report*, and other publications. The book's second appendix, "The E-mails of a Spy," was first published in *Insight* magazine. Hanssen's musings about his sexual fantasies in the third appendix of the book, and in other chapters, were posted on various Internet bulletin boards. I also relied on transcripts from CNN's *Larry King Live*, ABC's *20/20*, and Internet articles by journalists at ABC, CBS, NBC, and CNN.

A number of books helped me develop the narrative and also provided useful background, context, and dialogue. Notable among these were: the Bible; *The Man Who Was Thursday* by G. K. Chesterton; *The Annotated Thursday* edited by Martin Gardner; *Victory* by Joseph Conrad; *Moscow Station, Escape from the CIA*, and *The FBI: Inside the World's Most Powerful Law Enforcement Agency* by Ronald Kessler; *Tower of Secrets* by Victor Sheymov; *The Sword and the Shield: The Mitrokhin Archive and the Secret History of the KGB* by Christopher Andrew and Vasili Mitrokhin; *Confessions of a Spy* by Pete Earley; *Killer Spy* by Peter Maas; *Last Days of the Sicilians* by Ralph Blumenthal; *Molehunt* by David Wise; *Shadow* by Bob Woodward; *Main Justice* by Jim McGee and Brian Duffy; and *The FBI Story* by Don Whitehead. To understand Hanssen better, I also relied upon the 1962 yearbook from Taft High School in Chicago.

In addition, I referenced portions of Louis Freeh's *Report to the American People on the Work of the FBI, 1993–1998*, and Robert Hanssen's monograph on the use of "Soviet Active Measures."

If I have inadvertently failed to cite any published works or broadcasts that contributed meaningfully to this book, I apologize. I am greatly indebted to the many journalists and authors whose reporting and storytelling informed this book.

ACKNOWLEDGMENTS

I am extremely grateful for the strong support I received from the *Washington Post* throughout the writing of this book. The *Post,* where I have been a journalist since 1984, is an absolutely superb place for reporters and editors to work. My thanks to Washington Post Company Chairman Don Graham; Publisher Bo Jones; Executive Editor Leonard Downie, Jr.; Assistant Managing Editor for National News Liz Spayd; her deputy, Michael Abramowitz; my editor on the National desk, Lenny Bernstein; my partner covering the Justice Department, Dan Eggen; Assistant Managing Editor for Photo, Joe Elbert; and my mentor and friend, Assistant Managing Editor Bob Woodward.

A special thanks to Managing Editor Steve Coll, and Investigative Editor Jeff Leen, two incredibly talented journalists who encouraged me to delve into this subject and then took the time to share their thoughts about the best way to tell the tale.

My appreciation also goes to literary agent Rafe Sagalyn, who did a magnificent job of finding the right publisher for this book and gave me sage advice throughout the process. I also want to thank publisher Morgan Entrekin, head of Grove/Atlantic Inc., and my book editor, Brendan Cahill, who made excellent suggestions for ways to improve the first draft. Notwithstanding a tight schedule, he followed through despite canceled flights that left him stranded in Canada and London, and a kidney stone attack that left him hospitalized and in tremendous pain. Brendan's smart ideas and thoughtful line editing of the manuscript improved the book markedly.

Finally, I want to thank my wife, Lori, and our three daughters, Lisa, Allison, and Jennifer, for being extremely supportive and understanding while making the sacrifices that allowed me to write this book.

Lori was a constant source of encouragement, ideas, and love, a sounding board, and an astute reader of an early draft who saved me from making a potentially embarrassing error. Lori pointed out that I had written a sentence stating that Bonnie Hanssen had been in labor "for months."

"You can tell a guy wrote this," she said.